A *Short History of the*
CHINESE PEOPLE

L. CARRINGTON GOODRICH

ILLUSTRATED

DOVER PUBLICATIONS, INC.
Mineola, New York

Dedication

to ROBERT K. REISCHAUER

*First American casualty in the Second World War,
who urged the writing of this book*

Bibliographical Note

This Dover edition, first published in 2002, is an unabridged republication of the
1969 Fourth Edition of the work originally published in 1943 by Harper & Brothers,
New York.

Library of Congress Cataloging-in-Publication Data

Goodrich, L. Carrington (Luther Carrington), 1894–
    A short history of the chinese people / L. Carrington Goodrich.
        p. cm.
    Originally published: N.Y.: Harper & Bros., 1969.
    Includes bibliographical references and index.
    ISBN 0-486-42488-X (pbk.)
        1. China—History. I. Title.

DS735 .G58 2002
951—dc21

                                                                    2002071601

Manufactured in the United States of America
Dover Publications, Inc., 31 East 2nd Street, Mineola, N.Y. 11501

Contents

Preface to the First Edition

Preface to the Third Edition

   I. The Beginnings of the Chinese   I

       The Prehistoric Period

       The Historic Period; the Shang (*ca.* 1523–1028 B.C.)

       The Chou (*ca.* 1027–256 B.C.)

          The Early Chou—The Middle and Late Chou

  II. The First Empires   31

       The Ch'in (221–207 B.C.)

       The Han

          The Early (or Western) Han (202 B.C.–A.D. 9)

          An Interregnum: The Hsin Dynasty (A.D. 9–23)

       The Later Han (A.D. 25–220)

       Han Culture

 III. The Period of Political Disunion   58

       The Three Kingdoms and Western Tsin (A.D. 220–317)

       The Eastern Tsin and the Turkic—Hsiung-nu—Mongol Dynasties (317–420)

       The Wei in North China, and the Sung, Ch'i, Liang, and Ch'ên Dynasties in the South (420–589)

IV. A Reunited China: The Sui and the T'ang (590–
          906)   114
      The Sui (590–618)
      The T'ang Dynasty (618–906)
      Religion and Culture Under the Sui and the
          T'ang
  V. Disunion; the Sung and the Partition of the North
      and Northwest   143
      The Five Dynasties and the Ten Independent
          States
      The Sung (960–1279)
      The Khitan, Tangut, and Jurchen
 VI. The Mongols (The Yüan Dynasty, 1260–1368)   171
VII. A Chinese House (The Ming, 1368–1644)   189
VIII. The Ch'ing, or Manchu, Dynasty (1644–1912)   214
  IX. The Republic (1912–   )
Appendixes: 249
  Supplementary Readings
  Chronological Table
  Chronological Chart
  List of Chinese Characters
Index

Illustrations

ILLUSTRATIONS WILL BE FOUND FOLLOWING PAGE 140

PLATE

    I. Digging for the remains of Paleolithic man, near Peking

   II. Gorilla; Peking man; modern Chinese

 III.⎫
 IV.⎭ Prehistoric painted pot from Kansu

    V. Early bronze vessel, *ca.* 1300–900 B.C.

  VI. White pottery vessel, *ca.* 12th century B.C.

 VII. Earliest known form of Chinese writing, *ca.* 12th century B.C.

VIII. Documents on wood of Han date

  IX. Sundial, with a reconstruction of the suggested form of gnomon in place

   X. How an ancient Chinese book was assembled

  XI. House model (painted pottery) of Han dynasty (202 B.C.–A.D. 220)

 XII. Section of painting attributed to Ku K'ai-chih (fl. A.D. 350–400)

XIII. Avalokitesvara, Northern Wei dynasty (A.D. 386–535)

XIV. Detail, band of celestial musicians, from a stela, A.D. 551

 XV. Front of a stūpa, 7th century A.D.

XVI. Kneeling Bodhisattva from Tunhuang, 8th century A.D.

XVII. Bronze mirror, T'ang dynasty (A.D. 618–906)

XVIII. Wall painting: The fight for Buddha's relics, T'ang dynasty (A.D. 618–906)

XIX. Pottery figurines: Ladies playing polo, T'ang dynasty (A.D. 618–906)

XX. Part of oldest extant printed book: The Diamond Sūtra scroll, A.D. 868

XXI. Bowl, Ting ware, Sung dynasty (A.D. 960–1279)

XXII. Painting: Bare willows and distant mountains, by Ma Yüan (*ca.* A.D. 1200)

XXIII. A mountain scene in China

XXIV. The imperial palace library, Ch'ien-lung period (A.D. 1736–1795), Peking

XXV. Two varieties of ephedra

Maps

Paleolithic Sites in East Asia

Neolithic Sites in East Asia

Black Pottery Sites in China

Shang Dominion

Early Chou

Middle Chou

Late Chou

The First Empire: Ch'in

The Han Empire

The Three Kingdoms

Routes of Chinese Pilgrims

T'ang Empire

The Sung, Tangut (Hsi-Hsia), and Liao Empires

The Mongol Empire

Ming

Cruises of Ming Admirals

Empire of the Manchus

Preface to the First Edition

THE history of the Chinese people cannot often enough be told. Old as it is, new light is being shed on it every year. Meanwhile the Chinese are making history before our eyes. We need, as never before, to understand how they have come in our time to make such a sacrificial defense of a way of life that is theirs as much as it is our own.

The Chinese are different from us; at the same time they are more like us than the people of India, of Annam, or of Japan. At the conclusion of the last war, the writer served for a time with a Chinese labor battalion attached to United States forces in France. Again and again, puzzled American corporals and sergeants helping to direct the battalion remarked to him on the innate likenesses between themselves and the Chinese, despite the barrier of language and difference of custom. They wanted this phenomenon explained; so have others. It is worth while therefore to examine the record, and see how the Chinese people have traveled down the corridors of time from the Old Stone Age to the present.

Another good reason for a study of Chinese history is to make it serve as a foil for our own. Semi-detached from some of the other great civilizations of the world, the Chinese have yet evolved in some ways like ourselves, in some ways not. They have a great historical tradition. So had the Romans; but the Hindus have not. Why? The Chinese learned a great deal about the stars, devised a workable calendar, and made several praiseworthy achievements in mathematics, medicine, engineering, architecture, geography, and historical criticism, but did not arrive at a fully rounded scientific method. Again why? There are many such questions that one can pose. Not all the answers are in this book. It is the writer's hope, however, that the reader will have a fuller understanding of the background and a greater ability to get at the answers after he has concluded the last chapter than when he started. Naturally some of the questions can meet only with speculative replies, and these can never give general satisfaction. It seems to the writer, none the less, that a thorough study of Chinese civilization will give every student of history, whether of the peoples of Europe, of western Asia, of the Americas, or of any other region, a better basis for comprehension of that history. Indeed, this is the only way to reach a global understanding.

A final reason is to profit from the empirical knowledge of the Chinese in many fields. To give two examples: It is said of Vice-President Wallace that he has inwardly digested the monographic material on the policies of the eleventh-century statesman Wang An-shih,[1] together with their application and fruit. Another case is that of the United States Department of Agriculture which for years has been actively studying and endeavoring to exploit Chinese experience in afforestation, production of certain crops, soil enrichment, prevention of plant disease, and the like. Similar examples might be cited. They certainly should be increased.

The summary treatment of any subject of so vast a scope as the one under hand is bound to be uneven. Every general history of China yet undertaken suffers from that fault, and the writer is conscious that his is no exception. He hopes, however, that the suggestions made under the heading of Supplementary Readings will afford some remedy. One thing which he has consciously done needs explanation. The chapter on political disunion (Chap-

---

[1] It now appears that Mr. Wallace was primarily interested not in Wang An-shih but in Wang Mang (d. 23 A.D.). See his letter to Derk Bodde, quoted in the *Far Eastern Quarterly* V 412 (August 1946).

ter III) is long. The reason for this is threefold: first, a discussion of so confused a period can hardly be abbreviated without making it nearly meaningless; second, Buddhism and Taoism—particularly the former—came into their own then and vitally affected all areas of Chinese life; and third, this period is the trunk from which much of the culture of Korea and Japan and other contiguous areas sprang; to know them one must have more than a cursory knowledge of the four centuries beginning about A.D. 200.

It remains to acknowledge with gratitude the help the writer has received from many sources: from his students for much they have taught him; from his colleagues for their friendly criticism and aid; from Miss Dorothy Thompson of Harper & Brothers for editorial assistance on the book; from Mr. Henry C. Fenn, for permission to make adaptations of one of his charts; from several people and institutions for permission to use their photographs for illustration; from the writers of many books and papers whose translations he has used and acknowledged in the text; and from many Chinese friends of every age and station. The resulting work is unworthy of their aid, but it goes out with a prayer for indulgence from them all.

L. CARRINGTON GOODRICH

Preface to the Third Edition

SINCE this book was first published (in 1941) the Chinese, perhaps more than other people, have been subjected to remarkable pressures, which have resulted in profound changes in every field of their life, political, military, social, and cultural. This edition, like the second, takes account of these changes. Advantage is also taken of the opportunity to make a few revisions in the text in the light of recent scholarship.

L. C. G.

New York
September, 1958

CHAPTER I

The Beginnings of the Chinese

THE PREHISTORIC PERIOD

THE history of the Chinese is the story of the gradual peopling of the great river valleys and plains of China, and of this people's expansion and development in their own part of Asia and beyond, on both the mainland and the coastal islands. The legends of China, like the Hebraic, used to put the beginning of the story several millenniums before the Christian era, say five thousand years ago; but recent discoveries have pushed this back to a far earlier time and enabled us to picture the China of today before man ever fished or hunted or tried to wrench a living from its soil.

At a time variously estimated at one hundred thousand to half a million years ago, a species of pre-human animals called hominids appeared in north China. Fossils of these hominids, somewhat more primitive than most fossils of the same age found in other parts of the world, have been discovered in close association with thousands of stone, bone, and horn implements, with charred bones and charcoal ashes, with uneaten bits of food, and with the fossils of many animals, some of them now extinct. These hominids seem to have known how to walk on their two feet and hold their bodies erect. They were not unskilled in fashioning tools and they were familiar with the use of fire. Their brain capacity (850–1220 cc.) was about twice that of the gorilla, chimpanzee, and other higher primates, but somewhat less than that of modern man (average, 1350 cc.). They were capable of articulate speech. The remains of hominid skulls and teeth show five characteristics that are common to modern man in eastern Asia but much less common to man elsewhere. *Homo sapiens* in Asia seems to have slowly evolved from this or some related prehuman type to what is commonly known as the Mongoloid race.

The continuity of human evolution in north China and the large land masses to the north and west was broken by glaciation during the Middle Pleistocene. A tremendous ice cap, whose average thickness varied from 6500 feet in Europe to 2300 in the Ural Mountains and which leveled off gradually as it approached Mongolia, stirred up winds of greater velocity than have ever been known since. Coming from a colder to a warmer climate, these winds picked up the soil of such regions as the Tarim and Gobi plains (hence their desiccation) and deposited it over the entire Yellow River basin from Kansu almost to the Gulf of Peichihli. These conditions made life difficult, if not impossible, and may have driven man elsewhere for a time.

At the end of the glacial period man of a distinctly human type returned, for his remains have been found at the top of the primary loess soil throughout north China, Mongolia, Manchuria, and Siberia. It was at this time, twelve to twenty thousand years ago, that man began to migrate to North America and possibly also to Japan. His ability to make tools such as needles was superior; he often brought stone from great distances; he lived in small communities; and he was doubtless acquiring considerable knowledge of root and leaf crops, fish, and the animals that ran wild on the plains. One find suggests that he was working the surface iron ore for its red powder. By six or seven thousand years ago he was living in pit dwellings in larger communities, had domesticated at least one animal, the pig, and was manufacturing a coarse kind of pottery, some pieces of which were eighteen inches high with pointed bottoms. The stone-bladed hoe was his chief agricultural implement, and the bow

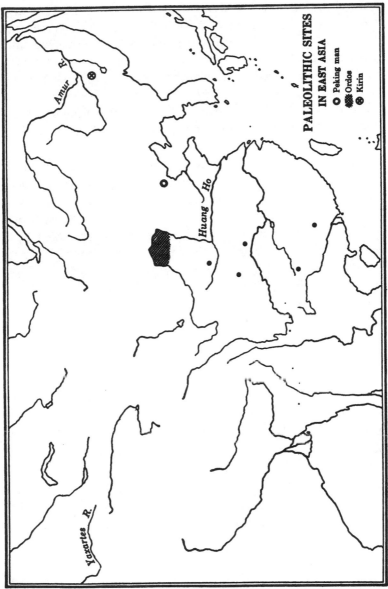

PALEOLITHIC SITES
IN EAST ASIA
○ Peking man
▧ Ordos
⊗ Kirin

Amur R.

Huang Ho

Yaxartes R.

and arrow were probably his chief means of defense and offense.

As the centuries passed he added the dog to his home complex. Millet became his chief crop and he may also have cultivated some wheat and dry rice. When his land became less productive he moved on to another area, burned off the tree cover, drained the soil, and put in his crops. He continued to fish and hunt. To aid in defense he devised a bamboo-headed spear. Clothing made from skins, bark, and perhaps hemp kept him warm. He ornamented his womenfolk with perforated shells. In certain areas, particularly in the middle and upper Yellow River valley and the north, pottery-making developed; a potter's wheel may have been used. Several forms of vessels were made, and some of them were painted, both monochrome and polychrome. Several of these forms may have analogues in western Asia, Russia, and India; the earliest, known as cord-marked pottery, may be peculiar to east Asia; it is characterized by pointed bottoms. Possibly for exchange purposes, and also as a decoration and a charm, these men of the Stone Age began to use the cowry, a little shell that may have come originally from so distant a place as the Maldive Islands southwest of the Indian peninsula.

In later centuries colonies sprang up from the Shantung headlands to Hangchow Bay and as far inland as Honan province. The many sites located before and after the outbreak of World War II indicate that these settlements averaged about 750,000 square feet in size and were commonly surrounded by walls of tamped earth. The partly subterranean dwellings were circular and set on flat earthen floors, in the center of which was the stove. The chief occupation of these people was farming,[1] but they also hunted, fished, and herded animals. In addition to the

---

[1] Their experience in the relatively treeless areas in which they lived doubtless proved that "agriculture can feed between twenty and fifty times as many people as the hunt." (K. A. Wittfogel, "The Society of Prehistoric China," *Zeitschrift für Sozialforchung,* VIII:169, n. 7 [1939].)

pig and dog, they had horses, sheep, and cattle. They divined the future by scapulimancy, the art of prophesying on the basis of the cracks formed when heat is applied to the scapulas of oxen and deer. They buried their dead face down in rectangular pits in the midst of their settlements.

They made a variety of implements from the shells of fresh-water mollusks—knives, scrapers, sickles, arrowheads, pins, and pendants. They are best known, however, for their black pottery, which was often thin and lustrous. They made bowls, basins, tumblers, cups, beakers, pots, jars, jugs, hollow-footed tripods, and even toys such as doll-sized vessels and rattles.

At this time, say 2000 B.C., there is as yet no indication of writing or of the use of metals, save for coloring matter. There may have been government of a kind, for law and order had to be maintained within these settlements if not between them; but we know nothing about it except through surmise.

The scribes who penned Chinese traditional history during the first millennium before our era fix the next five hundred years as the period of the Hsia, the first of the ruling dynasties of China. It began, according to one document, in the year corresponding to 1994 B.C. and lasted to 1523. (Another document, not so generally supported by scholars, puts the first date at 2205.) During these five centuries, again according to tradition, a succession of princes ruled a group of city-states, possibly from a point in Shansi, near the last great bend of the Yellow River. Their people knew the use of bronze weapons, went to war in chariots, engaged in agriculture and sericulture, and put down their ideas in writing. Actually there is no satisfactory evidence that this state existed; we cannot identify a single vessel or weapon or bronze inscription as being Hsia in date. Nevertheless, the many artifacts and inscriptions that have come to us from the next historic period are not primitive in the least and must have had a history in China of several hundred years. They make us willing to grant that, even if Hsia never existed, there

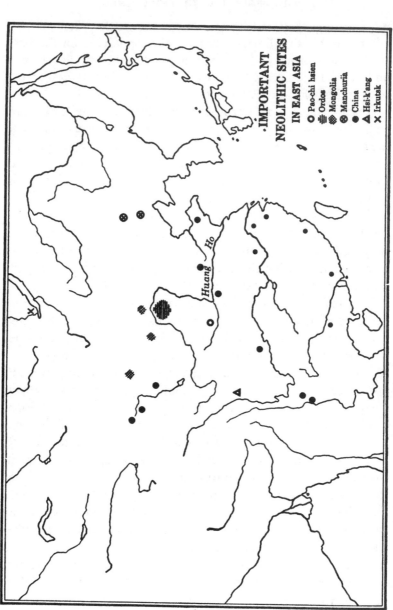

IMPORTANT
NEOLITHIC SITES
IN EAST ASIA

○ Pao-chi hsien
🏛 Ordos
⊛ Mongolia
● Manchuria
● China
▲ Hsi-k'ang
✕ Irkutsk

were centers near the banks of the Yellow River which knew the art of casting bronze, learned the value of the silkworm, used the wheel on the farm and in war, and began to use written symbols. The first steps toward civilization had been taken.

THE HISTORIC PERIOD; THE SHANG (*ca.* 1523–1028 B.C.)

The beginning of history in China coincides, more or less, with the latter half of the second millennium before the Christian era. As late as 1924 Professor Thomas Francis Carter made a chart of China's past which put this entire millennium in the prehistoric period. This was changed in 1928, when Chinese archeologists, cooperating initially with the Freer Gallery of Art of Washington, D.C., unearthed a series of highly important discoveries along the River Huan, a tributary of the Yellow River, in the northern part of modern Honan. There is one qualification of the word "historic," however. Though scientists are working on the problem of accurate dating,[2] we can as yet speak only qualifiedly of certain events occurring or certain articles being made during any part of this half millennium. Not until the ninth and eighth centuries B.C. do events in Chinese history have dates, and even they must be used with caution.

The Chinese call this period Shang (a later name is Yin), after the royal house that ruled over the region near its capital. The document referred to above fixes its dates as approximately from 1523 to 1028 B.C. The origins of the Shang dynasty can only be guessed at; however, we must certainly assume developments of fundamental significance that could produce a governing group which could command many lesser chiefs who in turn dominated the peasants, could make war with wheeled vehicles

---

[2] The important contribution on the calendar of Tung Tso-pin, entitled *Yin li p'u* (1945), has not gained general acceptance. Tung holds to the dates of 1751–1112 for the beginning and end of the Shang, but these are sharply contested by Bernhard Karlgren of Stockholm and Homer H. Dubs of Oxford University.

and sizable bodies of troops,[3] could initiate and carry on the construction of public works, and could perform religious rites apparently on behalf of the people as a whole. These developments must have included a population increase that required some centralization of authority; the storing of millet, wheat, and possibly rice against times of drought, flood, and siege; the collection of metals from a wide area for the casting of tools and weapons; and increased specialization in skills on the part of the people.

According to traditional history, the first Shang princes succeeded in subduing eighteen hundred city-states; that they had periodic difficulties with the more powerful aggregations of these city-states is clear. On several occasions they were forced to shift their capital, possibly because of raids or the difficulty of defending it, or because of some calamity like a flood. The exact location of the capital cities is unknown; possibilities are near modern Chengchou (Honan), Tsinan (Shantung), and Sian (Shensi), where archeologists have recently found extensive remains of early and middle Shang culture. Around 1300 B.C. one ruler and his court arrived near modern Anyang and slowly erected a city that contained government buildings, palaces, temples, and mausoleums.

The discovery of this capital city has thrown light on what was hitherto only dimly known, for the remains of its buildings and their contents have withstood the dampness and man's destructive hand better than less complex structures and furnishings. In addition to the exact knowledge about architecture, defensive weapons, and ritual vessels thus made possible, a great body of information has been acquired through the recovery of tens of thousands of inscriptions, most of them fragmentary and unquestionably representing only a small portion of the written documents of the period. There are a few laconic inscriptions on

---

[3] King Wu-ting in one period of three months is said to have called 23,000 men to arms. But most armies were much smaller, 3000 to 5000 men in all.

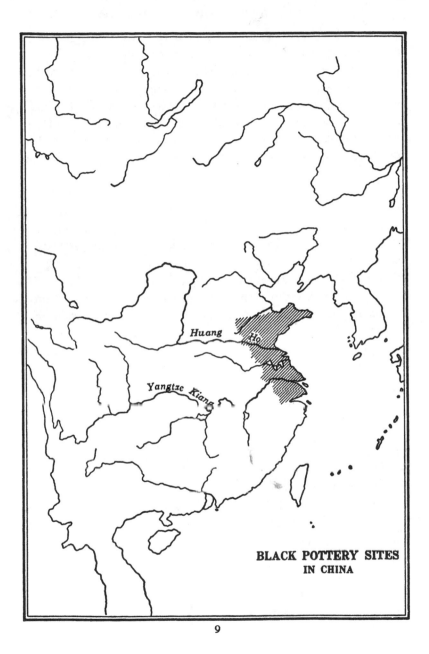

Huang

Ho

Yangtze Kiang

BLACK POTTERY SITES
IN CHINA

9

bronze, such as blades of dagger axes or the bowls of altar pieces, and on pieces of pottery and jade; but most of them are found on the bones of animals or the shells of a tortoise now extinct which derived from the valley of the Yangtze or farther south. They indicate that scapulimancy had become an art that may have been practiced by a special priesthood taught not only to divine but also to write down the prince's questions and the deity's replies. Some of these inscriptions indicate that there was a special group of men in the government whose duty was to keep records. In addition to writing on metal, shell, and bone, the inscriptions suggest that the Shang Chinese also wrote on wood, bamboo, and possibly silk. Depending on the writing surface, their tools included a knife or burin and a primitive brush; ink, probably made from soot, was used on wood and pottery; and the scratched lines were often filled in with cinnabar.

The non-primitive writing and the number of written words —around 3000 (about 1400 can be read)—argue a considerable history before the thirteenth century B.C.; but where writing originated is as yet unknown. Some scholars suggest connections with western Asia on the basis of the similarity between the pictographic forms of certain words used by both eastern and western scribes. It may be, but there is a gap of some two thousand years between the pictographs of, say, Egypt and those of China, and it is entirely possible that these early Chinese devised their signs for such words as they had for sun and rain independently, as did the Sioux and Ojibways in North America. Moreover, the arguments for an independent origin are reinforced by the fact that certain written signs, such as those for the numerals 5, 6, 7, 8, 9, 10 and for the twenty-two characters indicating the Chinese cycle, have no parallels elsewhere. Obviously there was some extended development within the Yellow River valley itself, for many of the signs have a purely Chinese connotation. As one of the principal English investigators has remarked, even in the Shang period these signs were "so greatly stylized

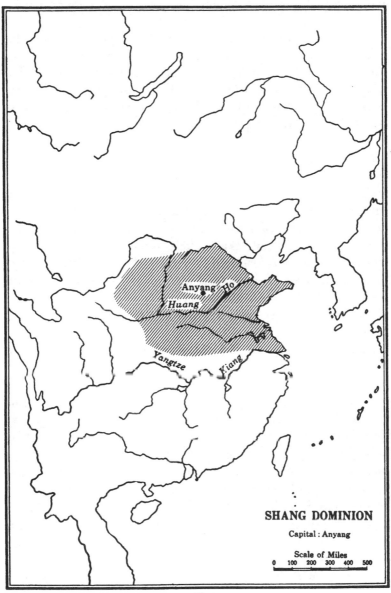

SHANG DOMINION

Capital : Anyang

Scale of Miles

0   100   200   300   400   500

and disguised as to presuppose the passage of a long, a very long past."

These signs are of different types. The pictograms indicate, in skeleton and fragmentary fashion, such common things as parts of the body, animals, birds, vegetation, streams, hills, rafts, weapons, and the heavenly bodies. The ideograms express ideas in pictographic form; thus "to shoot" is represented by an arrow laid across a bow, and the "west" by a bird nesting. The pictograms and ideograms, together with the artifacts found *in situ*, give us invaluable information on the material culture of the age, although most of the signs are so telescoped in form that their earliest significance can only be guessed at. The crude explanations given by writers unacquainted with this swiftly developing branch of science must be accepted with discretion. For example, some hold that trouble in the home is represented by two women under one roof; however, there is no such character in the Chinese dictionaries. Nevertheless, our knowledge has progressed far beyond what it was nearly eighty years ago when Dr. Herbert A. Giles, the learned compiler of a *Chinese-English Dictionary* (1892), asserted in the preface: "There does not remain to us one single genuine specimen of an inscription of a pictorial or pictographic nature, and it seems improbable that such ever existed."

In addition, these early Chinese frequently "borrowed" signs for words which were pronounced like words that already had signs. Thus, if the English language had a sign for "bang" as an explosive and a word with the same pronunciation was applied to a certain style of women's hair-do, the one sign might be used for both meanings. In later years, although some examples have been found dating from the Shang period, characters were formed on the principle of two elements, one giving a clue to the meaning and the other a clue to the pronunciation. The element 石, for instance, indicates things that have something to do with stones; the element 包 is pronounced *p'ao* or *pao*. When during the Middle Ages the Chinese invented the ballista—or borrowed it from abroad—they called it *p'ao*, and wrote it 砲. Later on, when the ballista evolved into a cannon, it too was called *p'ao* but it was written with the key for "fire," 火, thus: 炮. Even today Chinese chess on one side of a board include two ballistae marked 砲, and on the opposite side two marked 炮. This ancient "key plus phonetic" principle in constructing written sounds has enabled the Chinese to invent new characters almost as freely as scientists coin new words from the Latin or Greek. As Creel has well said: "Every important principle of the formation of modern Chinese characters was already in use, to a greater or less degree, in the China of . . . more than three thousand years ago." As time passed and writing materials changed, the characters were deformed or conventionalized—almost beyond recognition in some cases—and greatly supplemented. But the early scribes devised a system that not only was to last until our day but was also to spread to most of eastern Asia, including Korea, Japan, and Annam.

At first the direction of the lines of writing was not fixed, but generally they seem to have run vertically. The reason for this is not known; it may have been because of the narrow bamboo or wooden slips on which most of the writing was done, or because of the funeral slabs set up at the graves of dead ancestors. In any event, this vertical characteristic still continues and has affected the writing of the Uigur, Mongol, and Manchu peoples, who in other respects have adopted the alphabetical script of the Mediterranean peoples.[4]

Although recent discoveries have given us a great deal of

[4] For some unexplained reason the Tibetans, who, under the direction of Indian pundits in the seventh century of our era, used Sanskrit as the basis of their script, never adopted this arrangement despite their long and close association with the Chinese and their heavy borrowings from the latter's culture. It is equally difficult to understand why the Uigur, who flourished at about the same time as the early Tibetans, should first have adopted the horizontal arrangement of the west and then changed to the vertical of the Chinese.

knowledge about the written language, we have far less information regarding the spoken. The inscriptions show that the order of words was not unlike our own, that there were—to give Chinese parts of speech the same names as our own—pronouns and prepositions, that the nouns were not inflected to show number or gender, and that the verbs were not conjugated. The pronunciation, however, can only be guessed at from the study of groups of words of a much later date. Probably far more words were used in speech than have been preserved on bones and shells. There also must have been many dialects; intercommunication was slow and hazardous because of the many variations in the writing of certain words. The writing problem was solved by fiat ten centuries later when one dominant group forced the adoption of a single form, but the dialects have continued with modifications until our own day.

The scribes at the royal court and elsewhere were only one of several groups who provided for the functioning of the government. At the head was the king, with whom was associated one or more queens.[5] (The inscriptions contain the names of twenty-three of the thirty-one kings named in later documents.) There is a remote possibility that eunuchs officiated in his household. The king led in battle, in the hunt, and in special sacrifices as an intermediary between his people and nature—the latter to such an extent that he came to have a kind of priestly function. On questions that perplexed him he consulted his ancestors—the possible beginning of ancestor worship. The rule of succession was mixed, some being from father to son, some from elder to younger brother, with five deviations from both practices.

City government was well developed, for the titles of a number of functionaries in the capital city have been found. Their duties concerned the collection and expenditure of tribute, the

[5] The rulers and feudal lords in later time were encouraged to take nine (or twelve) wives in a single marriage, the women to come from states not their own. Cf. T. S. Tjan, *Po hu t'ung*, pp. 251–252.

construction of public buildings and defenses, and the care of irrigation works. The priests were important associates; they probably presided over all ceremonies and advised the king on everything to prevent him from offending the unseen world. They made sacrifices to the royal ancestors in the temples, and to the *shên*, or gods, both indoors and out. The sacrifices included sheep, pigs, dogs, cattle, and at times horses and humans, the latter probably captured on raids into enemy lands.

The determination of the calendar, which was then and has been throughout history a major function of the Chinese government as it is for any people who depend largely on farming, was also doubtless in the hands of the priests. The Shang calendar, though clumsy, was fairly stable and was frequently adjusted to make it agree with the seasons. The shortest period was ten days; three such periods (sometimes shortened by one day) made a month, the character for which was a moon. Six ten-day periods made a sixty-day cycle;[6] this was a fundamental unit and each day in it had a two-character designation. Six cycles made a year. (The character for a year, says one scholar, represents a man carrying a sheaf of grain on his back—in other words, the annual harvest in the one-crop country of northern China.) When necessary, the offices of the celendrical bureau added to the six-cycle year one, two, or more commonly three ten-day units;[7] there is one instance of the addition of a whole cycle, making fourteen months in all. This practice, which is called intercalation, was continued until modern times.

The men who managed the calendar must have been both knowledgeable and responsible, for on them in considerable measure depended the favor the king received from the people. Among a credulous people, the king was presumed to commune with the spirits; if he failed to preceive their signs, he had ob-

[6] There was no sixty-year cycle until the first century A.D.

[7] At first the additional unit (or units) was appended at the end of the year, but before the end of Shang it was found advisable to add the unit at the end of any month deemed most appropriate.

viously lost their favor. Hence his hold on his court and his subjects had to be maintained by calendrical accuracy as well as military success abroad and political adroitness at home. This accounts for the attention paid to this branch of science throughout thirty-odd centuries, and for the eagerness with which Chinese rulers welcomed astronomers from India, central Asia, Persia, and Europe, when they excelled the Chinese in these calculations. The men responsible for the calendar in the Shang period were probably less advanced than the Babylonians in their knowledge of the stars, but their performance was good and as a result they may have been entrusted with other record-keeping duties. In the second century B.C., the Grand Astrologer and his son who succeeded to this title were both official archivists and historians as well. This combination of offices in one man helps to explain why the earliest Chinese historical documents (down to 200 B.C.) include so many data on eclipses and other celestial phenomena.

Warfare during the Shang period, both offensive and defensive, was apparently frequent, for there are references to such struggles in the inscriptions. To collect tribute and supply the court with all its needs and luxuries—cattle, horses, slaves, copper, tin, furs, ivory, plumes—must have necessitated a great deal of "power politics" and foraging in regions far away from the capital. Similarly, outside tribes must often have looked with envy and longing at the growing wealth of the central plain and reached out in force to seize it. The people fought with the composite bow (a powerful weapon, widely used in northern Asia but not in Europe) and feathered arrows tipped with ribbed or barbed bronze or clay points. Other bows "shot" pellets of bone points or stone. Bronze spears, halberds, and battle-axes were used in close fighting. The common soldier or slave fought on foot; the noble, from a chariot drawn by two horses. Certain soldiers were protected by bronze helmets and possibly by armor and shields made of leather, wood, or bone.

Life in the country districts probably did not change materially from the Stone Age to the Bronze, although agriculture may have increased in importance. Hoes and mattocks were still bladed with stone, and the ground was still tilled with a foot plow. Some of the people tended cattle; others made coarse unpainted pottery. Everyone lived—at least in winter—in subterranean dwellings or loess caves. According to a poem of a slightly later date:

> Of old Tan-fu the duke
> Scraped shelters, scraped holes;
> As yet they had no houses.[8]

Life in the capital city, however, and doubtless in other urban centers became complex, and specialization appeared. Some of the city dwellers must have handled the sale and distribution of products coming in from the country districts and elsewhere. Others made clothes, cord, and pennants from silk and hemp. There were basket weavers, craftsmen in bone and wood and stone, potters who made incised white vessels, bronze casters, and builders of houses, temples, and mausoleums. Men will probably marvel for all time at the handiwork of this period that has survived—the great royal tombs furnished with ceremonial bronze and pottery vessels and pieces of sculptured marble; the wrought ivory, and the bone inlaid with turquoise; the small figures cast in bronze; the various musical instruments, such as triangular stones, bells, and ocarinas; the dagger axes, chariot fittings, harness ornaments, and box covers. They indicate a high degree of material culture. Some of them, like the *li* tripod and certain decorative motifs, are obviously descended from Late Stone Age prototypes; others raise serious questions about borrowings from other parts of Asia. Bishop[9]

[8] A. Waley (translator), *The Book of Songs*, p. 248. Two other ancient collections make similar assertions.

[9] Supplement to the *Journal of the American Oriental Society*, LIX:52–53 (December, 1939). See also Max Loehr, *Amer. J. of Archaeology*, LII:135 (June, 1949).

draws particular attention to the celt and spearhead, both sock-
eted, which have earlier forms in the west but not in China. A
puzzling factor, however, is the absence of any evidence of such
advanced work in bronze anywhere between the east and west.

The collapse of the Shang dynasty in the eleventh century
B.C. has been ascribed to the advent of the Chou, a new power
that developed to the west. In all probability the members of
the old ruling house had become effete and were unable to carry
on the hard fighting with frontiersmen born to war and welded
into an effective unit by an able leader. At all events, their capital
was ruthlessly destroyed by the invader and those who escaped
had to flee for their lives. This was an important moment in the
history of civilization in eastern Asia, for the defeat of the Shang
suddenly widened the range of Chinese civilization. Korean history traditionally begins with the overthrow of the Shang. For
over ten centuries the Fu-yü, a people of Manchuria, celebrated
annually a religious rite based on the Shang calendar. Some of
the fleeing Shang adherents too may have reached the Yangtze
state of Ch'u.

The Chou (*ca.* 1027–256 b.c.)[10]

The Early Chou.—The origin and early development of the
Chou people are as uncertain as the origin of the Shang. More
than one western scholar has been impressed with the number
of parallels between the Chou and the Aryans who conquered

[10] For convenience, the long Chou period is often subdivided. The Chinese commonly
divide the last two periods (middle and late) as follows: the *Ch'un Ch'iu,* or spring
and autumn (annals) period, 722 to 481–480; and the *Chan Kuo,* or contending states
period, 403–221. Both of these names are names of books of the period that have
survived. This time-honored subdivision seems artificial; in addition it does not include
the years 479–404. Consequently we shall use the following: early Chou, *ca.* 1027–771,
when the kings actually ruled; middle Chou, 771–473, from the removal of the capital
to the absorption of the Wu state by the state of Yüeh; late Chou, 473–256, when the
struggle for hegemony was narrowing to a contest between Ch'u in the south and Ch'in
in the northwest.

India: both were Bronze Age chariot fighters and both were roughly contemporary, the Aryan invasions taking place shortly before the twelfth century B.C. But the traditional Chinese accounts give no hint of a far-western origin, leading one to conclude—at least until there is proof to the contrary—that the Chou were as Chinese as the Shang and were simply less acquainted with the arts of civilization in the lower reaches of the Yellow River than with the life of the oases dwellers and nomadic peoples to their own west and north. That they were more pastoral than agricultural seems probable. That they stemmed from the region of modern Shensi and Kansu and were aware of the value of the great Szechuan plain to the south is quite clear. They brought with them into eastern China not only the ability to fight and destroy, but also religious and social ideas and customs that differed from those of the Shang. What started them on the road to conquest? It may have been merely lust for power and booty, the probable motivating force behind the Manchu when they conquered China in the seventeenth century A.D. But it is entirely possible that a great ethnic movement that had begun a few decades earlier in western Asia reached the chain of oases in central Asia and, like a ball in table pool, started the Chou moving toward a distant area of low resistance.

The conquest of Shang territory (some fifty states, it is said) lasted approximately twenty years and was accomplished with the aid of chronic enemies of the Shang. When it was completed, the surviving members of the Shang court who were still in central China were permitted to remain in a small section whose center was near modern Kwei-teh in Homan, and to continue their historic sacrificial rites. The Chou kings installed themselves in Shensi near modern Sian, and created a number of fiefs that were governed by relatives and those who had aided in the conquest. At its height, the Chou kingdom extended from south Manchuria in the north to parts of the Yangtze valley in the south, and from eastern Kansu in the west to the seacoast on the

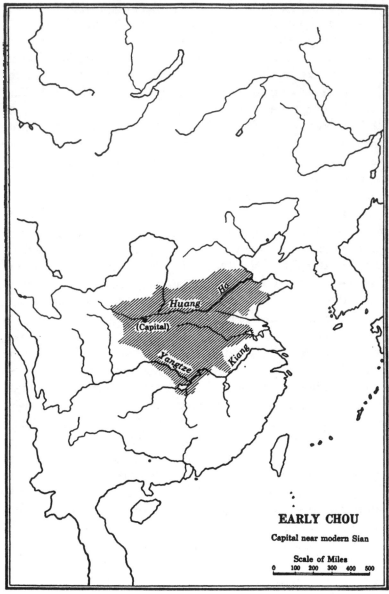

EARLY CHOU

Capital near modern Sian

Scale of Miles

0   100   200   300   400   500

east. On the periphery of this huge area lived small groups of people who long resisted conquest and absorption.

For the larger part of the first two and one-half centuries—about the average length of a strong dynasty in China—the Chou kings were able to maintain their hold on the country. The lords of the fiefs paid their liege lord tribute, both oral and in kind; and his prowess in the field, his skill in settling disputes, and his hold on the loyalty of the common people maintained their respect for him. But by the ninth century, approximately 800 B.C., the authority of the kings had begun to decline to such an extent that the heads of states who had strengthened themselves at the expense of their weaker neighbors dared defy their ruler openly. In 771, the head of the state of Shên, believing himself insulted by the king, asked for and received military support fom a non-Chinese horde.[11] These warriors slew the king, raided his capital, and forced the court to flee to the comparative safety of the Lo River Valley in western Honan. Whereas up to now the Chou kings had wielded both temporal and priestly authority, from then on until the extinction of the dynasty in the third century B.C., they were shorn of their military power and of their right to govern, and were consulted only on questions of legitimacy such as claimants to authority in this or that state. For five centuries China was divided into a number of more or less independent states at varying levels of civilization, which tried to solve the age-old problem of coexistence.

The Middle and Late Chou.—The middle Chou is signalized by the gathering of power on the part of a few princes in the north, by the expansion of the population into the Yangtze valley, and by the creation of Wu and Yüeh, two new states in the southeast where the Yangtze River emptied through three mouths into the Yellow Sea. The late Chou is characterized by the growing strength of Ch'u throughout the entire lower

---

[11] Possibly these warriors were being pressed from the west, for it was during this century that the Scythians invaded southern Russia.

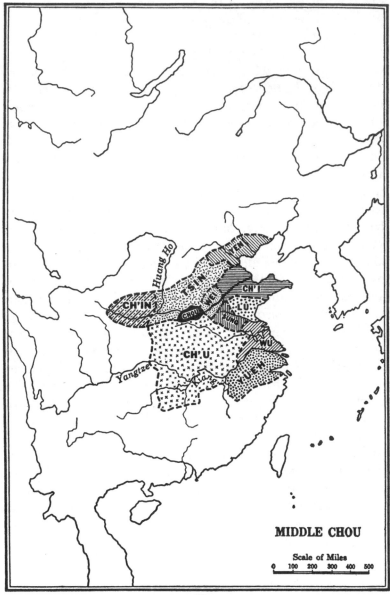

MIDDLE CHOU

Scale of Miles
0   100   200   300   400   500

Yangtze valley (Ch'u absorbed Yüeh in 334), and of the march state Ch'in in the north and west. In the resulting gigantic struggle for supreme mastery of China which continued after the disappearance of the royal house of Chou, the state with the better organization and discipline and the new tactics and weapons emerged victorious (223 B.C.).

Just as this was a period of social and political upheaval, it was also one of creativity and evolutionary development. The Chinese consider this their classical age—when some of their most memorable poetry and prose were composed; when the laws were written down for everyone to see; when market places increased and a money economy appeared; when advances in craftsmanship and methods of production, notably fertilizers, irrigation, and the traction plow, were made; when iron began to displace bronze in common tools and weapons; when science and thinking took great leaps forward, and increasing numbers of new ideas began to seep through the land barriers to the west and southwest to stimulate their own native genius. The very fact that China was in turmoil may have aided these developments. There was no set pattern, no orthodox church, no dominant policy.

The Book of *Odes* gives us, virtually untouched by later hands, the finest picture we have of social conditions of the eighth and seventh centuries B.C. Men sung of their courtship and marriage, women of their errant lovers, soldiers of their misery and the general devastation, princes of their unworthiness; all this and more, together with popular myths and legends, were gathered together, as were the Hebrew Psalms and the Song of Solomon, to form this book.[12] Other early works are omen and divination texts, histories of the royal house and of a few states, and the rituals practiced at court. These constitute a kind of *biblia*, transmitted orally from one person to an-

---

[12] One interesting feature in these odes is the constant use of rhyme, which does not appear in Latin or Arabic poetry until over ten centuries later.

other and then from manuscript to manuscript, often corrupted, that became the textbook for every statesman, seer, and school-boy for two thousand years. Both politicians seeking appoint-ment and the schoolmasters of the day knew much of it by heart and vied with one another in making apt quotations to please or confound their listeners.

Tutors settled in population centers to train boys for public service or wandered from one little court to another seeking ap-pointments as advisors to princes and feudal lords. Some gained a reputation and had large followings; others, disgusted at the chicanery and deceit of the charlatans, or unable or unwilling to make themselves heard above the clamor, retired to their homes to pour out their thoughts to small bands of loyal disciples. After filtering through the minds of a generation or two of their followers, some of the sayings, like those of Socrates or Jesus, were put down in books that are among the milestones of litera-ture and of thought. There are the words of Confucius, who emphasized man's duty to man; of Mo Ti, who championed the underdog, denounced war, and preached mutual love and asceticism; of Yang Chu, the individualist, cynic, and fatalist; and of Chuang-tzŭ the mystic, Lao-tzŭ the anarchist, and the Lord of Shang, founder of the "power and punishments" school of thought. Except for some of the ideas stemming from theo-retical mathematics and pure science, the Chinese of the middle and late Chou periods (the latter in particular) seem to have made most of the discoveries commonly accedited to their con-temporaries the Greeks.

The main accent, however, at least in the works which have been preserved, was on political thought. The school of Con-fucius emphasized the worth-whileness of manly virtue, the need of rites to make social relations possible, the value of calling everything by its right name, and the importance of preserving proper relations between husband and wife, father and son, elder brother and younger brother, ruler and subject, friend and

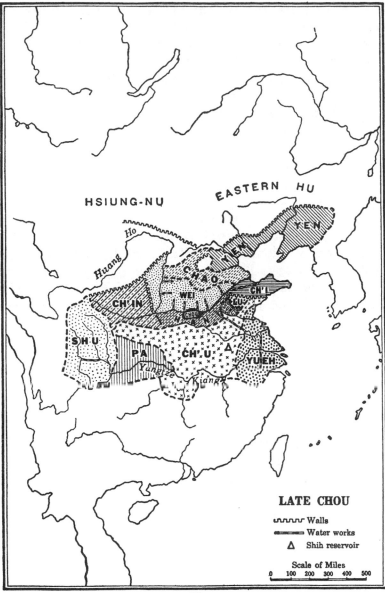

HSIUNG-NU

EASTERN HU

YEN

Huang Ho

CHAO

CH'IN

WEI

CH'I

LU

CHOU

SHU

PA

CH'U

YUEH

Yangtze

Kiang

LATE CHOU

〜〜〜 Walls

▦▦▦ Water works

△ Shih reservoir

Scale of Miles
0   100   200   300   400   500

friend. Applied to the state these ideals were supposed to result in political order. At a later day they were to become highly attractive to builders of empire as they tended to uphold the status quo. The school of Mo, which came closest to setting up a kind of ecclesiastical organization, measured everything in terms of utility to all people, hence the vehement objection to war and the call for simplicity and frugality. The Mo-ists wanted the responsibility for power placed in the hands of the ablest people and expected them to reflect the desires of the multitude; how this ideal situation was to be brought about, however, was not outlined. This school, closest in kinship to modern democratic thought, flourished for several centuries, but seems to have been virtually dead by the first century A.D. The Lao-Chuang school, absorbed by the Taoists a half millennium later, believed: nature dictates all; the way to order life is to do nothing contrary to nature; government is only for those not ordered by nature. Similarly, rites, morals, and the arts, lauded by the Confucians, were out of place in an ideal community. The legalists, of which group Lord Shang was such a forceful spokesman, insisted—in contrast to the followers of Lao-tzŭ— that there must be a rule of law which the state under an un-wavering monarch must obey at all costs.

The production of books on these and kindred topics and their preservation through the centuries argue a healthy intellectual condition among the people. In addition to all the time servers and rough warriors who thronged the royal court, many members both in and outside the slowly developing bureaucracy must have been stimulated and comforted by these writings and have tried to pattern their lives after some of the moral principles set forth. The officeholders, major and minor alike, were both the product and the creators of their environment. Several hundred miles of walls had to be built along the marches for defense against hostile peoples, and these kept constantly in repair. To maintain communities of any size in the river valleys, swamps had to be drained, flood rivers kept in check, waterways and roads built, and water tanks and reservoirs constructed. Some of these engineering projects which were built at the expense of neighboring peoples led to war; others became cooperative enterprises that covered considerable areas, the maintenance of which required a fairly honest and efficient administration. An elaborate protocol was developed to assure proper relations between the states, and a league was created to carry out provisions agreed upon by member bodies. Taxation, census-taking, prevention of famines—these and similar problems of that day which their leaders tried to solve, often with astounding prescience, indicate how rapidly Chinese society was maturing.

There is little question that the Chinese began to come into closer contact with other parts of Asia during the last centuries of the Chou dynasty. Much earlier, as we have seen, they were using the cowry shells that originated on remote tropical shores. Wheat, which was first cultivated in the Near East, appeared in China during the Bronze Age; and the domestic fowl, wet rice, and the water buffalo from around the Bay of Bengal were known by the beginning of the first millennium B.C., if not earlier. The Chinese were never isolated; from the fifth century on, however, such introductions seem to have become more frequent. Two factors are believed to account for this. The Persians under Darius (521–485 B.C.) extended their conquests beyond the Indus in the east and unified all the Iranian tribes under their dominion.[13] The Chinese, furthermore, had reached the point where they were more receptive to new ideas and institutions. Even though travel was enormously difficult and caravans went at great risk over mountain and desert trails, some articles and ideas could be and were transmitted.

Among the foreign cultural infiltrations were the following: The ox-drawn plow, developed in the Near East, appeared pos-

[13] These conquests were repeated by the Greeks under Alexander the Great (337–323).

sibly as early as the sixth century. In the fourth century the Chinese language used the Sanskrit word for lion, an animal that is not native to China. Instead of burying their dead wrapped in grass, the Chinese began to use coffins, an ancient practice in Egypt. Glass beads, similar in design to those of earlier Mediterranean manufacture, were recently discovered in tombs dating from around 400 B.C.[14] Cosmological and geographical ideas that are remarkably Hindu in spirit appear in fourth-century writings. The word *siap-d'iei*, the early Chinese name for one unit of the twelve-year cycle of Jupiter, is possibly derived from the Sanskrit *svāti*. The Chinese may have devised some of their military techniques and weapons, but others of their using were also known outside China. Examples of the latter are the diversion of streams against the mud walls of fortified towns and the use of mines. Horse archers like those on the steppes were used shortly before 300. Riding astride necessitated the adoption of trousers and boots known earlier to the Parthians, also the Scythian cap, and the belt buckle or clasp. Foreign motifs appeared in art—the Parthian flying gallop is an instance—and in science the so-called Pythagorean musical scale and western geometrical axioms. There are also at least two parallel ancedotes in Greek and Chinese literature. Mules, donkeys, and camels, first domesticated in middle Asia or beyond, were first used in China during the third century or earlier. These three animals were to assume extraordinary importance in the everyday life of the Chinese, the camel in particular, for without it the precious Chinese silk could hardly have been taken across the deserts to the rich markets beyond the Pamirs during the centuries immediately preceding and following the birth of Christ.

Far from merely absorbing the ideas and material culture of the people beyond the border, the Chinese underwent their most active intellectual development during this period, a develop-

---

[14] An interesting difference is that the Chinese beads, found in Honan, generally contain barium while the Greek beads do not.

ment so intense that a few brilliant minds seem to have gone to seed. The confusion was so widespread in the third century that the advocates of complete subservience to the state at the cost of all freedom and independence for the individual came into power, together with the most energetic military aggregation in the country's history down to that time. The Shang language, both written and oral, which had fulfilled all the poetic and descriptive requirements during the early Chou period, was showing signs of strain. But the "language crisis" was surmounted, as is shown by the well-ordered arguments of Mencius, who played "St. Paul" to Confucius, the colorful anecdotes of Chuang-tzŭ, and the soaring lyrics of Ch'ü Yüan—all writers of the latter half of the fourth century. Writing implements were improved by superior brushes and better ink and the wider use of silk in rolls. A painting with brush on silk, dating from about 300 B.C., is one of the major finds of recent years. There were other indications of China's native genius. Lacquer was "invented," probably in south China, as a surface for wooden furniture and was used with great skill and artistry, as surviving fourth-century examples show. Bronze mirrors, gold filigree, the use of gold and silver to decorate bronze vessels, and jade ornaments reflect both the wealth and the new demands of the leisured few, as do also the literary references to spacious dwellings and garden retreats. The use of iron resulted in many tools. One somewhat disputed text that probably describes conditions in the fourth and third centuries mentions plowshares, hoes, sickles, sledges, and scythes for the farmer; axes, saws, wheels, wheel hubs, drills, and chisels for the cartwright; and knives, awls, and needles for the women. (Some of the iron tools and molds to fashion them have actually been discovered in sites of this period.) Chopsticks, one of the most characteristic of tools, are first mentioned in the third century; their use marks a long step forward in the history of manners, for it shows that the people had progressed beyond eating with their fingers. The most powerful military weapon was the crossbow, long the Chinese soldier's major means of attack and defense. It enabled the Chinese later to defeat the Huns and the Parthians armed only with the compound bow, and its darts easily pierced the shields of the well-armed Roman legionnaires. The war chariot, a complicated mechanism, as hundreds of late Chou chariot fittings clearly show, was already doomed as in the west, especially after B.C. 133, because of the greater mobility of the horse archer. Progress is also evident in the sciences. By 444 B.C. the year was calculated to have 365¼ days. Other moderately accurate astronomical data, such as information on the planetary movements of Jupiter and Saturn, had been collected by 350. Halley's comet was first observed in 240 B.C.,[15] after which there is an almost unbroken succession of thirty observations down to 1910.

[15] There were two earlier observations in 611 and 467 B.C., possibly of the same comet. Dubs reports that the appearance of the comet calculated for May 163 B.C. is not recorded. Instead a comet appearing on February 6, 162 B.C. is recorded.

CHAPTER II

The First Empires

THE CH'IN (221–207 B.C.)

FOR a century before the final success of the Ch'in, certain princes of China were ambitious for empire or at least supremacy, and one by one they absorbed the weaker princes, including the head of the house of Chou. Scorned by the other states for their uncouthness and barbarity, the people of Ch'in absorbed some of their critics' culture and overlooked no opportunity to improve their military fitness. The teachings of a succession of statesmen who followed the Lord of Shang had made their government the best disciplined and most purposive of any east of the Gobi. In 318 the Ch'in, who dominated the northwest, moved into Szechuan and seized control of the great food-producing plain. The huge irrigation system which the governor and his son reputedly began there about 300 has banished serious floods and droughts for twenty-two centuries and is still in existence. A canal nearly one hundred miles long was cut across Shensi in 246 to enrich the alkaline soil with water laden with silt. The productivity of this region, says the annalist, promptly increased about twenty-eight pecks per square mile. Having thus assured a food supply, the authorities erected a grain station near modern Kaifeng to provision their troops. To break up the feudal system no fief was granted after 238. To guard against rebellion in the rear and to provide labor there was considerable transfer of the population from one province to another during 239–235 B.C. Powerful families—120,000 in all, according to the annalist—were required to move to the capital at Hsien-yang in modern Shensi. By 234 Chêng, who as a young boy had become head of Ch'in in 247, was ready to put his armies in the field and by 222 he had vanquished the last of the rival states. The combination of excellent preparation, constant pressure, and superb mastery of the newest arts of war, especially cavalry, proved too much for his enemies. He promptly created the first empire and assumed the title of First Emperor (Shih-huang-ti); his system of government lasted until the twentieth century.

With the help of Li Ssŭ (280?–208), a minister of outstanding ability, the emperor set to work to establish his house for ten thousand generations. In 221 he decreed that the whole country should be divided into thirty-six military areas; this was shortly increased to forty-one. Each had its military governor, its civil administrator, and its supervisory official. The people were disarmed but were given rights over their property, subject to tax. Promotions and demotions were used as rewards and punishments; other punitive measures were unusually harsh. Nobility was based on gifts and services to the state rather than on birth. Customs and laws, weights and measures were unified; even the axles of wheels had to be uniform. Artisans and farmers were benefited at the expense of merchants.

In 220 Shih-huang-ti began a network of tree-lined roads, fifty paces broad. The sectional walls in the north were joined together to form one long barrier (known to us as the Great Wall), thus for the first time indicating what was China and what barbarian. The Hsiung-nu (possibly the later Huns of the great invasions of Europe) had to be driven from the region south of the great bend of the Yellow River. Forty-four fortified encampments were built along the river (these were occupied by prisoners of war), the waterways deepened, and a long connecting highway constructed. Not content with a territory stretching from the new wall to the southern boundaries of Ch'u in modern Honan, the emperor sent his armies farther south. In a brilliant

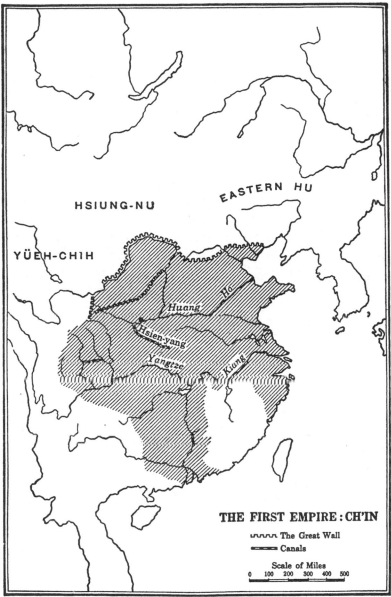

HSIUNG-NU

EASTERN HU

YÜEH-CHIH

Ho

Huang

Hsien-yang

Yangtze

Kiang

THE FIRST EMPIRE : CH'IN

ᴗᴗᴗᴗ The Great Wall

━━━ Canals

Scale of Miles

0   100   200   300   400   500

campaign during 221–214, they conquered the region of Fukien, Kuangtung, Kuangsi, and Tongking. This was achieved largely by the digging of a twenty-mile waterway called "the marvelous canal" which connected two streams and thus made possible water transportation all the way from the Yangtze to the West River.

The many styles of writing in different parts of the country Shih-huang-ti reduced to one. Because he found a large part of the literature of the past too worshipful of another way of life, he ordered it to be burned, except for the imperial archives and books on medicine, divination, farming, arboriculture, and the history of his own house. By this means he sought to destroy sectionalism and any lingering support of the feudal houses, and to unify the "hundred schools of thought." On one occasion he had 460 members of the lettered class, mainly magicians or charlatans, put to death.[1] The scholars whom he valued were unmolested, and he continued the office of Learned Doctor at the court. He himself worked indefatigably, handling "one hundred twenty pounds" of reports each day. He frequently made investigations in disguise, for he both feared assassination and tried to create the impression of divinity. His palace, completed in 212, was assuredly one of the wonders of the world; it measured 2500 feet from east to west and 500 feet from south to north and accommodated 10,000 people. Within a radius of some sixty miles there were 270 lesser imperial residences "connected by covered roads and roads bordered with walls" and furnished with "tents, canopies, bells, drums, and beautiful women."

All of Shih-huang-ti's measures did not spring from the brains of his own generation of leaders. Chinese pamphleteers had advocated some of them for a century and a half or so. Nor is it impossible that certain of them came in from the west. About three centuries earlier Darius had created an empire that de-

---

[1] This is denied by some. See *T'ien Hsia Monthly*, III:423 (November, 1936).

pended in large measure on provincial divisions, arterial roads to connect the provinces, a system of imperial posts, and personal representation. These were also features of the empire of Chandragupta (*ca.* 321–*ca.* 297) in northern India, as Carl W. Bishop has pointed out. Whatever their source, however, such measures in China awaited a man of the First Emperor's genius and absolute power. Although his empire was short lived—it crumbled in the third year of his son's reign—its founding was an event of large importance in world history. The First Empire put into practice for the first time the idea of unity for all the peoples "within the wall," an idea never lost to sight even during the long periods of imperial breakdown that followed. It established a centralized government charged with responsibility not only for law and order but also for public works, government monopolies of basic products, coinage, and the upholding of the rights of the common man as against those of the tradesman. It made the first sharp cleavage between the "we" group and the "they" group in the north and northwest, and sent exiles into Korea and probably elsewhere. The first contacts with the islands of Japan reportedly date from this time, when an expedition set out from Shantung in search of the isles of the immortals.[2] There seems scant doubt that the name of China is derived from the Ch'in because of the great influence of their state and empire on the peoples across Asia. The honor is well deserved.

In spite of its absolutism, however, the empire could not wholly silence two groups—the theorists, who disliked the state whose groundwork they themselves had laid, and the descendants of the princely houses and the ministers of state for whom the empire had no place. Besides these, countless people must have suffered indescribably from the forced labor, the frontier

---

[2] Actually expeditions in search of these isles were sent out as early as the fourth century B.C.; they remind a student of western civilization of the Carthaginian searches for the Insulae Fortunatae in approximately the same period. Cf. W. P. Yetts, *New China Review*, II:290–297 (June, 1920).

military service, and the heavy taxation. According to a later and perhaps biased historian who wrote in the first century A.D.:

> Having united the empire, Ch'in Shih-huang made public works within, and expelled the I and Ti tribes without. He received a tax amounting to the greater half, and sent forth as soldiers (all) to the left of the village gate. The men's exertions in cultivation were insufficient for the grain taxes, and the spinning of the women was insufficient for clothing. The resources of the empire were exhausted in supplying [Shih-huang's] government, and yet were insufficient to satisfy his desires. Within the seas there was sadness and dissatisfaction, and this developed into disorder and rebellion.[3]

When Shih-huang-ti died in 210 while on an expedition far from the capital, his body had to be brought back to Hsien-yang in a closed carriage for fear of a revolt. The removal of his iron hand and his inept son's succession to power resulted in the overthrow of the empire by the various dissatisfied groups in 207. There followed several years of anarchy which ended when the country was reunited by a military officer who had risen from the ranks and who overcame all rival claimants to the throne.

THE HAN

The Early (or Western) Han (202 B.C.–A.D. 9).—Vast problems confronted the new emperor, Liu Chi (or Pang), later known as Han Kao-tsu. Fragments of beaten armies were preying on the countryside; many cities had been looted and some destroyed—the capital had been burning for three months; dikes, dams, granaries, and other public works were in a serious state of deterioration and disrepair. All the new southland deserted Liu at the beckoning of the Ch'in military governor; the peoples north of the Great Wall seized the opportunity for an attack; and only a handful of officers and sycophants proclaimed their loyalty to him.

---

[3] Translation by Derk Bodde, *China's First Unifier*, p. 172.

Although a commoner and a man who might have devoted himself to prolonged orgies in celebration of his final victory over his rivals to the throne, Liu was astute enough to continue most of Shih-huang-ti's measures. He discarded one important feature, however, when he renewed the feudal system and granted fiefs to relatives and favorites throughout the empire. Half a century later (154) they had risen to such power that seven of the princes revolted. Though the revolt was ruthlessly suppressed within a few months the danger to the throne was obvious. Thereafter the policy was adopted of depriving a prince of some territory whenever he offended the court and (in 127) of requiring the eldest son of each prince to share half his father's fief with all his younger brothers. (From then on subdivision of property in every generation became the practice.) Liu was equally astute, when the need for barracks rule was over in 196, in searching for capable men to aid in the complex tasks of government and in the rituals of office. These men made Confucian ideas, somewhat modified by time and custom, dominant at court. This they were able to do both because of their weight in council and because, as tutors to the heir apparent and others of the privileged class, they could influence the next generation. Their progress, however, was slow, for old pre-Confucian superstitions mingled with the *laissez faire* of Lao-tzŭ and Chuang-tzŭ long remained in decided favor among both high and low and among many of the women, and plagued the learned doctors especially in periods of imperial weakness.

Most serious of all problems was that on the northern marches. From one end of the Great Wall to the other Liu was flanked by rising non-Chinese peoples—the Yüeh-chih in Kansu, the Hsiung-nu in Mongolia, and the Tung Hu in Manchuria—peoples whom his predecessors had insulted by their policy of exclusion. Although earlier under the Chou rulers these peoples had occasionally had a part in royal conferences and leagues, they now had the status of barbarians. The Hsiung-nu, who had consolidated their empire at the same time as the Ch'in, were the greatest threat to Han China. Their first chief (d. 210 or 209) had been powerless in the face of Shih-huang-ti's might, but the second, by legend a ruthless, exacting leader and a superlative horseman, swept the Yüeh-chih from the west country and then drove his hordes down on the Yellow River plain from which his people had been expelled a few years earlier. Trapping Liu in a fortified town—something his Chinese contemporaries had been unable to do—he forced the Han emperor to conclude a treaty. Liu secured his freedom by giving the Hsiung-nu chieftain a Chinese princess in marriage, in addition to large quantities of silks, wine, grain, and food. This was the first of many times that the Hsiung-nu asserted their military supremacy—or at least equality—and drove sharp and sometimes humiliating bargains with various Chinese rulers.

Not until near the end of the second century B.C. were steps taken to stabilize relations with the Hsiung-nu. After consolidating his empire, a successor of Liu (d. 195), Wu-ti (r. 140–87), first tried an alliance with their historic enemies, the Yüeh-chih, most of whom had fled westward about 200 B.C. The Hsiung-nu had defeated the remnants of the Yüeh-chih in 176 and again a decade later, killing the latter's last chief and forcing his people to flee to the highlands in northern Tibet. By 128, when Wu-ti sought an alliance with them, the Yüeh-chih had invaded Sogdiana and Bactria beyond the Pamirs and had lost interest in the politics of central Asia. Although Wu-ti's envoy was unsuccessful, his report on conditions in middle and western Asia gave the emperor the courage to send one of the most brilliant young cavalry officers in Chinese history on a campaign against the Hsiung-nu (121–119). While a general attacked on the border, defeating or killing 19,000 of the enemy and capturing a million sheep, this officer penetrated deep into Hsiung-nu territory and seized more than eighty of their chiefs. This campaign firmly established the authority of the Chinese and resulted in great prestige for them. Similar defeats, however, had to be inflicted repeatedly for a century, partly because certain officers of mixed origin who lived in the no-man's-land on the frontier sided now with the Chinese, now with the Hsiung-nu, as their own best interests dictated. A little later (115) Wu-ti sent his first ambassador and other envoys to western Asia; they were followed by armies that subjugated Ferghana and other countries in 101. China's sovereignty continued to be enforced until after 36 B.C., when Chinese soldiers apparently for the first and only time confronted Roman legionnaires in Sogdiana.

Wu-ti's desire to expand his empire sent his armies north and south as well as west. He penetrated Korea to the north or northeast by land and sea and established a colonial administration, centered near modern Pyong-yang, which ruled at least as far south as Seoul, if not beyond. This region was divided into four provinces, the chief one of which, Lo-lang, had a Chinese colony of nearly 63,000 households, or approximately 315,000 people.[4] According to contemporary records, this colony was even more populous and prosperous than those in Liaotung and Shantung, a fact borne out by recent excavations. Here developed a center of culture that penetrated beyond Korea to the still shadowy islands of Japan. In 111 one of Wu-ti's expeditionary forces recaptured the southern kingdom of Nan Yüeh, the center of which was Canton; and for over a century the Chinese ruled this region through local tribal chiefs. Not satisfied with conquest, the emperor sent representatives by boat to seek tribute and homage for their master. By A.D. 2 a few Chinese may have traversed the Indian Ocean; certainly they brought back handsome gifts from far-off lands—pearls, glass, rare stones, curios, and rare birds and animals, including a live rhinoceros—in return for the gold and silk that they offered.

[4] In the great census of A.D. 2, from which these figures are taken, the total population of China is given as 12,233,062 households and 59,594,978 individuals. (*Han shu* 28B/19b.) These figures probably must be corrected upwards to include certain uncounted members of society.

The expense of these expeditions precipitated a financial crisis. The tax on land had been halved around 150 B.C. Since any additional land tax would injure the farmers, who constituted the majority of the population, the court had to seek other means of raising revenue. In 129 a tax was imposed on vehicles and later on boats; this probably affected chiefly the merchant class and the wealthy. In 123, after the emperor rewarded his troops for a series of successful raids against the Hsiung-nu with 200,000 catties of gold (approximately 50,000,000 grams—a huge amount by ancient standards), the court put military titles up for sale, seventeen ranks in all. Four years later the monopolies on salt and iron were again strictly enforced, a practice followed by the Ch'in but sharply criticized in a forum at the court in 81. That same year (119) the currency was cheapened and was likewise made an absolute monopoly of the central government; in 115 death was made the penalty for disobeying this decree. A price regulation board was established in 110 for the twofold purpose of eliminating private speculation in grain and luring the middleman's profits to the imperial treasury. High-ranking nobles were forced to make ill-disguised donations by presenting their scepters of investiture on deerskins which could be purchased only from the government at high cost. It was customary for every man of high rank to make gifts at the annual autumnal sacrifice at the temple of ancestors, and the treasury saw to it that the contributions in 112 were of proper value; 106 lords are said to have been disgraced for shoddy offerings on this occasion. Artisans and merchants were required to declare their personal wealth and were stripped of 4.75 and 9.50 per cent respectively. The manufacture and sale of salt and iron were made a state monopoly in 110 B.C.; the monopoly of fermented drinks was added in 98, only to be given up in 81.

These measures tided the house of Han over the immediate crisis but created new problems. Selfish officials lined their own pockets, and unworthy men achieved high office through mere purchase. Complaints became widespread and led to the gradual repeal of these decrees. It is possible also that by the end of Wu-ti's reign the foreign tribute was sufficient to pay some of the immense costs of empire, as is indicated by the following rebuttal of the charges of his critics made by the Lord Grand Secretary at the above-mentioned forum in 81.

Now the treasures of the mountains and marshes and the reserves of the *equable marketing* system are means of holding the balance of natural wealth and controlling the principalities. Ju Han gold and other insignificant articles of tribute are means of inveigling foreign countries and snaring the treasures of the Ch'iang and the Hu. Thus, a piece of Chinese plain silk can be exchanged with the Hsiung Nu for articles worth several pieces of gold and thereby reduce the resources of our enemy. Mules, donkeys and camels enter the frontier in unbroken lines; horses, dapples and bays and prancing mounts, come into our possession. The furs of sables, marmots, foxes and badgers, colored rugs and decorated carpets fill the imperial treasury, while jade and auspicious stones, corals and crystals, become national treasures. That is to say, foreign products keep flowing in, while our wealth is not dissipated. Novelties flowing in, the government has plenty. National wealth not being dispersed abroad, the people enjoy abundance.[5]

An Interregnum: The Hsin Dynasty (A.D. 9–23).—At the end of Wu-ti's reign (87) China's domestic and tributary empire was at one of its three high points in history.[6] The prestige of Chinese arms remained high until near the close of the century, although the restless states in cental and western Asia had constantly to be disciplined. There was no competent successor to Wu-ti. The dynasty, weakened by court and palace politics and by interference from members of the harem and the eunuchs, succumbed in the first decade of the Christian ear to an extremely able minister, the nephew of the late empress, who served as regent from 1 to 8.

The first and only emperor of the Hsin dynasty was Wang Mang, who ruled from 9 to 23. Although his foreign policy was

[5] Translated by E. M. Gale, *Discourses on Salt and Iron*, pp. 14–15.

[6] The other two occurred in the first and eighth centuries A.D., if the Mongol and Manchu eras are excepted as non-Chinese.

at no time significant—in fact, colonial areas largely freed themselves from China during or shortly after this period of domestic upheaval—his reign left its mark on internal politics. Carefully wrapping himself in a mantle of Confucian righteousness and, like Shih-huang-ti ably served by a state counselor, Wang at once initiated a series of reforms. His first step was to nationalize the land and redistribute large holdings, and to free male slaves[7] and make them private retainers. Finding that these two acts could not be enforced, he repealed them three years later. In 17 he taxed slave owners at the rate of 3600 cash for each slave. He reenacted Wu-ti's monopolies on salt, iron, wine, and coinage, although the monopolies on the last were greatly modified. Wang cheapened the currency, but he also introduced many new coins; and by insisting that gold be turned in for bronze he succeeded in cornering almost all the gold in circulation both within the empire and abroad. Even faraway Rome felt the drain, Tiberius (A.D. 14–37) prohibiting the wearing of silk because it was bought with Roman gold. On Wang Mang's death his treasury was officially reported to have accumulated the equivalent of about five million ounces of the metal, estimated at more than the total supply in medieval Europe.[8] Another of his monopolies concerned the revenue from forest and wild products and from hunting and fishing. Finally he endeavored to stabilize prices by purchasing surplus goods and storing them in warehouses, to impose on certain professional people a tax of one-eleventh of their income, to make officials take a voluntary salary reduction in lean years, to triple the taxes on uncultivated fields, and to make loans either without interest or at 3 per cent per month.

These measures were partly in the Confucian manner, designed not so much to improve the people's lot as to gain politi-

---

[7] Male slaves probably never constituted more than about 1 per cent of the Chinese population, as against some 50 per cent of the population of ancient Greece.

[8] H. H. Dubs, *Journal of Economic History*, II:1, 36–39 (May, 1942).

cal and fiscal control. With a subservient and honest bureaucracy Wang Mang might have succeeded; but sharp and clever officials took advantage of them, capitalists were driven to desperation, and the population, stricken by a Yellow River flood as well, suffered. The antagonisms his actions created and his inability to rely on his court and military officers proved his undoing. When rebellion broke out, practically no one came to his support, and he was cut down by a soldier.

The Later Han (A.D. 25–220).—Several aspirants to the throne appeared on Wang Mang's death; the ensuing struggle lasted for two years until a distant cousin of the former Han emperor emerged victorious. He continued the Han dynastic name. The capital was moved from Ch'ang-an, which had been burned and looted during the struggle for the throne, to Loyang, the ancient capital of the Chou kings.

By the end of the first century China had almost regained its earlier position in world politics. It took a decade or more to pacify the various parts of the country. The area south of Canton rebelled in 40, and in 42–43 an expedition was sent there which subjugated Hainan, Tongking, and Annam. Instead of being made a simple protectorate, this region was incorporated into China as an actual province and remained so almost continuously for nine centuries. Through the ports of near-by Cochin-China, certainly after 120, came envoys and merchants from India, Iran, Syria, and the Roman empire, some of whom ventured northward to mingle with the Chinese.[9] The southwest (modern Yünnan) too, which had drifted out of the imperial orbit some time after its absorption by Wu-ti in 111 B.C., was reconquered in A.D. 69 possibly because of its importance as the terminus of the trade route to India. The population figures of A.D. 140 show decided increases for a large part of south China, some

[9] For discussion of finds made since 1944 at one of the seats of the old kingdom of Phnom, which dominated southeast Asia from the first to the sixth centuries of our era, see G. Coedès, *Artibus Asiae* X:193–199 (1947).

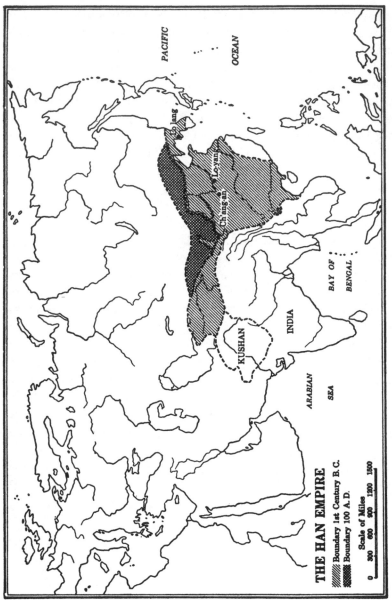

THE HAN EMPIRE

Boundary 1st Century B.C.
Boundary 100 A.D.

Scale of Miles

0   300   600   900   1200 1500

PACIFIC

OCEAN

Lo-yang

Lo-yan

Ch'ang-an

BAY OF

BENGAL

KUSHAN

INDIA

ARABIAN

SEA

nine million all told, as against the figures for A.D. 2, and even greater decreases for the northwest and northeast.[10] China was in active contact with Japan at least as early as 57, and parts of Korea and south Manchuria remained in its hands throughout the Han period. In central and western Asia a series of able commanders aided by small bodies of cavalry and by agricultural colonies established by the army succeeded in keeping the Hsiung-nu and other northern tribes at odds with each other, forced the petty kingdoms centered around the oases of the Tarim basin to capitulate, and even exacted tribute after A.D. 90 from the newly founded Kushan kingdom.[11]

Palace intrigue wreaked havoc with imperial rule toward the close of the first century as the families of the empresses, and even the eunuchs, became all-powerful. The resulting misgovernment, together with an agrarian crisis in Szechuan, brought on a peasant revolt in 184 which marked the beginning of the end for the Han dynasty. This uprising was suppressed, but not until the lust for power had put the warlords, not the emperor, in the saddle. The attempts to oust the eunuchs, who had made a puppet of the emperor years earlier, resulted in a palace revolution in which the ruler was dethroned. His successor became the tool of Tung Cho, an able but ruthless west China general and chieftain. As an indication of the low estate to which the emperor had fallen, Tung is said to have arrogated to himself the privilege of entering the imperial presence at a slow pace, fully booted and armed with his sword, and to have refused to permit anyone to address him by his personal name. The warlord, realizing that his position at Loyang was scarcely tenable, ordered the evacuation of the city and then destroyed it—

[10] Cf. *Hou Han shu* 33/17b and the illuminating discussion and charts of Hans Bielenstein, Museum of Far Eastern Antiquities *Bull. No. 19*, p. 139 (1947).

[11] The heads of this state, which resulted from the Yüeh-chih conquest of Sogdiana and Bactria, ruled from Afghanistan to northwest India during the first two centuries of our era. The use of the classical Chinese title, Son of Heaven, by the Kushan kings reflects their ancestors' long residence on the Kansu border.

palaces, temples, government buildings, and private homes. This did incalculable cultural damage, for the city had been the center of Chinese civilization for two hundred years. Though some of the archives (seventy cartloads of them) are reported to have been removed with the young emperor to Ch'ang-an, the former capital, only half of them were saved. Even the tombs of the Han emperors, the mounds of which can still be seen on the ridge above the Lo valley, were rifled of everything then considered valuable—an act which indicates in no uncertain terms the regard in which the house of Han was held. Other warlords raised the banner of rebellion in other parts of the country, with the result that China was shortly divided into a number of armed camps and the emperor's power hardly extended beyond his throne. A group of the rebels brought about Tung Cho's assassination in 192, the most brilliant of them, Ts'ao Ts'ao, emerging as dictator. Finally, on the latter's death in 220, his son deposed the emperor, thus ending the fiction of the Han dynasty.

Han Culture

If the Chou is the classical age of China, the Han is the imperial. This period has so fired their imagination and flattered their ego that the Chinese often call themselves "men of Han." Institutions may have had their start under the Chou and Ch'in emperors, but they attained their greatest height under the Han. There were new developments, enriched by intrusions from the outside, in science, art, literature, music, industry, and sport. A great deal of exact knowledge of the era is available not only through a large amount of historical and other writing that has survived but also from the recent discoveries in China or near the borders (Korea, Liaotung, Japan, Vietnam, Mongolia, central Asia) and beyond. All indicate a new atmosphere and the great expansion of China.

Precisely marked sundials of the second century B.C. show that Chinese timekeepers divided the day into 100 equal parts; water-clocks were graduated in 120 divisions in A.D. 8, but prior to that also in 100 divisions. In this they were far ahead of the Europeans, for the latter did not use equal units until the thirteenth century. In 104 B.C. the Grand Astrologer and Archivist, Ssŭ-ma Ch'ien, and others ordered reforms to be made in the calendar; their method was as follows: "Thereupon they determined the points east and west, set up sundial and gnomons, and contrived water-clocks. With such means they marked out the twenty·eight 'Mansions' according to their positions at various points in the four quarters, fixing the first and last days of each month, the equinoxes and solstices, the movements and relative positions of the heavenly bodies, and the phases of the moon."[12] The first, fourth, seventh, and tenth moons inaugurated the four seasons, and the second, fifth, eight, and eleventh moons contained the equinoxes and solstices. This was the official calendar until 1912, and continued in use unofficially. Liu Hsin, Wang Mang's distinguished counselor, reckoned the year at $365^{385}\!/_{1539}$ solar days. Galileo was the first European scientist to discover sunspots, publishing his work in 1613—while the Chinese had observed them with some regularity since 28 B.C. In the first century A.D. the Chinese devised special instruments to observe the ecliptic and measure its obliquity. About the same time two scholars remarked that the moon's orbit was elliptical and that the moon makes a complete revolution once in nine years. (Actually one complete revolution takes 8.85 years.) In 132 a scientist at the capital invented a remarkable instrument which registered earthquakes so faint that people at the court did not notice them, but no further improvements were made on this primitive seismograph. This scientist, Chang Hêng (78–139), deserves to be mentioned too for an equally remarkable

[12] *Ch'ien Han shu,* chap. 21; translated by W. P. Yetts, *The Cull Chinese Bronzes,* p. 162.

statement made in his book *Ling hsien:* "There are 124 stellar configurations within the circle of perpetual apparition. Altogether stellar groupings with names assigned amount to 320, containing 2500 stars. This does not include stars in the southern sky which have been reported by navigators in remote regions. If we count the fainter stars, the number may be increased to 11,520."[13]

In mathematics the Chinese used the place value system in the first century B.C., if not earlier. The number 16448664375 was written | ⊥ ||| ≡ ⫴ ⊥ T≡ ||| ⊥|||||. A zero was not used, but the space left empty. Also during the early Han, mathematicians wrote that 1 could be elevated to 100 by shifting its place two spaces. Not until later did India use the place value system.

A scientific attitude also appears in the writings of Wang Ch'ung (*ca.* 27–100), who fought against current superstitions that almost constituted a theology. Popular belief held that such catastrophes as fires, floods, famines, and earthquakes, and such anomalies as eclipses and comets were heaven-sent manifestations of displeasure and warning to the emperor. Well schooled in astronomical knowledge by the leading historian of his day, Wang Ch'ung refuted this in saying: "On an average, there is one moon eclipse in about 180 days, and a solar eclipse in about every 41 or 42 months. Eclipses are regular occurrences and are not caused by political action. All anomalies and catastrophes are of the same class and are never dependent upon political events."[14] Actual observation and a critical spirit seem to have been gaining headway around the end of the first century and the beginning of the second century A.D., but political and social deterioration cut them short.

That sculpture in the round was known is apparent from a few life-sized monuments around tombs which strongly indicate Assyrian or other counterparts. Most of the sculpture, however,

13 Translation of Y. C. Chang in *Popular Astronomy* 53:124 (1945).
14 Translated by Hu Shih, in *Symposium on Chinese Culture*, p. 44.

was in low relief in funerary chambers; it is so delicately chiseled as to suggest painting in stone. There are all too few remains of actual paintings, but they must have been familiar sights in cultural centers for all the materials and instruments we know now were in use in China by the second century A.D. From early literature we learn that by the first century of our era painting had risen from an artisan's job to the accomplishment of a professional of some standing; and the emperor Ming (58–76) patronized the art. There remain today only a few representations on tiles, lacquer, and the walls of sepulchers. One basket unearthed in 1931 in a tomb near Lo-lang in Korea is decorated with ninety-four sitting and standing figures painted in lacquer. Lacquer itself must have been extremely popular, for it has been found by archeologists almost everywhere that was settled by the Chinese—in Mongolia, the Altai Mountains, Indo-China, and Korea. One vessel found in a Korean tomb and bearing a date corresponding to A.D. 4 contains the names of two artists that also appear on another lacquer vessel of 2 B.C. found at far-distant Noin-Ula near Ulan Bator. That high-born Han ladies were not unlike their modern sisters is shown by a Lo-lang lacquer case that contains a mirror and six little boxes of varying shapes for rouge and paint,[15] Some of these lovely trifles were made in the western province of Szechuan—another startling evidence of the mobility of the age. Glazed pottery appeared and, at the end of the Han period, the first faint attempts to work in porcelain. Certain vessels with collars and bands showing naturalistic scenes in low relief are highly prized as giving documentary evidence of contemporary life; so also are the clay figures of people, animals, houses, barnyards, stoves, and the like that have been unearthed in tombs.

Architecture, particularly that of the palaces, is elaborately

[15] Archeologists have even turned up some of the carbonate of lead that was used as face powder in the first centuries of our era: Harada working in Lo-lang, and Bergman in Lou-lan in central Asia. See *Lolang* (1930), p. 33, and *Sino-Swedish Expedition*, VIII:1, 126 (1939).

described in both poetry and prose—pillars inlaid with jade; walls and cornices decorated with precious stones; woodwork carved, painted, and gilded (partly for preservation); ceilings covered with latticed floral designs; stairs built of carved marble. Except for a few foundations, however, clay models and bas reliefs are the only surviving evidence. The Mediterranean area had long known how to make bricks; knowledge of the process spread during this period, bricks being used particularly in building tombs. Wu-ti's imperial garden was world-famous. It contained new products which he brought in from the west, notably alfalfa for an imported breed of horses, and grapevines to provide his table with fruit and wine. After his conquest in 111 B.C. he also introduced southern products—oranges and areca and litchi nuts, among others.[16] His woods were stocked with animals for hunting, and two artificial lakes were equipped with pleasure boats and craft for war maneuvers. One poet wrote of his empress "gazing about her from the high Orchid Terrace. Amid the perfume of cassia trees, peacocks flocked together, monkeys screamed, kingfishers gathered, and phoenixes flew about."[17]

Commerce with distant lands breathed new life into some of the minor arts. Chinese lapidaries had long made knives and pendants from the jade found in certain river bottoms, but now the stone was brought from distant mines in Khotan and carved in new and curious shapes, including seals for state documents. Jewelers sought the pearls, glass, and rare stones (among them, diamond points) in ports on the southern seas and the Indian Ocean. After reaching two high points during the Shang and late Chou periods, bronze work declined. One form, however, the bronze mirror, is in evidence in outposts of Chinese civilization. Supposedly envoys valued these expertly cast reflectors into

---

[16] This practice was continued in later centuries. For example, the walnut tree, first cultivated west of China, seems to have been planted in the palace gardens at Loyang in the second century A.D.

[17] Ssŭ-ma Hsiang-ju (d. 117 B.C.). See A. Soper, *Art Bulletin*, XXIII:2, 144 n. (June, 1941).

which the emperor may have glanced; they had mystic significance as well. Silk, both plain and embroidered with grotesque
animals and symbolic Chinese characters, was made not only for
domestic consumption but also for foreign trade. The Scythians
and Hsiung-nu craved it before 200 B.C., as did the western
peoples after Wu-ti's campaigns. Examples of early silk have
been discovered in the frozen soil of the Altai, northern Mongolia, and Siberia, in the sands of the Takla-makan, and in
Palmyra, Kirghizia, and the Crimea.

Literature had new modes of expression resulting from the
common language and script, the long periods of domestic peace,
the larger leisure class, and the growth of education among the
privileged. This last is due to the fact that, after 165 B.C. and
especially after 124, many members of the growing bureaucracy
were selected on the basis of written examinations.[18] A Confucian
college of doctors had only fifty students when it was established
in 84 B.C.; 250 years later there were thirty thousand. The books
used there were strictly classical;[19] hence the desire to secure
correct texts and to copy and interpret them became one of the
most important tasks of the learned. By the close of the first
century before our era it was found that fewer books had been
lost in the strife at the end of the Ch'in dynasty than was generally believed. The first national bibliography dates from these
years; prepared by a corps of specialists in medicine, military
science, philosophy, poetry, divination, and astronomy, it lists
some 677 works written both on wooden tablets and on silk. In
spite of the hazards to which it was subjected in the destruction
of the capital in A.D. 23–25, the imperial library was at least
partly saved. Two thousand cartloads of books were borne away

---

[18] Actually there seems to have been no *system* of public examination during the
Han. The majority of the candidates for official positions were recommended to the
capital by provincial authorities. A prime requisite for such candidates was a comfortable
fortune.

[19] They generally included the *Odes*, the *Document of History*, the *Canon of
Changes*, one of the *Rituals*, the *Spring and Autumn Annals*, and sometimes the
Analects of Confucius.

to Loyang. So far as is known these have since completely disappeared, but fortunately several thousand fragments of manuscripts on wood, and a complete volume of seventy-seven tablets bound with the original thongs, have recently been recovered from the refuse heaps near the ancient watch towers of central Asia. Those of the latter that have been examined are not scholarly tomes but reflect the needs of soldiers on campaign—treatises on divination and astrology, primers, calendars for 63, 59, 39 B.C., and the like. Paper was invented about A.D. 100, and it gradually began to displace bamboo and wood, and to a less extent silk, as a writing material. Great as the invention was, it is an open question whether, from the standpoint of literature, it did not come too early; for if the invention of printing had followed it closely, Chinese books would have been available in greater numbers and have had a wider distribution. As it is, too many have been lost through either disintegration or catastrophe.

Archivists are as old as Chinese history, but not until the Han period were there historians. The earliest annals are concerned solely with factual matter which in the later chronicles is interspersed with imaginative stories. The *Shih chi*, Memoirs of an Historian, the first history in which truth was sifted from fancy, did not appear until 100 B.C. Its author, Ssŭ-ma Ch'ien, was the son of a Grand Astrologer who himself bore the same title; he was one of the best-traveled scholars of his day. He wrote modestly about his history: "My narrative consists of no more than a systematization of the material that has been handed down to us. There is therefore no creation; only a faithful representation."[20] Historians of later times did his work the high compliment of following its pattern fairly faithfully.

The family of historians whose work succeeded his a century and a half later achieved almost equal reputation. They differed

---

[20] Edouard Chavannes has translated, or given in abridged form, the first 47 of the 130 chapters of this history. This translation, with prolegomena and other aids, appears in *Les mémoires historiques de Se-ma Ts'ien*, 5 vols. (Paris, 1895–1905). For the life of the author, see Burton Watson, *Ssŭ-ma Ch'ien: Grand Historian of China* (1958).

mainly in the fact that they dealt only with the 230 years from the collapse of the Ch'in empire to the founding of the later Han,[21] whereas Ssŭ-ma Ch'ien regarded the entire past as his field. Only by reading these two histories can one hope to obtain insight into the method and treatment of these writers. Of value in this connection is a critique written by Pan Piao (3–54), the father of Pan Ku and Pan Chao and the teacher of Wang Ch'ung, who was mentioned earlier. It must be remembered, however, that literary criticism was still in its infancy, and that the freedom of thought of the second century B.C. had given way, by the middle of the first century A.D., to a fairly rigid dogmatism among the men at the Han court. Pan Piao wrote:

. . . The work of Ssŭ-ma Ch'ien is most valuable for the period from the origin of the Han up to the emperor Wu, but as for the manner in which he has collected classical texts, reassembled commentaries on them and given extracts of the writings of the hundred schools, he is, in a very great number of cases, negligent and incomplete, and does not give proper value to the original texts. His preoccupation and his desire are to make his memoirs as abundant as possible; it is the amplitude of his work which is its glory. In his critical discussions he is superficial and not sure; when he discusses points of doctrine he venerates Huang-ti and Lao-tzŭ and treats lightly the five canonical books. When he speaks of commerce he makes of little importance kindness and justice, and makes of poverty and misery something shameful. When he discourses on vagabonds who have paid for their misdeeds, he speaks slightingly of those who only did their duty, and praises a bold fellow of low degree. These are grave faults by which he has injured the true and right; that is why he was made to suffer so frightful a punishment. Nevertheless he exposes facts and their meaning; he is a clever writer without being florid; he is full of matter without being coarse; form and substance are in him in proper balance. These are the qualities of an excellent historian. In truth, if one could have made Ssŭ-ma Ch'ien depend on the rules of the five classics and if he might have been in accord with the sage [Confucius] in his judgments of approval and disapproval, his genius would be then very close to perfection.[22]

---

21 Dr. H. H. Dubs has made a translation of the basic annals of this text, three volumes of which have appeared: *The History of the Former Dynasty by Pan Ku* (Baltimore, 1938, 1944, 1955).

22 Cf. Chavannes, *op. cit.*, I, pp. ccxl–ccxli.

In addition to history and criticism, other forms of literature achieved some importance. After a tentative beginning in the *Literary Expositor* by an unknown author of about 200 B.C., lexicography was given a definite place by the *Shuo wên chieh tzŭ* in A.D. 100. It was compiled by one scholar after years of preparation during which he traveled to many parts of China, and it contains an explanation of 9353 characters and of 1163 which have a double use. This scholar was primarily concerned with the written forms of characters, but he also indicated the sounds given to the words in the different regions. From this and other sources modern investigators have ascertained that most Chinese dialects were monosyllabic but that a polysyllabic language was spoken by the people of Wu in the Soochow-Shanghai-Hangchow triangle. This helps to explain the marked dialectal break that exists even today in the language spoken around the mouth of the Yangtze and that spoken along the littoral down to Canton. Special forms of poetry (perhaps of southern origin, for they abound in the myths and legends of the Yangtze River), stories about supernatural beings, and codes of law should be mentioned;[23] so too highly moral "Lessons for Women" that remind a Westerner of St. Paul's letter to Timothy, treatises on geography, and the first commentaries on the canon.

Music, which had long been enjoyed by both high and low,[24] was enriched by two and possibly three new instruments. One was a kind of lute or mandolin that the Chinese called *p'i-pa;*

[23] The code when complete was immense, running to 960 volumes in 7,732,200 words. It is no longer extant, but modern compilations, based on ancient sources, exist. See J. Escarra, *Le droit chinois* (Peking, 1936), pp. 95, 470, 495.

[24] On one occasion Confucius is alleged to have said (*Analects*, XV:10): "For music one would take as model the Succession Dance, and would do away altogether with the tunes of Chêng, . . . for the tunes of Chêng are licentious. . . ." (Translation by Waley.) Waley draws attention to the following passage from the *Li Chi*, XIX, about two contemporaries of Confucius: " 'How is it,' the Prince of Wei asked Tzu-hsia, 'that when I sit listening to old music, dressed in my full ceremonial gear, I am all the time in terror of dropping off asleep; whereas when I listen to the tunes of Chêng and Wei, I never feel the least tired?' "

its appearance probably resulted from China's contacts with Bactria. (The name for a similar instrument in Persian is *barbat* or *barbud;* in Greek, *barbiton.*) According to Gandharan monuments of the first and second centuries, its body was round and it had a board of four strings; the player held it against his breast and sounded the strings with a plectron. This was essentially the first Chinese lute, and was first mentioned by two second-century Chinese writers. Another instrument, probably stringed, was called the *k'ung-hou* or *k'an-hou.* Although there is little definite information regarding it, one writer who died in A.D. 126 said that "it produces a soft amorous tone, and later appeared in place of music which was obscene." A third may have been a kind of fourteen-stringed zither with a bamboo body; this was possibly of southern origin.

Industry must have seen wide advances over such a long period as the Han, as the Chinese came in contact with the peoples to the west and south and put their own ingenuity to the solution of new problems. One scholar[25] has drawn attention to the introduction of the following in agriculture: drought-resistant rice; intertillage; early and late crops; improved crop rotation with beans;[26] the utilization of slopes for bamboo, fruit, vegetables, wood, and fuel; and strip ditches to reclaim waste land for at least partial productivity. One especially active commissary official who was appointed about 87 B.C. made a practice of assembling the "prefects, chiefs, petty chiefs, and vigorous cultivators together with hamlet elders who were good farmers" and giving them special implements for plowing, planting, and hoeing, and instructions in the best methods of using them.[27] Of major importance in agriculture, industry, and war was the development of the breast strap by the Chinese for their draft animals. As is often the case with such things, there is no men-

[25] Mabel Ping-hua Lee, *Economic History of China,* pp. 149–151.

[26] The well-known soybean had probably been known for a long time, although it is not definitely mentioned until the second century B.C.

[27] Cf. C. Martin Wilbur, *Slavery in China During the Former Han Dynasty,* p. 343.

tion of this in any of the writings of the period, but it appears unmistakably in bas-reliefs of the second century A.D. Animals in the west were not so harnessed until ten centuries later.

One passage in Ssŭ-ma Ch'ien's history (also translated by Dr. Wilbur[28]) lists the commodities consumed annually in a trade center and thus throws light on the products of his time (100 B.C.): "1000 horses, 1000 oxen, 1000 brace of sheep and hogs, 1000 (slave) youths and . . . wine, pickle, pickle juice, butchered cattle, sheep and hogs, grain, fuel, boats (by total length), planks of lumber, bamboo, light carriages, oxcarts, lacquered wood utensils, bronze utensils, plain wood and iron utensils, . . . delicate or colored cloth, thick cloth, lacquer, wine mash and salt beans, salt- and fresh-water fish, jujubes and chestnuts, furs of fox and sable, pelts of kid and lamb, mats, fruits. . . ."

Data on the amusements of the Han period have come both from literature and from representations on pottery, brick, and stone. The art of falconry probably originated among the nomads of the north, as may also the many forms of acrobatics on horseback. Circus-like performances on a pole with a crossbar—one performer sitting astride and two others swinging from the ends of the crossbar to the accompaniment of music—is thought to be Chinese, as is also miming in a chariot. Juggling with balls is mentioned as early as 300 B.C.; but about 110 B.C. the king of Parthia sent to the Chinese emperor "fine jugglers from Li-chien" (which may be an attempt to name Alexandria in Egypt, then famous for this form of entertainment). Stilts are referred to by the philosopher Wang Ch'ung. Football, which was used to keep soldiers in fighting condition, is mentioned in several pre-Christian texts and depicted on a second-century slab. Dancing was common for both men and women. The dancers usually wore long coats with long sleeves which they waved as they stepped in time to the music of flutes, hand organ, zither, mando-

[28] *Ibid.*, p. 336.

lin, and drums. Bull and cock fights and tugs-of-war were probably of southern origin. Archery, foot and dog races, fishing and
hunting were all of ancient lineage but still had many devotees.
The more sedentary among the Chinese enjoyed such games as
wei-ch'i, a kind of draughts played on a square board, and various
gambling devices such as pitch-pot and knuckle bones. Both the
shadow play and puppetry are thought to have originated in this
era; in the long history of the stage they may have exercised
considerable influence on the drama of the Middle Ages.

CHAPTER III

The Period of Political Disunion

THE THREE KINGDOMS AND WESTERN TSIN (A.D. 220–317)

FOR some three hundred years the people of China had lived a relatively stable existence. There had been upheavals, particularly during periods of imperial weakness, but in general the governing group had weathered them fairly successfully and maintained a remarkable continuity. By the end of the second century of our era, however, the growing discontent became uncontrollable and the house of Han was overthrown.

The extinction of the Han dynasty was followed by half a century of contention for the throne among the three royal houses in the three chief economic and political areas—the Wei in the north and northwest, with Loyang as their capital (220–265); the Wu in the southeast and south, their capital being moved from Wu-ch'ang to Nanking (222–280); and the Shu or Shu Han in the west and southwest, with Ch'êng-tu as their capital (221–264). Every prince and adventurer strove to restore the empire. The Wei were successful, largely because of their astute use of military agricultural colonies, the enlargement of their own irrigated supply bases, and their policy of submitting the enemy to prolonged starvation instead of meeting him in open combat. In 264 one of their officers subdued Shu; in 265 he usurped the power of his own master, and in 280 he crushed the Wu. The new imperial house which he established—the Tsin—had a somewhat hazardous existence until 420.

Changes of considerable importance resulted from the Chi-

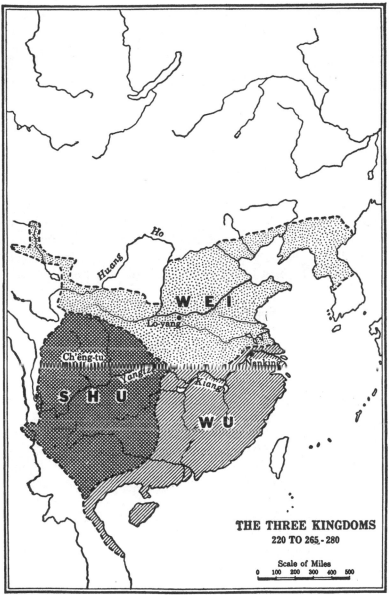

THE THREE KINGDOMS
220 TO 265 - 280

Scale of Miles
0   100   200   300   400   500

nese penetration south and west and their military activities. The long destructive wars brought famine to many areas and drove the impoverished farmers into banditry or to the support of some one of the great families; thousands of people, aristocrats among them, were forced out of their ancient holdings in the Yellow River valley to newly opened regions elsewhere. Feudalism reappeared; the great landowning class resorted to fortresses and walls as a means of defense. The disintegration of the central power meant corresponding gains for local self-government and officialdom. The sectionalism that was one of the immediate effects was accentuated by the increased merging of Chinese with non-Chinese. Many of the latter drifted into north China or entered as allies, and many Chinese married into the hitherto unassimilated non-Chinese peoples in the south and southwest. In addition, people were deliberately shifted from one region to another. In 225, for example, after a memorable expedition into the southwest, the Chinese commander moved "ten thousand families" of an aboriginal tribe from Yünnan into the western province of Szechuan. The lack of currency made barter common again. This was an age of transition from stability to anarchy, from the solid bases of living to complete insecurity.

Such conditions, difficult as they were for all classes of people, were better suited than any other for the infiltration of new ideas, new institutions, new customs, and new products. Of all these new influences, Buddhism had the most enduring effect; it is the most deeply rooted of any foreign religion in eastern Asia today. No one knows just when it appeared. Alexander's campaign late in the fourth century B.C. may have brought Buddhism into Bactria and elsewhere west of the Pamirs. The Indian empire of Asoka extended it not only to the northwest but also to Ceylon. Undoubtedly the Chinese envoys who went to Afghanistan or ventured into the Indian Ocean between 128 B.C. and A.D. 6 saw evidences of this religion and may have brought back word of it on their return home. Similarly the foreign envoys who came to the Chinese court at Ch'ang-an or Loyang may have told the emperor or a courtier about it. In fact, one of the earliest references, although an obscure one, tells of an ambassador of the king of the Yüeh-chih (their land later became part of the Kushan empire) orally instructing a Chinese official in the Buddhist sūtras in 2 B.C. By A.D. 65 there was a community of Buddhist monks and acolytes (whether any of them were foreign will probably never be known) in what is now northern Kiangsu, near the estuary of the Yangtze; they were under the protection of the reigning emperor's brother. A decree issued by this monarch contains transliterations of the words for Buddha, śramana, and upāsaka—an example of linguistic borrowing which was to expand greatly in the next few centuries.

Between A.D. 148 and 170, a Parthian prince(?), whom the Chinese called An Shih-kao, voluntarily abdicated his throne to enter the church. His missionary activities in China reached from the capital to the coast; the Buddhist center which he reported finding at Loyang must have developed considerably during his ministry. He not only taught, he also brought together groups of scholars to translate certain sūtras into Chinese. Their method of handling the extremely difficult problem of putting alien ideas expressed in unknown terms into another language is illuminating. For example, one group of these scholars included an Indian monk who knew no Chinese, a Parthian monk who could speak both Sanskrit and Chinese, and four or five Chinese scholars. The Indian recited the sūtras and explained them orally; the Parthian translated them orally into Chinese as well as he could, and the native Chinese put his translation in writing. As might be expected, the scholarship was not of the best, and many of the earliest translations had to be done two or three times. The influence of An Shih-kao's missionary work extended beyond the scholars into the imperial court but failed to convert the emperor completely. Adopting a cautious role, he not only erected a temple to Lao-tzŭ and Buddha in the palace and worshiped there in 166, but he also put up a flowered canopy to the legendary Yellow Emperor. His hypocrisy was evident, for an official boldly informed him that the abuses in the palace were not in keeping with Buddhist and Taoist doctrines and urged him "to respect life and despise killing; to lessen his desires, abandon excess, and esteem Non-interference."[1]

In addition to its growth in the capital which the destruction of the city, already mentioned, failed to halt, Buddhism was spreading elsewhere. A bas-relief dating from A.D. 76–83 showing six tusked elephants—an early Indian motif—was sculptured in southern Shantung. During the 170's a stūpa or reliquary was placed on a tomb near the present capital of Shantung province. A few years later another stūpa several stories high was constructed in a temple near modern Hsü-chou in northern Kiangsu; the temple contained a gilt statue of Buddha. When the statue was baptized, the donor of the stūpa distributed food to the multitude (the temple area held three thousand people) and also provided them with straw matting covering four to five square *li* (a square of about half a mile on each side). Allowances should perhaps be made for some of these figures, but they were reported by a writer (whose book dates from *ca.* 220) and hence may well have a basis in fact. The first Chinese monk whose name has come down to us came from what is now Anhui province; he worked with a Buddhist missionary from Parthia. There are also indications that Buddhism appeared in southwest China: late Han cave reliefs at Ma Hao, Szechuan, brought to light recently, include a figure of the Buddha.[2]

The third century saw an increase in Buddhist activity both north and south, and a not surprising deepening of interest in Buddhism on the part of the people. Pious and intellectual men in India, Sogdiana, Khotan, Ceylon, and nearby centers of the new faith must have realized that the Chinese were worthy of

---

[1] Translation by Ware, *T'oung Pao*, XXX:121 (1933).
[2] See R. Edwards, *Artibus Asiae*, XVII:103 (1954).

their missionary efforts; and the Chinese, torn and embittered by the sectional warfare at home and probably also disgusted at the depths to which official morals had fallen, were ready to welcome a faith that brought comfort in a time of stress and seemed to answer every need. As Reichelt has written: "Confucianism never succeeded in satisfying the deeper religious needs of the Chinese; it gave no answer to the deepest questions of existence; it gave neither strength for the battle of life nor comfort in the hour of death." Clenell characterizes Buddhism "as a faith for the multitude, as a rule of life for the devout, as a consolation, much more than as a philosophy, for the cultured." Buddhism in part substantiated Chinese religious ideas and in part supplemented them. But its most important appeal lay in the fact that it introduced the idea of karma and of transmigration of the soul which replaced the old notion of fatalism, of the retribution of good and evil; it ushered in the worship of ideas symbolically represented in clay and stone, some of which are treasures of loveliness; it gave to a people whose religion had hitherto contained neither heaven nor hell not one of each but many; and it showed the way to immortality after death through attainment of arhatship or Buddhaship. In short, Buddhism gave to China all that India and neighboring lands had to give. Some of it was good, and some was bad, as for example "the ideas of the world as unreal, of life as painful and empty, of sex as unclean, of the family as an impediment to spiritual attainment, of celibacy and mendicancy as necessary to the Buddhist order, of almsgiving as a supreme form of merit, of love extended to all sentient beings, of vegetarianism, of rigid forms of asceticism, of words and spells as having miraculous power."[3]

Many of the missionaries were marked by their breeding and culture, and they came from every Buddhist region. One of

[3] Hu Shih, in *Independence, Convergence, and Borrowing*, p. 225. One may question whether the Buddhists of India regarded sex as unclean. Actually, like all Indians, they thought that descriptions of natural processes could do no harm. It took the Chinese, raised in the Confucian tradition, several centuries to understand this.

them, a translator who worked in Nanking from 223 to 253, was descended from a Scythian family established in China in the last quarter of the second century. An Indian in 250 made the first translation of the 250 articles in the monastic rules (this is important because it implies a growing demand on the part of Chinese congregations). One missionary working in Loyang in 252 came from the region of the Oxus River; he revised the *Amitâyus sûtra* of An Shih-kao. Another, who was active in Nanking from 247 (or 241) until his death in 280 (or 276), came from a family of Sogdian origin that had established itself in Tongking in the interests of the South Seas and Indian trade; he succeeded in converting the king of Wu and persuaded him to erect a stūpa. A prince of Kucha in central Asia served as a missionary at Loyang in 259. Other instances could be cited to show the diverse backgrounds of the Buddhist missionaries and the varied forms of Buddhism they introduced.[4] Both Hinayāna (or Theravada) and Mahāyāna, were well represented, as well as other forms of Indian and Iranian worship and thought. One reason for the striking success of the Buddhist missionaries was probably the fact that they captured both the minds and the hearts of the Chinese without resort to force.

The influence of the Indians spread into other fields. Medicine was greatly enriched and Indian influence on architecture was evident. The stūpas that began to dot the Chinese landscape were probably patterned after the Mahābodhi temple of Bodhgayā or the stūpa of Kanishka near Peshawar, or other similar buildings. There are practically no extant remains of the earliest ones; however, a pillar discovered by a French explorer and

---

4 According to a recently published list of those who served in China and helped in the translation of Buddhist texts from the second century to the eleventh, 76 came from India, Kashmir, and Ceylon; 30 from Parthia, Sogdiana, Gandhara, and other regions in western Asia; 16 from Khotan, Kashgaria, Kucha, and Turfan in central Asia; and 3 from Java and Cambodia. This of course is only a fraction of the total Buddhist missionary population. Professor Pelliot is authority for the statement that almost all the first translators were Iranian, not Indian (*La haute Asie*, p. 10).

bearing a date equivalent to 209 was copied from indubitable Irano-Indian models. By the end of the century, according to a sixth-century author, there were forty-two stūpas in Loyang alone. Many of the furnishings of these buildings must have been of foreign origin or been copied from foreign models.

New forms of writing appeared in Chinese literature as a result of the translation of the sūtras. The *jātaka* tales added new material to the folklore of China; two collections of these stories were translated into Chinese around 250 by the Sogdian missionary Sêng-hui at Nanking.[5] The first Chinese catalogue of Buddhist literature dates from about 260. The new language, Sanskrit, had an immediate effect on the Chinese language. Besides introducing new ideas and new terms—the number of the latter has been put at 6000 by Eitel and at 7000 by Ogihara —it created a demand for the devising of methods to transcribe the unknown tongue. Indian chants began to enrich Chinese music. The ceremonial burning of incense may have come in from the south by the end of the third century, if not much earlier. During the Han period the śramana had shaved their heads and worn red clothing, but after 220 they adopted habits of various colors. One of the most important causes of the spread of Indian ideas over China was the fact that the Buddhist religion led the most devout to undertake extensive pilgrimages to the sacred places of Buddhism. The first pilgrim of whom there is a record was a Chinese monk who left in 259 for Khotan where he remained until his death a half century later. He was the forerunner of some 186 known individuals, according to a recent Chinese scholar, who made such pilgrimages between 259 and 790. The stories told by those who returned to China added new information, particularly regarding geography, to China's store of knowledge.

At the same time that Buddhism was being adopted, an im-

[5] Chavannes even considered one Han bas-relief to be the depiction of a jātaka tale. *Mission archéologique dans la Chine septentrionale*, I:152–153 (1913).

portant school of native thought and practice was slowly developing into a religion. It was sometimes named for Huang-ti, the legendary emperor, and the author of the great prose poem, *The Lao-Tzŭ*, and sometimes after two pioneers, Lao-tzŭ and Chuang-tzŭ; but it is best known as Taoism. During the early Han dynasty many of the people were helping to establish cults aside from the official religion. Granet and more recently Dubs have drawn attention to the movement that arose about 3 B.C. in Shantung as the result of a drought, in which crowds drifted from place to place singing and dancing to propitiate the mysterious Mother Queen of the West who later became one of Taoism's most beloved divinities.[6] This mystery cult is known to have found favor in high circles from the time of the emperor Wu to that of Wang Mang the usurper, and the literature of both Han dynasties contains hints of its growing popularity.

Tradition assigns the actual establishment of Taoism to a member of the Chang family who lived during the second century A.D. in the region of Szechuan, and who is said to have "manufactured writings on the Tao to deceive the people," supporting himself by exacting five pecks of rice from each of his disciples. Actually there was an equally strong but somewhat different Taoist center in the first two centuries A.D. in the coastal areas of Shantung and northern Kiangsu. Dubs has made the interesting suggestion that the western cult may have received strong impulses from the great Iranian religion of Mazdaism. However that may be, the western cult finally lost its particular savor in the fifth century under the leadership of K'ou Ch'ien-chih (d. 442). The new religion gained headway during the troubled years at the end of that century; its cohesive strength was bound to increase as the power of officialdom waned. About 190 Chang Lu, another member of this family, succeeded in setting up a small independent state in Shensi province, and here the church took visible form, "with a hierarchy possessing both

[6] Cf. the mass hysteria which developed in Europe after the Black Death.

spiritual and temporal powers: the faithful called themselves demon-soldiers; instructors called libationers[7] [i.e., officials] explained the holy books and administered a department; above them there were great libationers; lastly Chang Lu himself had assumed the title of Prince Celestial Master."[8] When Ts'ao Ts'ao swept through the country in 215, the "Prince Celestial Master" was taken into protective custody and sent to the capital, where he devoted himself to the study of alchemy until his death in about 220. The church managed to survive—it always has prospered during periods of imperial weakness and collapse; and the alleged descendants of the Chang family carried on the tradition of Chang Lu for seventeen centuries from the center they later established in Mount Lung Hu in Kiangsi province. This so-called papacy was not officially recognized until 748, but it wielded vast power from time to time. The Chinese republicans discarded it in 1927.

This new faith, the third of the three great religions, did not merely follow the teachings of *The Lao-tzŭ* and *The Chuang-tzŭ*, although these and other early works, including the *Classic of Changes,* became part of its canon. They were too difficult to be understood easily, and only the best-read and the best-fitted temperamentally were capable of applying their doctrines. Instead Taoism organized into a corporate whole the original primitive beliefs and customs, those that centered about the worship of nature, which was considered animate. Some precepts were discarded in the process, but many new ones were constantly incorporated. The *Tao,* or Way, was the road one traveled in order to obtain three ultimate aims: happiness, wealth, and long life. The intellectuals could do this by meditating on the writings of the masters and following their ethical teachings, and by consciously seeking longevity through studying alchemy

[7] A curious fact is that at first the Buddhist monks were called *Tao-shih* (scholars of the Tao, a term later applied to Taoist adepts), whereas the term libationers was derived from a title used in the civil government.

[8] Maspero, *Asiatic Mythology,* p. 258.

and observing certain physical requirements such as a selective diet, breathing exercises, calisthenics, and sexual practices. The common people could believe in the existence of ghosts and in the magic of charms; they recited parts of the slowly accumulating scriptures, and were taught to confess their sins and receive absolution by doing such good deeds as repairing a road for a length of one hundred paces. They could follow the practices prescribed for the intellectuals if they could master them. Faith in the power of magic to cure illness was held out. The Taoists often dispensed charity in the regions under their control, rice being stored at certain stations for wayfarers. Demoniac possession was used to bring the unbelievers into the fold and to punish certain crimes.

It was inevitable that two such parallel movements, each with a wide following, should have much in common and enrich each other in a period when the official religion was in disrepute. Buddhism, incomparably the richer, was the greatest giver. The Indian priesthood gradually became the model for the Taoist, except for the Buddhist requirement of celibacy; this ran counter to one of Taoism's popular practices. The doctrines of the transmigration of the soul and of causal retribution through successive existences were accepted, and India's thirty-three heavens and eighteen hells were taken over and given Chinese names and Chinese presiding deities. Numberless sūtras were composed. The Indian cosmological term Kalpa (432,000,000 years) was applied to huge divisions of time, and other technical terms were adopted unquestioningly. The idea of a life of seclusion is common to the teachings of both Buddha and Lao-tzŭ. Two aspects of the Buddhist teachings, however, their asceticism and their prohibition against using fermented liquors, are quite foreign to the Chinese. A cult of city gods, first mentioned in 230, reflects the eclecticism of the times, for some of its features suggest the ancient Chinese land and grain deities and others suggest the Buddhist purgatory. Buddhism later broke up into numerous sects, one of which, the Ch'an or meditative school, drew heavily from Taoist tenets and practices and probably represented the finest flowering of Indian culture in Chinese soil.

The earlier tolerance shown by the adherents of the two sects toward each other became hostility from the third century on.[9] Shadowy evidence of this is a dispute in 247 at Nanking between the builders of a temple for the Sogdian Buddhist Sêng-hui and the members of a nearby "illegal cult," as a Buddhist historian of 519 called them. More convincing evidence is afforded by a second-century memorial and two third-century works, one Buddhist and one Taoist, which revealed a controversy that eventually assumed menacing proportions. Popular belief held that after Lao-tzŭ supposedly left China he went among the barbarians in the west and became the Buddha. One Buddhist, finally deciding to spike this legend, wrote *The Record of Central Asia,* in which he maintained that Lao-tzŭ had come to Kashmir and paid homage to a statue of the Buddha. A Taoist who refused to accede to this assumption of priority rewrote this book about 300 under a different title, *The Conversion of the Barbarians;* according to it, Lao-tzŭ went to India and there became the teacher of Sakyamuni. The Buddhists answered this with the assertion that the Buddha preceded Lao-tzŭ by more than two centuries. And so this quarrel continued and widened, finally becoming so fierce that *The Conversion* was repeatedly proscribed, even as late as 1281. Both groups presented the dispute pictorially to the people; scenes showing Lao-tzŭ among the barbarians decorated the Taoist phalansteries and the walls of Buddhist temples.

A fundamental difference between the two religions was their divergent attitude on sex. The Buddhists preached asceticism and banned marriage for their priests. The Taoists, however, believed that continence was contrary to human nature—had not

[9] A seventh-century Buddhist tradition fixes the date of the first struggle between them at A.D. 71, but this can probably be disregarded.

the Yellow Emperor, Huang-ti, had twelve hundred women in his harem and become immortal? Both sexes were encouraged to live in common in the Taoist phalansteries, and certain festivals were celebrated by bestial orgies, to the horror of the Buddhists and doubtless of many other outsiders. When in their search for the secret of long life the Taoists realized that some form of continence must be practiced, they promulgated a set of rules; the penalty for not observing them was the loss of a year of life. But more than rules apparently was required. The innate morality of the Chinese and the shocked complaints by people of other faiths as well as the imperial court forced discretion in these practices about the seventh century, but they were continued *sub rosa* until the twelfth. Discussion of them was dropped from the great sixteenth-century edition of the Taoist canon by imperial proscription.

No consideration of the Taoists is complete which excludes their activity in the field of science. The study of alchemy, the conversion of base metals into gold, not to create material wealth, but to find an elixir which would confer immortality, dates back at least to the second century before the Christian era. Despite threats of public execution in 144 B.C., the alchemists continued their work. In the first half of the second century A.D. Wei Po-yang wrote a book describing the process of preparing the pill of immortality. This process so resembles that for the preparation of the philosopher's stone in *Speculum Alchemiae*, ascribed to Roger Bacon, that it has given rise to the suspicion that European alchemy may have derived from the Chinese.[10] Alchemy furnished—perhaps by accident—the steppingstone for important discoveries in medicine and industry. At this time, says a sixth-century official chronicle, "efficacious recipes and marvelous formulae existed by thousands and tens of thousands."[11] Un-

[10] For the controversy, see the papers of Davis and Hopkins in *Isis*, February and May, 1938, and the conclusions of Dubs, *Isis*, November, 1947.

[11] Ware, *Journal of the American Oriental Society*, LIII:223–224 (September, 1933).

doubtedly there were grotesque and impractical features. It is only recently that the Chinese have understood the anatomy of the human body; the official annals record only two dissections— one in A.D. 16 and the other in 1106—before the Europeans came. But they discovered many valuable herbs and experimented with sulphur, arsenic, mercurial substances, compounds of zinc, of lead, and of copper, and iron. Their skill in "metallurgy, their brilliant dyestuffs and manifold pigments, their early knowledge of gunpowder and pyrotechnics, their asphyxiating and anaesthetic compounds" all bear testimony to "a commendable proficiency in many matters which pertain to practical chemistry."[12] Laufer and others have pointed out the probable help of the alchemists in the production of the fine glaze during the Han period and of the porcelain ware in the third century of our era. The first *Materia Medica* that has come down to us was prepared by a Taoist who lived in the first part of the third century. In addition to listing the medicines in use at that time it gives instructions for making pills, powders, and poultices from drugs.

The penetration of Buddhism, the growing systematization of Taoists beliefs and practices, and the deterioration of governmental authority at the end of the second century combined to dim the luster of the official religion and to make serious inroads upon it. The growing anarchy of the third century must have brought widespread destruction of liberties, schools, and places of worship, and scant opportunity for men to be trained in literature, history, law, and ritual. The civil examinations, the backbone of the Confucian system of correct government, partially collapsed; at least the prince of Wei (in modern Honan) ordered them to be drawn up anew in 237–239. Examinations were held at one place and another sporadically, but they came under the control of those close to power and many officials were chosen for other reasons than passing an examination success-

---

[12] Johnson, *A Study of Chinese Alchemy*, pp. 103–104.

fully. The temper of the times permitted no longing glances at the past; it was opposed to manners and morals. "A situation in which Chinese gentlemen surrendered themselves to drink, did not mourn for their parents, took no thought of funerals, neglected etiquette, and went naked, indicates a collapse of the Chinese moral structure."[13] Confucianism, which depended on bookishness, a leisured class, settled times, and general prosperity, survived by some miracle. A member of the K'ung family, to which Confucius belonged, was honored by a marquisate in 221; both the annals and local monuments give evidence that the master's shrine, till then sadly neglected, was repaired; the prince of Wei sacrificed at this shrine, and dormitories for students were ordered built. Only three figures, however, were of sufficient importance to be included in the Confucian hall of fame during the four centuries following 220, as against eleven contributed by the Han in the preceding four centuries.[14]

Between 240 and 248 three items of the Confucian canon were carved on stone and set up at Loyang near those authorized sixty-five years earlier. Interestingly enough, these were the historical classics—the *Document of History* and the *Spring and Autumn Annals;* the *Tso chuan* was the only new item to be included. The characters of these canonical works were written in three classical forms; hence the twenty-eight fragments of the stones that have been recovered during the last half century are invaluable. Together with a few recent archeological discoveries in the sands of central Asia, they preserve not only the texts then current (many alterations and interpolations were made after 248, particularly in the *History*), but also the forms of writing, two of which were even then archaic. This attempt to preserve certain parts of the canon in stone is significant, for it points to the continuing strength of Confucianism at the northern capital. Wang Su (195–256), a Wei scholiast and official, was at this

---

[13] Shryock, *A Study of Human Abilities*, p. 16.
[14] *Id., The Origin and Development of the State Cult of Confucius*, pp. 265–266.

time engaged in writing classical commentaries, making new versions of *The Family Sayings of Confucius* and the *Document of History* by means of which he introduced theories of his own, attacking the dogmas of Later Han theologians. He refused to accept their belief that Confucius was more than Sage—an uncrowned King—and helped to re-establish him as great but human. Other writers of Wei were laboring on the *Book of Filial Piety* and the *Canon of Changes*. The chief center of learning of this time was Ching-chou (in modern Hupeh) where some three hundred scholars are said to have been engaged in drawing up a revised edition of the Confucian canon. But in other places far away scholarship also survived. So Ching (239–303), a native of the remote western oasis of Tun-huang, a military leader and the finest calligrapher of his day, made a study of the five elements of nature outlined in the *History*. This has been lost, but facsimile specimens of his brush work that have been preserved still astonish admirers of this art.[15]

The growing eclecticism of the period is shown by the interest in Lao-tzŭ and the sayings attributed to him; the *Analects* also attracts interest. Wang Pi (226–249) made some of the most brilliant interpretations of these works that have survived, in spite of the fact that he lived only twenty-three years and was said to have been as interested in pleasure as in literature. He seems to have believed that the systems of Confucius and Lao-tzŭ had a common basis, and though the latter's ideas harmonized with his own he considered Confucius the ideal man. He did not preach conservatism, but he did maintain that men must behave uprightly. Kuo Hsiang (d. 312), another independent thinker whose commentary on *The Chuang-tzŭ* is standard, in-

---

[15] Ou-yang Hsün (557–641) is said to have seen a tablet bearing So Ching's handwriting which was ancient even then. "Reining in his horse, he looked at it for a long time and then rode away. A hundred paces off he stopped, turned back, and remained gazing at the tablet until he was exhausted. Then he sat on a blanket and continued to gaze. He slept at the foot of it and remained there for three days." Edwards, *Chinese Prose Literature*, I, p. 89.

veighed against the institutions and morals of his day; they were out of date and hence artificial. A group of courtiers and officials at Loyang who called themselves "The Seven Sages of the Bamboo Grove" (a scenic spot nearby) extolled the virtues of wine and inaction to their many followers. One of them, Hsi K'ang, who married into the imperial family, and whom van Gulik characterizes as "an artist in the best and truest sense of the word," left a poetical essay on the lute; another, Liu Ling, a military officer, wrote on the virtue of wine; Margouliès says of his essay: "It is absolute liberty, complete independence, the contempt for all the most fundamental laws of the world which wine brings to him."[16] The age was unsuited to the rigid moralism of the *Analects*, but in harmony with the lighter touch of the belles-lettres, folk literature, and poetry that began to appear.[17]

None of the literature of the third century A.D. that has sur-

---

[16] *Le Kou-wen Chinois*, p. lix.

[17] The influence of one or two developments in literary history of the time that were closely allied to Confucianism has remained to our own day. In 220, when the Wei prince who inherited the power of his redoubtable father Ts'ao Ts'ao was about to inaugurate his rule over north China, he ordered his ministers to compile an imperial survey which would aid him in carving out an empire as great as the Han. Although earlier rulers, such as the First Emperor, had endeavored to encompass all the existing knowledge themselves, the son of Ts'ao Ts'ao realized the impossibility of doing this himself. Thus the first general compendium, or summary of each subject, came into existence; it had many successors for both imperial and private use. The survey made for the Wei prince has long since been lost but was said to run to over 8,000,000 words.

Another important event occurred in 281 when the tomb of a prince or some other person of rank who had died nearly six centuries earlier was opened. Over 100,000 bamboo tablets covered with writings were discovered. Fifteen different works and fragments of other writings were said to have been found in the tomb, among them a copy of the *Canon of Changes*, the *Romance of Mu, Son of Heaven*, and the official chronicle of the state of Liang or Wei that ended in 299 B.C., the state of Chin, and the royal houses from legendary times on. This find was extremely important, for these works obviously had escaped the great burning in 213 B.C. and the tampering of schoolmen or copyists. The scholars of that day began at once to compare the current texts with the original chronicles. One result of their work was the conclusion that the *Tso chuan* should be restored to the place it had lost in the Han; another, that the chronology of ancient events followed by the chronicle of Liang was perhaps more reliable than any hitherto accepted. An entirely unexpected result was the fact that the sorting and cataloguing of these bamboo tablets led to a classification system that has been used by Chinese librarians ever since.

vived shows concern over the penetration of Buddhism. These authors may have expressed their feelings in conversations or possibly in fugitive writings heavy with irony and sarcasm. Undoubtedly, however, the traditionalists among them looked with scorn at the foreign cult's "hesitant terminology, the confused mass of its texts, its too florid style, its over-subtle metaphysic, its naïve legends, its incomprehension of the practical aspect of things, its ignorance of human ethics and the daily experience of life, its disdain for social conventions, the excesses of certain of its monks, the ostensible disinterestedness of others."[18] One probably authentic evidence of their attitude is indicated in a spirited defense of Buddhism written about 197 by a youthful Chinese convert. This young man and his mother had fled to Tongking from their home in what is now Wu-chou in Kuangsi to escape the troubles that were engulfing China. Returning home at the age of twenty-five, he married and devoted himself to a comparative study of the official ethic, the budding Taoist cult, and Buddhism. This converted him to the foreign faith and in defense of it he wrote the treatise which has come down to us. Confucianism, of course, was not to be won over or even modified by any isolated rebuttal of its arguments. For many centuries it tried by every means to stem the overwhelming tide from peninsular and central Asia, but it was not until the eleventh and twelfth centuries that, baffled and undermined, it made peace and established a new official faith.

China's knowledge of the world and her contacts with foreign peoples in other than religious fields had steadily increased. We may recall the successive conquests of Tongking in 214 and 111 B.C. and in A.D. 42, and the many missions from the South Seas that bore tribute to Ch'ang-an. During the first six years of our era a Chinese mission was sent to the Indian Ocean and may have crossed it. In 120 the Han emperor received musicians and jugglers, natives of the Mediterranean Orient whom a Burmese

[18] Aurousseau, *Bulletin de l'école française d'extrême-orient*, XXII:277 (1922).

prince had sent; in 132 the king of Java rendered tribute. In 166 "envoys" from Marcus Aurelius Antoninus reached the court by way of Tongking. Chinese Buddhist records tell of Sogdian businessmen in Tongking at the turn of the century. In 226, the year when this area submitted to Wu, Ch'in-lun, a merchant from the Roman Orient, arrived in Tongking and was sent by the local prefect to the prince of Wu at Nanking.

It was natural, therefore, for this prince, whose state lay south and whose way to the north and west was barred by the houses of Wei and Shu, to expand his power in a southerly direction. Such a policy was undertaken some time prior to 231, when the Chinese governor of Kuangtung and Nanking sent officers to subdue the areas to the south. As a result, according to the official chronicle, "the kings beyond the frontiers, of Fu-nan [southern Cambodia and Cochin-China], of Lin-i [Champa], and of T'ang-ming [north of Cambodia], each sent an embassy to offer tribute." Fifteen or twenty years later this same prince dispatched two ambassadors on a reconnaissance mission that took them over almost the entire Indian Ocean. Identification of all the "one hundred and several tens of countries" visited and reported on is still difficult, but Ceylon and India must have been included, as well as western Asia. The fragments of their reports that have come down to us contain many interesting items, perhaps the most outstanding being the revelation of regular trade routes, knowledge of the monsoons, a description of the great junks, and the extensive Hinduization of wide areas throughout the South Seas. The chief ambassador, who may have come from Sogdiana in central Asia, reported that while he was in Cambodia the envoy of an Indian king presented four Scythian horses to the king of Fu-nan. The junks hoisted seven sails and could stay asea for weeks at a time; one contemporary report asserts that they carried over six hundred men and more than one thousand tons of merchandise. These figures may be exaggerated; but the precise information about these ships and the fact that envoys and Buddhist monks continued to travel on foreign craft for some time show that the Chinese lagged behind their southern and western neighbors as a seafaring people. Only after the third century are there indications of their beginning to venture beyond sight of land with some regularity.

In addition to learning about the peninsular and island countries and peoples to the south and southwest, the Chinese were acquiring new knowledge of central Asia, Mongolia, Manchuria, Korea, and Japan. The northern court of Wei and its successor, the Tsin, maintained official relationships with Lob-nor, Kucha, Khotan, and even Ferghana; with the Hsiung-nu of the Ordos and Alashan regions; and with the Hsien-pi of eastern Mongolia. Chinese outposts were still located in southern Manchuria and northern Korea, and missions were exchanged with the queen of the Wo in Japan in 238 and 240. One of the most reliable accounts of the early Japanese is found in the records of the state of Wei kept by Ch'ên Shou (233–297), although at least three older ones exist.

All of these activities called for geographers. So far as we know, there were no maps encompassing all these regions that were comparable to the map of Marin of Tyre (*ca.* 110) corrected by Ptolmey (*ca.* 170); by this time, however, there must have been maps of areas under Chinese control for the local officials, maps showing the campaigns of the imperial armies, and possibly even some devised for the caravan trade. In 99 B.C. General Li Ling, for example, sent the emperor a chart that indicated the line of his great march into Hun territory (thirty days north from western Kansu into Mongolia) and showed mountains, watercourses, and the configuration of places through which he passed. More interesting still is the deduction made by Herrmann[19] that a Chinese guide, indicating the caravanserais of Chinese Turkestan and the length of stages between them, must have existed on which Marin based his distances. His fig-

---

[19] *Das Land der Seide und Tibet im Lichte der Antike* (Leipzig, 1938).

ures do not fit Greek stadia or parasangs, but they are exact when calculated in Chinese *li*. These early maps were undoubtedly crude, but they paved the way for the more scientific maps that appeared in the third century.

The chief cartographer of the age was P'ei Hsiu (224–271), minister of works in 267 under the first Tsin emperor. Dissatisfied with all existing maps, both general and local, because of their lack of rectilinear divisions, of correct orientation, and of completeness in showing mountains and rivers, he set down in the preface of his work (only the preface has survived) six rules for map-makers, on which he based his map of China. If we may believe his own words, this map indicated "the mountains, seas, and watercourses, the highlands, lowlands, slopes and fens, also the nine ancient divisions and the present sixteen divisions, the boundaries and outlying districts of their provinces, states, prefectures, and towns, together with the old names of the places where the ancient states made their treaties or held their assemblies, as well as the various routes by water and by land."[20] P'ei's map was done in eighteen sections on a scale of 500 *li* (about 125 miles) to one inch. The most remarkable of his innovations is his use of rectilinear subdivisions, or the grid system. This may, of course, date from an earlier period; but whether this is an independent invention of the Chinese is a moot point.

The increasing knowledge of the great subtropical areas to the south of the Yangtze River[21] gave rise to an entirely new type of literature, works on botany. The first book in this field is *Nan-fang ts'ao-mu chuang* (Flora of the Southern Regions) written by Hsi Han (fl. 264–307), one-time governor of Kuangtung. It groups plants into four classes—herbs, forest trees, fruit trees, and bamboos—and treats a total of eighty species; it mentions some two dozen other plants, and lists those that foreign

[20] Translation by Soothill, *Geographical Journal*, LXIX:541 (June, 1927).

[21] Other works on this region—*I wu chih* (Record of Strange Things) by Yang Fu (end of second century A.D.), a native of Kuangtung, and *Kuangchou chi* (Notes on Kuang-chou) by Ku Hui (fl. 170–250) of Kiangsu—deal only in part with plants.

countries sent to the Tsin court as presents. Although there are many unfortunate interpolations, this book is a rich mine of information for historians of cultivated plants.

One of the most beneficent results of the occupation of this southern area was the discovery of tea. Tea drinking may well have been common long before the third century, but no mention of tea occurs until this time. The earliest definite reference is in the biography of an official who was born in Szechuan and died in 273: "They made a gift to him of leaves of tea to take the place of wine."[22] This is the old story of a substitute displacing the original article in popularity. Tea did not achieve immediate favor, however; it was identified with the southern and central provinces for centuries. Of Wang Su (464–501), a native of Shantung who fled to the T'o-pa in northern Shansi, it is said: "He is noted for his love of koumiss, of which, he told the emperor, tea is only fit to be the slave."[23] Tea did not come into general use in the north until some time during the eighth to tenth centuries, at about which time it reached Tibet; a Buddhist monk made it popular in Japan after 1200. The Mongols, now among the heaviest tea drinkers, apparently ignored it during their period of occupation in the thirteenth and fourteenth centuries, as did all the medieval European travelers to Cathay—at least in their journals. The Arab traders were more alert, one of them describing tea and the way it was infused as early as 851. The herb did not become widely appreciated in Europe until the seventeenth century.

Tea must be mentioned in any history of eastern Asia because of its widespread effects on the life and habits of the Chinese and neighboring peoples. The tea plant apparently was never cultivated on large plantations; rather, each household raised its own supply, producing a wide variety of leaves some of which were rare and very expensive. By 780 the author of the *Tea Classic*

[22] Pelliot, *T'oung Pao*, XXI:436 (December, 1922).
[23] Giles' *Biographical Dictionary* #2228.

could write: "The best quality leaves must have creases like the leathern boot of Tatar horsemen, curl like the dewlap of a mighty bullock, unfold like a mist rising out of a ravine, gleam like a lake touched by a zephyr, and be wet and soft like fine earth newly swept by rain."[24] The porcelain industry owes a great debt to the Chinese delight in wine and food and ritual, and undoubtedly as great a debt to tea. It is not without significance that both this industry and the cultivation of tea began about the same time, that both center in much the same localities (Kiangsi and Chekiang), and that these are the areas in which a chosen few could afford both the finest leaves and the loveliest cups and covers. The first mention of Yüeh ware, made near Shao-hsing in Chekiang and highly prized, occurs in the *Tea Classic*, the author recommending that tea be drunk from these bowls of "ice and jade . . . which impart a tint of green to the tea." The Chinese have long recognized the therapeutic value of tea. Some claims may be exaggerated, but there is no doubt that a strong brew is efficacious when applied to burns, that its almost universal use instead of unboiled water has saved the people from countless intestinal diseases,[25] and that it has soothed the nerves of mankind in every imaginable circumstance.

Other significant additions to material culture in this period are the wheelbarrow and water mill, the use of which in grinding grain and irrigating fields freed Chinese farmers of an enormous burden. Although Chinese take credit for the invention of water-driven mills and wheels in the first century A.D. there is no reason, as Laufer points out,[26] why they may not have derived from some region between China and the Roman empire, where they were known in the first century before the Christian era.[27]

---

[24] Ukers, *All About Tea*, p. 3.

[25] Cf. Stuart, *Chinese Materia Medica*, pp. 81–87.

[26] *Chinese Pottery of the Han Dynasty*, pp. 33–35. See also L. S. Yang, *Harvard Journal of Asiatic Studies*, IX:118 (1946).

[27] See Bloch, "Avènement et conquêtes du moulin à eau," *Annales d'histoire économique et sociale*, VII:538–563 (1935).

The wheelbarrow is another now universal contrivance whose past is little known. Its invention is assigned to the warrior Chu-ko Liang (181–234); it did not appear in Europe until ten centuries later.[28] As someone has said, it halved the number of laborers needed to haul small loads by substituting a wheel for the man at the front end of the hand-barrow. It is particularly useful in China on the narrow paths separating fields and it is used to carry pigs and humans as well as ordinary freight. In a favoring wind it is helped along by sails in parts of China.

Two older machines which underwent improvement in the third century are the drawloom and a crude sowing machine, both of which go back in origin to early Han times. The loom, which made possible the execution of complicated designs in silk, now had its treadles reduced from fifty or sixty to twelve, thus simplifying the operation. The sowing machine spread widely throughout farming areas from 265 on.[29]

The Eastern Tsin and the Turkic—Hsiung-nu— Mongol Dynasties (317–420)

Except for a few decades after its founding in 265 to 280, the Tsin empire, as we said earlier, led a hazardous existence until 420. Its troubles began at the turn of the century with an uprising in the west which deprived it of the rich province of Szechuan from 302 to 347. Serious as this was, it was small compared with the losses in the north which for years had been swarming with various peoples of Turkic, Mongol, and Tungusic blood. None of their chiefs during the third century seems to have commanded sufficient support from the west to challenge the authority of the Chinese emperor at Loyang. On the con-

[28] Lynn White, *Speculum*, XV:2, 147 (April, 1940). Yang, *op. cit.*, thinks there were two varieties. Possibly Chu-ko took them over from the peoples he encountered on his campaign into the southwest in 225.

[29] Yang, *op. cit.*, pp. 118, 155.

trary, they fought furiously among themselves, and the Chinese rulers encouraged first one side and then another, striving in this way to keep them divided. This state of affairs might have lasted for a considerable period had not the court become corrupt, its reputed masters sunk into debauchery, the country afflicted by banditry, drought, floods, famine, and plague, and its armies grown weak in comparison with swift-striking mounted bowmen of the Hsiung-nu, Ch'iang (Tibetans), and T'o-pa. The envoys and even the chieftains (*Shan-yü*) of the various hordes who were stationed in Loyang could not refrain from scheming to take advantage of such conditions.

One of these chieftains as a boy had been a hostage at the court and had became thoroughly acquainted with the rudiments of Chinese government and history, as well as with the local situation. In 304 he founded the kingdom of Han in the T'ai-yüan region of Shansi province, shrewdly laying claim to the glory of that great name by letting it become known that he was descended on his mother's side from the earlier imperial house. After completely reconstituting the tribal organization of his people along standard Chinese lines, he four years later proclaimed himself emperor at T'ai-yüan, backed by an army of fifty thousand. On his death in 310, his son continued this ambitious scheme, invading Loyang in 311 and Ch'ang-an in 312, and dethroning and then executing the Chinese monarch Huai. Practically all of north China had now fallen into Hsiung-nu hands. The fitful glimmer of Chinese resistance that flickered for a time was extinguished in 316 with the capture and subsequent execution of Huai's successor. For the next two centuries and a half north China was lost to the Chinese empire. Although it was ruled by a succession of dynasties of nomadic origin, it remained basically Chinese in agriculture, language, mores, and religion. Each house and each tribe that shifted its base south of the Great Wall and stayed there for two or more generations tended to adopt Chinese ways—ruling as the Chinese ruled, modifying their own customs, adopting Chinese religious beliefs, and exchanging their polysyllabic clan names for orthodox Chinese surnames. The great Chinese ocean "salted every river that ran into it."

One non-Chinese practice that became standard in China was the adoption of the costume worn by the mounted nomads. As early as 307 B.C. the mounted officers and soldiers of the Chinese prince of Chao were wearing clothes like those of the Hu so that they could better resist their fast-riding enemies. Court officials and many of the other men, however, long continued to wear the loose upper garment, long skirt, and low shoes of a chariot-riding people. The belted tunic, trousers, and boots of a people born to the saddle did not become common until the fourth and fifth centuries of our era; their use was firmly established by T'ang times (seventh to ninth centuries). The aristocrats also adopted the large hats worn by the nomads; these were ornamented in front with a gold or silver cicada and on either or both sides by tails of sable, and the whole was surmounted by two long pheasant feathers. The ancient Chinese knotted girdles were replaced by leather belts decorated with as many as thirteen links or rings, or appliqués of bronze or iron, sometimes encrusted with gold, silver, or turquoise, and fastened with a metal buckle; various objects were suspended from the links.

The highly confusing political picture of the period, as far as north China is concerned, may be summarized to some advantage as in the chart on page 85.

Throughout the fifth century and the first half of the sixth (about 403 to 552) the Avars, a Mongol people variously called Jou-jan or Juan-juan, maintained a great empire that extended north of the Great Wall from the boundaries of Korea to Lake Balkash. The Tungus ruled in eastern and northern Manchuria; the T'u-yü-hun in Kokonor. Unquestionably this was a great period for the Turkic, Hsiung-nu, Mongol, and Tungusic peoples, and one during which they brought both the Chinese and the Roman empires to their knees at virtually the same time. Eastern Asia had both earlier and later counterparts of Attila, chief of the Huns in eastern and central Europe.

While these various peoples were fighting for supremacy north of the Yangtze, the Chinese empire of the eastern Tsin, founded at Nanking by a prince who escaped from Ch'ang-an, maintained itself south of the great river at first weakly and then more strongly. At times it extended north almost to the Yellow River and south as far as Tongking; it penetrated Szechuan after 347. If its rulers had any real capacity for leadership, social conditions and court intrigues prevented it fom appearing. Eleven emperors occupied the throne during the fourth century; most of them died in their twenties or thirties. Their subjects were increased by the Chinese refugees—Dr. Li Chi[30] estimates that there was a fivefold population increase from 280 to 464—who fled from the Yellow River basin. According to one annalist: "During the Tsin dynasty, from the time when Emperor Yüan moved to the left of the Yangtze River on account of disturbances in the central domain, all those who voluntarily fled to the south were called immigrants. They established districts and prefectures and called them by the place-names of their native land. They scattered and moved about and did not settle at one place."[31]

The Tsin empire also continued the process, already well established, of assimilating the non-Chinese people within its borders, encroaching on foreign territory and on previously uncultivated tracts of land in the south and west, and exacting tribute from local chiefs. Negritos whom the Chinese historians called "black dwarfs" are reported in the mountainous districts south of the Yangtze; after the third century of our era, however, they are not mentioned. Some emigrated, but others remained and were assimilated by the dominant southern Mongo-

---

[30] *Formation of the Chinese People,* p. 233.
[31] Translation by Chi Ch'ao-ting, *Key Economic Areas in Chinese History,* p. 109.

Ruling Group	Race	Domain	Result	Dates of Rule
The Chao				
Early Chao, or northern Han	Hsiung-nu	Shansi	Ended by founder of the later Chao	304–329
Later Chao	Hsiung-nu	Hopei	Absorbed by early Ch'in	319–352
The Liang				
Early Liang	Chinese	Kansu; central Asia as far as Turfan	Ended by early Ch'in	313–376
Later Liang	Turkic or Mongol	Kansu	Subdued by Tsin	386–403
Southern Liang	Hsien-pi or Turkic	Kansu	Annexed by western Ch'in	397–404, 408–414
Northern Liang	Hsiung-nu	Western Kansu; Central Asia as far as Kao-ch'ang	Defeated by Wei	397–439
Western Liang	Chinese (?)	Western Kansu	Ended by Northern Liang	401/5–421
The Yen				
Early Yen	Hsien-pi or Mongol	Hopei and Honan	Absorbed by early Ch'in	349–370
Later Yen	Hsien-pi	Hopei	Ended by northern Yen	384–408
Western Yen	Hsien-pi	Shansi	Absorbed by Wei	384–396
Southern Yen	Hsien-pi	Shantung	Capitulated to founder of Chinese house of Liu Sung	398–410
Northern Yen	Chinese	Northern Hopei and southern Manchuria	Absorbed by Wei	409–436
The Ch'in				
Early Ch'in	Mongol	Shensi; and into central Asia at one time	Absorbed by western Ch'in	351–394
Later Ch'in	Mongol or Tibetan	Shensi	Conquered by Tsin	384–417
Western Ch'in	Turkic or Mongol	Kansu	Destroyed by Hsia	385–390, 409–431
The Wei Northern Wei	Turkic	Shansi; then Loyang after 494	Subdued by eastern Wei	386–535
The Hsia	Hsiung-nu	Shensi	Subdued by T'u-yü-hun (Mongol?)	407–431

loid stock, as witness the kinky hair and swarthy skin noticeable today among a few southern Chinese. The Thai (T'ai), whose best-known representatives now occupy Thailand (Siam) is another people who became intermingled with the Chinese.

A few people of the original Yellow River valley stock, conscious of these ethnic developments, tried to combat the infusion of foreign blood into their own families, and with true pride of race began to compile genealogies that traced their ancestry back to a mythical Yellow River emperor. The national bibliography in the history of the Sui dynasty (prepared about 629 to 636) records four such treatises, the longest one containing 690 chapters, that appeared during the third and fourth centuries; there were undoubtedly many others of which no record has survived. But this effort to keep the stock pure was unavailing, for Chinese men who pioneer in new territory have never been averse to intermarriage. The custom of concubinage, for all that can be said against it, has insured the enrichment of the aristocratic lines with new blood of peasant, aboriginal, or foreign origin.

This was another age quite unsuited to the official religion. But Confucianism was not dead; at worst it was merely quiescent. Its classics still appealed to the intellectuals and to the quasi-ruling class. In 409, for example, when the eighteen-year-old T'o-pa Ssŭ ascended his father's throne at what is now Ta-t'ung, he commanded Ts'ui Hao (381–450), a rising young scholar who later became famous as the Taoist foe of Buddhism, to give him a course in Chinese literature. This course, which took three years, included the Han vocabulary and exercise book *Chi chiu chang*, the *Classic of Filial Piety*, the *Analects*, the *Odes*, the *History*, the *Spring and Autumn Annals*, the *Book of Rites*, and the *Changes*. Such a list is revealing for it shows that even the rude northern court, where the military arts had a strong hold, considered the distilled wisdom of the Chinese ancients essential for the governing group.

Buddhism and Taoism nevertheless increased their hold on

the people and on Chinese and foreign rulers as well. In fact Buddhism really came into its own after 300 A.D. and more than ever put the Taoists on their mettle. One of the main figures responsible for its spread was Fo-t'u-têng (d. 349), a learned and widely traveled missionary of Indian parentage [?] from central Asia who reached Loyang in 310. Had the country been at peace he might have settled down, as others had before him, to a life of translation and religious education. Instead, seeing the breakdown of Chinese authority and the usurpation by unlettered hordes of the regions round about, he attached himself to the house which was to found the Later Chao and for thirty-seven years shrewdly used his connections and employed his talents to found a church which would appeal to both his patrons and the masses. He persuaded the emperor (Shih Hu, r. 334–348) to issue an edict tolerating monasticism, built many temples with government support, and trained disciples, several of marked ability and influence. He also made for a close association of monks in the life of the court. In time to come, when the Buddhism of the south, designed for the cultured, blended with that of the north, we see, as Arthur Wright puts it, "the full maturity of Sinicized Buddhism."[32]

In the latter half of the fourth century Buddhist missionaries were sent to Korea. (Paekche, one of the three kingdoms into which Korea was then divided, officially adopted Chinese writing in 374; from here all forms of Chinese thought and belief flowed into Japan in the course of the next century and a half.) Tao-an (314–385), one of Fo-t'u-têng's disciples, was a priest of importance in both the Yangtze and Yellow River valleys; he compiled the first Buddhist catalogue (374) of which extracts of any size have suvived. He believed in evangelization, in spreading the story and teachings of Buddha to the people by sermons, debates with the learned, and pious submission to toil and suffering. He sent his disciples in all directions; one went to

[32] *Harvard Jo. of As. Studies*, XI:326 (1948).

the great province of Szechuan. Hui-yüan (334–416), his most important disciple, was formerly a Taoist who continued to use Taoist figures of speech after his conversion. He is credited with founding one of Buddhism's most important sects, the Pure Land, Lotus, or Amidist school. Scholars have pointed out its many non-Indian influences, influences both Nepalese and Iranian, which nevertheless were blended with Chinese thought to such a degree that this is the only sect that persists today among the common people. It was valuable because it taught reliance on faith rather than on action; but in urging the constant invocation of the name of Amitabha with faith which it promised would be rewarded by rebirth in the Pure Land or Western Heaven after death it gave exaggerated emphasis to the efficacy of mere repetition. It required insufficient moral effort of its followers, but the comfort it gave was beyond measure.

Another great sect that appeared in this era was the Ch'an (Chinese for Dhyāna), the meditative or contemplative school that appealed deeply to people of intellect and devotion. Its teachings certainly resemble certain passages in the Upanishads, but it too was harmonized with the best in Taoism. This sect was probably founded by Chu Tao-shêng (fl. 397–434), a Chinese who came under the influence of Kumārajīva (350–409?) during the latter's extraordinary career as missionary at Ch'ang-an from 401 on. This sect, as someone has said, taught that "(a) the only true reality is the Buddha nature in the heart of every man. (b) All that man needs to do is to turn his gaze inward and see the Buddha in his heart. Prayer, asceticism, good works are vain. (c) The final vision is an intuition which comes in a moment; it cannot be taught or learned, teaching can only prepare the way for it." This doctrine of sudden enlightenment that Chu advocated exerted a profound influence at least until the twelfth century; some of the masters of the brush of Sung and even later times owed their inspiration to it and left immortal documents that attest its power.

The fame of Kumārajīva was probably and justly due to his skill as a translator. His father was an Indian, his mother a Kucha princess. He himself was dedicated to the church at the age of seven, and studied the Hinayāna faith at Kashmir from 352 to 354 and the Mahāyāna at Kashgar and Kucha after 354. In a city that already boasted ten thousand monks he was famous early in life; he was well traveled, and well taught in languages, "the four Vedas, the five sciences, the heretical *shastras*, and astronomy." It must be acknowledged, however, that he honored his church's interdiction against sexual indulgence in the breach rather than in the observance.[33] In 382 or 383 he was taken captive by a marauding expedition in central Asia led by Lü Kuang, who later became emperor of the Later Liang, and was taken first to Liang-chou in Kansu and thence to Ch'ang-an. His knowledge of the essential languages enabled him to make more competent translations than his predecessors; as a result, working with a large corps of assistants, he translated ninety-eight works (in 421 or 425 rolls), of which fifty-two (in 302 fascicles) have survived in the current *Tripitaka*, or Buddhist canon. That Kumārajīva recognized the difficulty, if not the impossibility, of his task is evident from the statement ascribed to him. "Translating Sanskrit into Chinese is like feeding a man with rice chewed by another; it is not merely tasteless, it is nauseating as well."[34] Nevertheless, one reason for Buddhism's appeal from this time on to certain scholars in China is the beauty of his translations and those of some of his successors.

Another translator of note, but one more famous for his record of his travels in Asia, was Fa-hsien, who came from the northern province of Shansi. After his ordination into the church he decided to make a thorough study of Buddhism. Finding materials incomplete, he set out for the holy places with several others in 399, determined to obtain all the scriptures in Sanskrit.

[33] S. Lévi, *Journal asiatique*, II:337 (1913).
[34] Translation by T. K. Chuan, *T'ien Hsia Monthly*, VII: 5, 456 (December, 1938).

The pilgrims traveled through central Asia via Tun-huang, Karashar, Khotan, and Gandhara, and arrived at Magadha in 405, after a total of 259 days actually on the march. Fa-hsien's itinerary in India included very region except the Deccan. He settled down at Pataliputra for three years, collecting and copying the sacred texts of various schools. In 411 he returned by sea (in a foreign boat) via Ceylon and Java, landing on the Shantung coast because his boat was carried hundreds of miles off its course by a terrific storm; according to one account, he spent 330 days on the water. Somehow he was able to reach Ch'ang-an in 414 with his books and relics more or less intact, and there and in Nanking in 416 he worked at the laborious task of translation and of outlining his memoirs. This memorable travelogue,[35] which described vividly the places he visited, the hardships he endured, and the legends he heard, was the forerunner of other Chinese books about India which are invaluable for their precise information. It is a curious fact that the people of India, known for their lack of interest in exact historic data, failed to transmit this quality to the Chinese to whom they carried the evangel of Buddha; the Taoists, on the other hand, nourished on an indigenous faith and culture, were as uninterested in history as the Indians.

One field in which the Buddhists seem to have been increasingly active at this time was medicine. This may have been due to the growing rift between themselves and the Taoists, some of whom were discovering, in their search for the elixir of immortality, many things that were useful for the Chinese pharmacopoeia. Or perhaps the Buddhists found that an ability to heal the sick was an important accomplishment for monks, for many of even the well-educated people with whom they worked were extremely credulous. Or medical work may have been an inseparable part of Buddhist missionary labors. As early as the second century An Shih-kao is said to have translated a Bud-

---

[35] See translations into French and English by Rémusat, Beal, Giles, and Legge.

dhist text that dealt with 404 maladies. A century later an Indo-Scythian missionary named Dharmaraksa listed the medicines and formulas helpful in disease of the eye, ear, and foot, in demoniacal possession, etc.; he is also responsible for a short sūtra on hot baths, which he maintained cured ills due to wind, humidity, cold, and warm air. About 300 a certain Jîvaka is reported to have effected a number of miraculous cures, among them one on a court official whose legs were twisted by paralysis. His most famous successor in the fourth century was a Kuchan priest who served at Loyang from 310 to 349; he halted an epidemic and did other miraculous deeds that endeared him to the later Chao princes. One of his disciples, an Indian, even had women patients. Yü Fa-k'ai, another Buddhist, probably Chinese, became famous for favoring such Chinese methods of prognosis as acupuncture and examination of the pulse. His reputation was so great that the Tsin emperor called him to Nanking in 361 for consultation. Yü diagnosed his disease as incurable and, in accordance with the law of India as of ancient Greece, refused to treat him. A scholar of that period declared that Yü had done much to spread Buddhism by exercising his talents as a physician.[36]

The Taoists were no less active than the Buddhists during this period. They penetrated the houses of the mighty, both north and south, realizing full well the political advantages of these connections; their continued search for the elixir of life and for a process of transmuting base metals into gold aroused the interest of both Chinese and barbarian rulers. But more interesting perhaps is the effect of Taoism on various fields of culture, particularly literature. One of the Taoists, Ko Hung (293–363), wrote an important book on the nature-philosophy of his time. T'ao Yüan-ming (or T'ao Ch'ien, 375/6–427), like many other men of the lettered class, presented an official and moral front that was Confucian but he followed Taoist

---

[36] Cf. *Hobogirin*, fasc. 3, p. 244.

precepts in his personal and spiritual life. The descendant of a long line of officials, he was born near P'oyang Lake in modern Kiangsi province. After serving as magistrate for a short time under the Tsin dynasty he retired to his home to enjoy the world of nature—the birds, domestic animals, and cultivated plants—which he loved so well and to devote himself to writing. He held the old-fashioned Chinese virtues in deep respect, and he maintained that the farmers with whom he often worked between long periods with his beloved books made the most satisfactory neighbors and companions. Considered the greatest poet of his age, he also wrote short stories, a fairly novel genre at that time. His "Peach Flower Paradise" is in reality a satire in which he depicted his dejection over the conditions of his time. It describes the utopian existence in an ideal world created by a group of families who had fled from political exploitation and military upheaval.

An earlier nature lover of this period who was also Taoist in spirit was Wang Hsi-chih (321–379), China's greatest calligrapher as well as a distinguished officer and scholar. His script, specimens of which are worth a fortune today, has been described as being as

> light as floating clouds
> vigorous as a startled dragon.[37]

For us, brought up in an age of type, the art of calligraphy is strange; but it would not have been strange to European monks before Gutenberg's time, nor to the Moslems until very recently. They would have appreciated this coruscating passage written by Sun Kuo-t'ing who lived during the T'ang dynasty:

I breathed and lived in this wondrous art for more than two decades, ever with hopes of improving my hand by ceaseless practice, albeit not to the extent of excelling that master of masters, Wang Hsi-chih. Of the wonders of *shu-fa* [art of writing], I have seen many and many a one.

[37] Giles, *Biographical Dictionary*, No. 2174.

Here, a drop of crystal dew hangs its ear on the tip of a needle; there, the rumbling of thunder hails down a shower of stones. I have seen flocks of queen-swans floating on their stately wings, or a frantic stampede rushing off at terrific speed. Sometimes in the lines a flaming phoenix dances a lordly dance, or a sinuous serpent wriggles with speckled fright. And I have seen sunken peaks plunging headlong down the precipices, or a person clinging on a dry vine while the whole silent valley yawns below. Some strokes seem as heavy as the falling banks of clouds, others as light as the wings of a cicada. A little conducting and a fountain bubbles forth, a little halting and a mountain settles down in peace. Tenderly, a new moon beams on the horizon; or, as the style becomes solemn, a river of stars, luminous and large, descends down the solitary expanse of night. All these seem as wonderful as Nature herself and almost beyond the power of man, though they all the more glorify the union between ingenuity and artistry, and reflect the delight of the artist when his hand moves at his heart's desire. The brush never touches the paper but with a purpose—the miens and tones of the strokes and the dots all lying in wait, as it were, at the command of the tip of the brush.[38]

Wang Hsi-chih was taught the art by Wei Shuo (272–349), a lady who was the successor of several outstanding calligraphers of the second and third centuries. Although trained along classical lines—Wei Shuo denounced "modern" art—Wang broke with the past and he and his son, Wang Hsien-chih (344–388), set the fashion that has lasted a millennium and a half.

Master of an associated art—that of painting, for both are done with the brush—was Ku K'ai-chih (*ca.* 344–*ca.* 406), who also served as a government official for almost forty years but was a Taoist at heart. His great roll, now in the British Museum, is called "Admonitions of the Instructress of the Palace," and represents nine of what may originally have been twelve scenes of court life; it may be a T'ang copy. Laurence Binyon of the Museum, who gave it close study over a long period, speaks of its "marvellous subtlety and distinction" and of the "consummate grace and expressiveness of the tall and slender figures, and the air of a mature and fine civilization which they seem

---

[38] Translation by Sun Ta-yü, *T'ien Hsia Monthly*, I:2, 194–195 (September, 1935).

to breathe. Far from being primitive," he adds, "the figure drawing seems to belong to the close of a tradition rather than its beginning; and we may conjecture behind it the ruder, masculine style of Han gradually subtilized and transformed in the direction of elegance and charm."[39] This painting, so famous for its figures, is truly primitive in the depiction of the landscape. Not until several centuries later did landscape painting come into its own, as is shown by the paintings recently discovered in Korea, south Manchuria, and elsewhere. A remarkable feature of this roll is the fact that it reveals none of the Indian influence that was already becoming evident in the sculpture and painting of central Asia and that soon overwhelmed north China.

Although the region governed by the Tsin was culturally not at a low ebb, such artists as these three could not have flourished in the north, hostile and embittered as it was during the fourth century. The fertile valley formed by the Yangtze delta, with its pleasant climate, its semi-tropical vegetation, and its hills and lakes, enabled an easier life than was possible in the north. Part of the secret of the valley's habitability is the fact that it was artificially developed. Irrigation was introduced at least as early as the fifth century B.C. and was continued by the later settlers. Two great reservoirs were built and a lake was deepened near modern Chinkiang in Kiangsu in A.D. 321, and a little later the Yangtze was connected with another fertile valley, the Huai, by two canals. Such conditions made the Yangtze valley the home of scholarship and the arts within a few centuries, where the Chinese of substance and learning—like the forty-two friends of Wang Hsi-chih who joined him on a perfect spring morning in 353 to celebrate by a river near Shao-hsing—could rejoice in heaven's bounteous gifts.

Far to the west, in the kingdom of Ch'êng or Shu (modern Szechuan) which in 347 yielded to the brilliant Tsin com-

[39] *Encyclopaedia Britannica,* 14th ed., sub Chinese painting.

mander, Huan Wên (312–373), a new type of record—local
histories or gazetteers—was evolving which was to be invaluable to modern historians. The earliest example, only twelve
chapters long, describes the region that is today incorporated in
southern Shensi and northern Szechuan, and touches on such
interesting subjects as the building of the capital (Ch'êng-tu)
in 310, the biographies of famous local people, native customs,
monuments of note, both wild and domestic animals, birds and
fish, and such commodities as copper, iron, salt, honey, drugs,
fruits, grain, bamboo, fine cloth, tea, face powder, and the like.
A later record, dated about 750, was recovered in manuscript
by Pelliot from the walled-in library of an ancient Buddhist
sanctuary at Tun-huang. It covers the area around the frontier
district of Tun-huang at the western terminus of the Great Wall
and includes water control, dikes, post stations, schools and
temples, marvels, and even the popular songs of the year 689.
For centuries one after another of these local records were compiled, sometimes as a labor of love by a retired scholar of the
district, sometimes by official order to provide all the necessary
information about the local governments in which there was a
succession of men from outside. For over ten centuries outsiders
regarded these gazetteers lightly; only during the last three
has their importance begun to be fully recognized. Not until
all of them have been studied and reported on in detail will the
history of China in all its phases—political, social, economic,
biographical, and cultural—be adequately told. More than 7500
of them, covering provinces, prefectures, and districts, are now
known, one of the largest collections being in the United States
at the Library of Congress.

New additions to the material culture of this period are of
some importance. Six-sided dice appeared around the third century, possibly an intrusion from the southwest. From China they
spread to Japan where eighth-century dice, dice boxes, and gam-
ing sets are still preserved. Mica, mined extensively in Shantung,

came to be used during the third and fourth centuries for lantern windows, fans, screens, watch-tower windows, and decorations for vehicles and boats.[40] The sedan chairs that until recently were a familiar conveyance in many parts of China are first recorded in the biographies of the great calligrapher Wang Hsi-chih and of Fo-t'u-têng. By that time they were used as a mark of privilege, although, as Arthur Hummel suggests, they may have been first employed to carry the old and the sick.

Of more importance than dice, mica, and sedan chairs is the fact that coal began to be used during this period. Some scholars believe that coal was used to smelt iron in the last centuries of the Chou kingdom or in the early Han when what is apparently coke is mentioned; but no definite reference antedating the fourth century A.D. has come to light.[41] Its use spread, and by the thirteenth century Marco Polo astonished his friends and readers by describing "large black stones which are dug from the mountains as veins, which burn and make flames like logs and consume away like charcoal. . . . And you may know that these stones are so good that nothing else is burnt through all the province of Catai [north China] as far as possible, though it is true that they have wood enough, that is logs."[42] Perhaps unconsciously, the use of coal made for an enormous saving of timber in China; this was not true of Europe until ten or more centuries later. The Chinese may have discovered this fuel at such an early date because of the close association of coal and iron ore in such long-settled places as Shansi province and the surface outcroppings near well-traveled highways, but the scarcity of timber throughout the loess belt in China made a substitute imperative.

[40] Cf. E. H. Schafer, *T'oung Pao,* XLII:265–286 (1955).

[41] T. T. Read, "The Earliest Industrial Use of Coal," *Transactions of the New-comen Society,* XX:119–130 (1939–1940). See particularly a letter written by Lu Yün to his brother Lu Chi, both of whom were executed in A.D. 303.

[42] Translation by Moule and Pelliot, *Marco Polo,* I, p. 249.

The Wei in North China, and the Sung, Ch'i, Liang, and Ch'ên Dynasties in the South (420–589)

During the century and a half after the collapse of the eastern Tsin in south China in 420 and the overthrow of the last competing houses in north China by the Wei in 439, the country continued to be divided into virtually two parts. The south was ruled by the Chinese, the north by the Turks. To the northwest beyond the Great Wall were the Avars; on the western border were the T'u-yü-hun, on the northeast, beyond the Liao River, were the three Korean kingdoms of Koguryŏ, Paekche, and Silla; and on the south lay Annam, which remained part of the empire except for a short period of independence in 541 to 547. Although south China seems to have been quite unstable politically—the (Liu) Sung (420–479), the Ch'i (479–502), the Liang (502–557), and the Ch'ên (557–589) dynasties followed each other in quick succession at Nanking—the administration held to the same pattern throughout this period and the social and cultural patterns were apparently not seriously disturbed.

The ruling houses in the Yellow River valley in the north were mostly non-Chinese. After 535, when the Wei split into two sections, the east and west, they were succeeded by the Northern Ch'i (550–577), the Northern Chou (557–581), and the Later Liang (555–587). But these people were essentially Chinese and Chinese civilization continued to flourish without marked changes. The Wei, under their clan name T'o-pa, had drifted into Shansi as early as the second century A.D. and hence were familiar with things Chinese. Far from imposing a foreign language or manners on the natives, they deliberately cultivated Chinese names, customs, dress, and institutions, except in military matters. There is no trace of their written language, although a number of early written documents from one or another of their seats of residence have survived. (Louis Bazin has recently examined the 160 T'o-pa words written with Chinese characters found in the Wei records, and considers that although they are preponderantly pre-Turkic a substantial number are pre-Mongol, two are pre-Tungusic, and one is basically Indo-Iranian. The first Turkic and Mongol texts known date, respectively, from the seventh to eighth centuries and the thirteenth.)[43] Their own rule and that of their successors seems to have been generally pacific; their enemy Tardu, the supreme khan of the Turks, spoke of them in a message to Maurice, emperor of the Romans, as follows: "The nation practices idolatry, but they have just laws, and their life is full of temperate wisdom."

There is no doubt that, however much they encouraged Chinese modes of life, T'o-pa were as aggressive and as resolute in war as any of their nomadic neighbors. Their success in clearing north China of all rivals was in itself a great achievement, but they went much further when in 402 they crossed the Gobi in a drive against the new menace on their frontiers, the Avars. Counterattacks followed but were successfully repulsed. Another Wei monarch, T'o-pa Tao (b. 408; r. 424–452) crossed the Gobi to strike deep into enemy territory in 425, and again in 429, 443, and 449. To defend his northern border against retaliatory attacks the Great Wall was repaired (423–440) and a protective loop was built north of modern Kalgan. In 445 and 448 his troops penetrated central Asia as far as Kucha. Here were generalship and cavalry action at their best. Such deeds and similar ones on the part of his immediate successors so impressed their neighbors in central Asia that for several decades after the fall of the Wei dynasty north China was known to Turks, Arabs, and Byzantines by some form of the name T'o-pa.

The importance of cavalry detachments that could ride hard and strike swiftly had long been recognized by the Chinese as well as the nomads. As far back as the fifth and fourth centuries

[43] *T'oung Pao* 39:228–329 (1950).

B.C. the chariot-riding Chinese nobles found themselves at the mercy of the mounted bowmen of the northwest. Speedy cavalry units accounted in part for the success of the Ch'in. Wu-ti, the Han emperor, paid special attention to horse breeding and was thus able to defeat the frontier peoples of his time. In the fourth century A.D. the Chinese rulers lost the fertile grazing grounds that Wu-ti had developed and without which they could not hope to defeat their enemies, for the climate and fodder south of the Yangtze were unfit for horses raised on the steppe. All they could do was to defend the great river at all costs, for the terrain to the south of it was not suited to cavalry action. This they did successfully in December, 383, when two of their generals, Hsieh Shih and Hsieh Hsüan, repelled the early Ch'in northern army led by Fu Chien on the banks of the Fei in modern Anhui.

How much horseflesh the government required during the fifth and sixth centuries is difficult to determine. Dr. T. C. Lin, who has studied this problem, estimates that the T'o-pa needed two million head which were pastured in the Ordos region. After 439 they probably also used the Kansu feeding grounds which were famous even before Emperor Wu's time. The latter grounds were used again in the seventh century when the T'ang established eight centers to handle three hundred thousand horses. A thousand later years, during the reign of a Manchu monarch, (1662–1722), Jehol and Chahar were set apart for this purpose. Feeding was a tremendous problem and many people were driven away from their land so that the horses could have sufficient pasturage. The Chinese realized that each horse required, on the average, about fifty *mu* (some seven acres) of grazing land.

The harness used during this period differed in only one respect from its earlier counterpart in Ch'in and Han times, which had included bit, bridle, and saddle, but no stirrups, at least as far as can be determined.[44] This extremely useful adjunct to the mounted soldier shooting a crossbow at full gallop is first mentioned in Chinese literature in the biography of an officer who was born in Honan and flourished in 477. No authenticated stirrup before that year has been unearthed, but representations of them on figurines of the Tsin period (265–420) have recently been brought to light. We may therefore conclude that certainly by the fifth century, and possibly even earlier, the Chinese and Koreans had learned the use of the stirrup from the Hsiung-nu. In like manner at a somewhat later date the nomads of the steppe (possibly the Avars?) passed it on to the peoples living along the Danube and in the Balkan peninsula. The stirrup enabled the Chinese better to combat their traditional foe, for people of a village culture like China's and Korea's are not naturally good horsemen.

The T'o-pa failed to maintain their military supremacy. Shifting their seat of residence from the mountainous block of northern Shansi to the Lo valley (modern Honan) in 494, they made their last great—and unsuccessful—effort to conquer south China in the spring of 507. Their dynasty came to an end soon after 534, when they were divided into two houses, an east and a west. Their great foes, the Avars, were weakening at the same time. Subdued in 551 by a group of their own serfs, a number of the Avars apparently pushed on across the Urals around 558 and reached the Danube some seven years later; others went to China where they were absorbed by the Northern Ch'i.

These former serfs, whose specialty had been work at the forge, were known to the Chinese as T'u-chüeh, and to the Avars as Türküt (the plural form of Türk), i.e., Turks; this is the first time in history that this name appears. For the next fifteen years they were engaged in building an empire patterned on that of the Avars. It stretched across all northern Asia, includ-

---

[44] For an excellent discussion of the appearance of the stirrup in the old world, see Lynn White, Jr., *Medieval Technology and Social Change* (Oxford 1962), pp. 14–28, 140.

ing Mongolia, part of Chinese Turkestan, Russian Turkestan, and northern Afghanistan, and exchanged ambassadors with Byzantium, Persia, and China. Its very size brought about its downfall in 582, when it was divided into two parts. Of these, the eastern Turks remained in power for a longer period (until 745), their domain extending from the Manchurian border to Hami and touching China at the Great Wall. From their base on the Orkhon River they often dealt with the Son of Heaven on terms of embarrassing equality, a fact that helps to explain why, of all the literatures in the world, that of China contains the fullest records of the early Turks.

Political unrest was augmented by social unrest in the years 420 to 589. The principal cause of this discord concerned land and taxation. Natural catastrophes or political disruption often forced the smaller landowners to sell their holdings to the rich and strong at a low price. To escape the inevitable taxation, the latter commonly put their land under the protection of a Buddhist temple or a Taoist phalanstery, or arranged to have a member of their family enter the church. In despair, some of those stripped of their holdings entered religious establishments to escape military service or forced labor. Wei Shou (506–572), the sympathetic historian who reported in about 554 on the situation in the north, wrote; "After 520–525 the empire suffered much anxiety, and the services demanded of the people became increasingly oppressive. Thereupon they everywhere entered religion pretending a love for the śramanas, but in reality avoiding assignment for military service. Abuses and excesses attained a peak unequaled since the introduction of Buddhism into China. Calculated in round numbers, the monks and nuns were estimated at a total of two million; and their monasteries thirty-thousand-odd. The disorders have not abated even down to this time, and, accordingly, the wise heave sighs of regret."[45]

[45] Cf. translations by James R. Ware, *T'oung Pao*, XXX:178–179 (1933), and Arthur W. Hummel, *Report of the Librarian of Congress, 1933–34*, pp. 5–6.

Despite all checks—such as sharp conflicts with the Taoists, particularly in the north in 438 to 446, and with Confucian scholars, particularly in the northwest in 574, Buddhism flourished; this period has even been called its golden age. Various sects to suit nearly every need developed apace; Chinese women, permitted to enter the church after 357, took orders in increasing numbers; and sutras and other parts of the canon were translated and retranslated with fervor. T'o-pa Hung, son of the northern emperor T'o-pa Chün (r. 452–466), abdicated in 471 to devote himself to reading books on the mystery of Buddhism, and each successive dynasty in the south played into the hands of the church, in spite of a few sharp protests from powerful officials. Loyang, the Wei capital, is said to have sheltered three thousand foreign monks between 500 and 515. Under the Liu Sung rulers thousands of pagodas, Buddhist temples, and statues are reported to have been erected; Buddhist priests became wellnigh supreme in government councils under the Southern Ch'i; although a Taoist in his youth, the first Liang emperor (Wu, 502–549), became the promoter and protector of Buddhism to such an extent that he has been called the Chinese Asoka; and under the Ch'ên seven hundred Buddhist monuments that had been damaged during a rebellion in 547 were rebuilt, and two emperors and one heir apparent took the vows of priesthood.

Of all the features of this great religious invasion and its active acceptance by the Chinese, the artistic is today the most revealing. Few paintings of consequence have survived except an occasional mural in a tomb or in such Buddhist grottoes as those at Tun-huang, although there is sufficient contemporary Chinese evidence to suggest that painting did not lag behind sculpture. Mute evidence of the artistic ardor still remains in Shansi, Hopei, Shantung, Honan, Shensi, and Kansu; and there is scarcely a general cultural museum of importance anywhere in the world that does not contain some lovely object from one of these sites. The northern emperor T'o-pa Chün and his successors promoted sculpture and architecture so effectively that some of these works still survive in spite of man and the elements. During the period from 414 to 520 the T'o-pa cut grottoes in the limestone caves near the first Wei capital near modern Ta-t'ung in Shansi, decorating them with statues and other ornaments carved out of the living rock. Other grottoes were cut by the T'o-pa and under later dynasties in many places, notably at T'ien-lung hill in Shansi, at Li-ch'êng in Shantung, at Lung-mên near Loyang, at Tun-huang, and Mai-chi hill in Kansu. The carvings in these chapels differ, although there are comparable themes as in the Christian art of the churches of medieval Europe. Progressive modifications and many outside influences, especially from Taxila, Peshawar, Mathura, and other western Asiatic centers, are naturally quite evident; it is possible that some of the artisans employed were brought in from outside of China.[46] But in spite of all the alien influences—Indian, Iranian, central Asiatic, and even faint traces of Siberian and Greek—the most massive contributions to architecture and sculpture were Chinese; as the French writer René Grousset has put it, the chapels near Ta-t'ung and Loyang are the equivalent of the French cathedrals at Chartres and Reims. The great foreign cult was becoming increasingly Chinese.

Music, particularly psalmody, had its part in chapel and monastery. The primitive Buddhist chants in India were accompanied by stringed and wind instruments, but in China as a rule there was only vocal music, as is true today for the most part. That instruments did figure to some extent is evident from the small orchestras depicted on stone and other surfaces from the sixth century on. The following instruments are shown: a *ch'in*, or psaltery; a *shêng*, or reed mouth organ; a four- and five-stringed *p'i-pa*, or balloon guitar; a *so-na*, or clarinet; and a

---

[46] The *Wei shu* tells us that in 439, when the Tun-huang country came under the T'o-pa, 30,000 families were moved bodily to the capital at Ta-t'ung; "at this time the monks and Buddhist paraphernalia all came east." (Ware, *T'oung Pao* XXX:135 [1933].)

vertical flute, harp, cymbals, gongs, whistle pipes, clappers, and drums. The clarinet and harp were apparently importations from western Asia; even the names are probably transliterations of the Persian: *so-na,* from *zourna* or *surna* (the clarinet); and *k'ung-hou,* from *čank* (the harp). From about 400 on the northern courts also patronized the music of other Asiatic peoples.[47]

The early missionaries soon discovered that it was no easy matter to adapt their hymns to the Chinese tongue; no one could even recite monosyllabic Chinese with the intonations used in polysyllabic Sanskrit. To a large extent a new idiom was needed, and both native and foreign members of the church joined in creating it. Ts'ao Chih (192–232), a Wei prince, reputedly composed as many as forty-two psalms, of which six were still extant in the seventh century. Missionaries from Kucha and Sogdiana, among others, composed other psalms. Compositions are ascribed to an emperor and a prince of the Southern Ch'i at the end of the fifth century; the history of their short dynasty dryly records that in 487 the prince invited several monks to his palace to discuss Buddhism and "to elaborate new melodies for the chanting of sacred texts."[48] From this and other sources we deduce that the art of psalmody was fluorishing at this time. Still very much alive, it deeply impressed Japanese pilgrims who visited the great monastic houses on the continent three centuries later.

The remains of the architecture, statues, and temple furniture of the fifth and sixth centuries, together with the writings of Chinese Buddhists, give a fairly clear picture of Buddhism at its apogee. One of the most remarkable of the writings is a book entitled *Kao sêng chuan* (The Lives of Eminent Buddhist Priests) compiled in 519 by Hui-chiao, who was himself a member of the Buddhist clergy. This contains biographies of nearly five hundred monks, both foreign and native, and covers a period

[47] Cf. Kiyohide Masuda, *Shina-gaku kenkyu,* XIII:43–53 (September, 1955); and Curt Sachs, *The History of Musical Instruments* (1940), chap. 10.

[48] Cf. *Hobogirin,* fasc. 1, p. 93, to fasc. 2, p. 97.

extending from the Han to the Liang. Among these monks were the translators and expositors of the sacred canon, whom we have already mentioned; there were also the miracle workers like Fo-t'u-têng, the central Asian who could produce lotus flowers in a vase filled only with water, to the great astonishment of the barbaric founder of the Later Chao dynasty. The biographies of the seven self-immolators that are also included reveal a body of thought that was entirely foreign to the Chinese mind before the advent of Buddhism. The twenty-third chapter of the Saddharma Pundarīka sūtra taught that the sacrifice of one's own person outranks all other sacrifices—that even burning one's finger as a sacrifice is superior to rescuing all the people of a state. As Dr. Hu Shih puts it, Bhaiṣajya-rāja, the hero of that chapter, therefore "perfumed his whole body, anointed it with fragrant oil, soaked all [his] clothing in oil, and finally burned himself as a sacrifice to Buddha." To attain salvation and with this model before them—this sūtra seems to have been extremely popular— a number of monks followed in his footsteps, generally in a public place and to the plaudits of the crowd. In 463, for example, the priest Hui-i climbed into a large cauldron before the palace in Nanking, poured oil on his head, ignited the oil, and died while repeating the legend of Bhaiṣajya-rāja.[49]

Pilgrimages abroad continued. In 511 Emperor Wu of Liang welcomed with great pomp a Chinese mission which returned from western India, whither it had been sent to receive a sandalwood statue of the Buddha made by special order of the Indian king. The most noted pilgrimage was the one in 516 ordered by Hu, the dowager empress of the Wei, herself an ardent Buddhist. The layman Sung Yün and several companions and the priest Hui-shêng left in 518 for Gandhara via central Asia, returning to Loyang in 522 with 170 sūtras and shastras of the Mahāyāna branch of the faith. The two accounts of this pil-

---

[49] Cf. Hu Shih, *Chinese Social and Political Science Review*, IX:148–149 (January, 1925); Chuan, *T'ien Hsia Monthly*, VII:5, pp. 464–467 (December, 1938).

grimage which have survived through a secondary source dated 547 give valuable descriptions of the places visited, particularly Uddiyana and Gandhara, then flourishing under the rule of Indo-Scythian princes.

Of the new Buddhist schools during this period, the most important was the T'ien-t'ai, named for a range of hills in north-eastern Chekiang province and founded in 575. One of the two founders was Chih-i or Chih-k'ai (538–597), who strove hard to give it a strong foundation. A pupil of the great monk Hui-ssŭ (d. 577), who came from Hêng-shan in modern Hunan and who worked so laboriously to save Chinese Buddhist literature from destruction (Hui-ssŭ is sometimes considered the co-founder of the school), Chih-i himself was a man of literary ability, great influence, and enormous energy. He is said to have dictated many commentaries and treatises on Buddhism, raised funds for the transcription of fifteen complete copies of the sacred canon, made some four thousand converts, and built thirty-five monastic establishments. Small wonder that he received many imperial honors during his lifetime.

In contrast to the Pure Land sect, which emphasized the invocation of Amitabha's name with faith, and the Ch'an or meditative sect, which believed in the attainment of Buddha-hood through sudden intuitive enlightenment, the new school stressed the importance of studying the sacred canon. The mind of Buddha, said the T'ien-t'ai, is in every living thing, but instruction is imperative if one is to be aware of it and able to put it to service. Such a doctrine, it may well be imagined, appealed strongly to the intellectual classes. The school, however, was not one-sided, for it also approved of such diverse elements as ecstasy, ritualism, and self-discipline and thus created a fine spirit of tolerance among the many social groups that constituted the Buddhist world from the sixth century on. Although the T'ien-t'ai became so scholastic that it was eclipsed by the Ch'an school, it still exists.

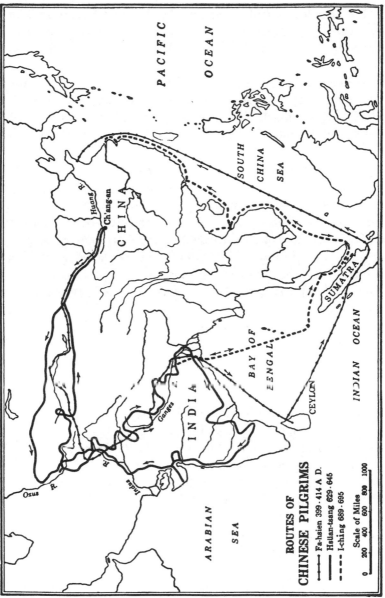

ROUTES OF
CHINESE PILGRIMS

——— Fa-hsien 399 - 414 A.D.
········· Hsüan-tsang 629 - 645
- - - - I-ching 689 - 695

Scale of Miles
0   200   400   600   800   1000

PACIFIC   OCEAN

SOUTH
CHINA
SEA

CHINA

Huang R.
Ch'ang-an

SUMATRA

BAY OF
BENGAL

INDIAN   OCEAN

CEYLON

INDIA

Ganges

Indus

Oxus R.

ARABIAN
SEA

Ever goaded as well as enriched by the great foreign religion, the Taoists succeeded in 446 in proscribing Buddhism in the northern court of Wei, but the proscription was lifted a few years later. It also had to face the criticism of the Confucian scholars who lamented the great cost of building stūpas, the waste of time on ceremonies, and the shallowness, chicanery, and deceit of much that was practiced in the name of Tao. But people could not be divided into rigid categories in those days any more than they can now. The most representative famous men of that period embraced the two Chinese faiths and at the same time reached out their hands to grasp the invading faith, just as the Han emperor had done in 166. Chang Jung (444–497), a one-time envoy to Annam and a favorite at the court of the Southern Ch'i, requested on his deathbed that the *Classic of Filial Piety* and the *Tao-tê-ching* be put in his left hand and a Buddhist sūtra in his right. Similarly, because of his well-known syncretism, Fu Hsi (497–569), the reputed inventor of the revolving bookcase, is always represented as wearing a Taoist cap, Confucian shoes, and a Buddhist scarf across one shoulder.

Alarmed by the new philosophical ideas of Buddhism which were often so contrary to the fundamental beliefs of ancient China, a few assailed the church in pamphlet and memorial. One tenet that was rooted deep in the Chinese mind was predetermination. The early Confucians and Taoists, including such masters as Confucius and Chuang-tzǔ, believed in fate and resigned themselves to its dictates. The karma principle taught by Buddhism was thus a revolutionary doctrine to the Chinese; faith and right conduct, said the missionaries, would win salvation, if not in this life, then in later ones. From this it followed that man had a soul which was indestructible. Hence their belief in a paradise and one or more hells, where man would be rewarded or punished according to his deserts. For all the comfort such ideas might give the masses and some of the intellectuals, these tenets were proper subjects for debate by the learned. Dr. Hu Shih[50]

---

[50] *Chinese Social and Political Science Review,* IX:146–147 (January, 1925).

tells of Fan Chên (fl. 510), a high official of the Liang, who wrote an essay entitled "Destructibility of the Soul" in which he tried by homely analogy to undermine the Buddhist teachings. Seventy Chinese converts, including the Lord High Chamberlain and the emperor himself, sprang to the defense of Buddhism. The results of the wordy contest that raged for centuries were for a time inconclusive. As late as the eleventh century Ssŭ-ma Kuang (1019–1086), a great historian who was familiar with all the arguments on both sides, chose to ally himself with his fellow Confucian Fan Chên. In reality during all these centuries the Chinese, face to face with the tremendous innovations of the Indian religion, were merely trying to find the elements which they could understand and accept.

The scholars of this period were by no means wholly occupied with religious disputes; on the contrary, their interests were as varied as ever. Geographical knowledge was increased by such works as Shên Huai-yüan's *Description of South China* (fifth century); the *Commentary on the Water Classic*, which covers a considerable portion of east Asia and was written by Li Tao-yüan, an adviser on frontier affairs who died in 527; and by Yang Hsüan-chih's description of Loyang (dated 547), which was then the religious, social, and political center. An agricultural treatise by Chia Ssu-hsieh (fl. 532–549) of Shantung was so popular that after the invention of printing it had over 20 editions. *The Thousand Character Classic* by Chou Hsing-tz'ŭ (d. 521) troubled millions of school children from that day to 1912 with its 250 lines, each of four different characters on nature, emperors, man, high officers, illustrious figures, agriculture, domestic government, education, and the like. Later versions of this book appeared in Korean, Japanese, Mongol, Manchu, and Jurchen. The first approximately correct calculation of π (the ratio of 355 to 113 which equals 3.14159 . . .) was made by Tsu Ch'ung-chih (429–500), who also invented automatic contrivances including a form of compass. The earliest general critique of Chinese letters was completed by Liu Hsieh in about

480; in it he discusses some thirty-five different forms of literature. Hsiao T'ung, a Liang prince (501–531), made the first
purely literary collection; it contains thirty-six different types of
literary composition but excludes the canonical, and in influence
on later generations it is surpassed only by the Taoist and Confucian classics. Of high antiquarian interest is a collection of
anecdotes about scholars, high officials, and bureaucrats, most
of them omitted from contemporary official records, which was
compiled by Liu I-ch'ing (403–444). The first book to deal
exclusively with painters and painting was written by Sun
Ch'ang-chih (fifth century), and the canons of painting were
enunciated for the first time by Hsieh Ho (fl. 500). For all the
gullibility of the age, some of the authors exhibited a remarkably
healthy skepticism. The Taoist Wei Wên-hsiu (fl. 440), for
example, was quite incredulous regarding the elixir of life and
the transformation of base metals into gold.

This spirit of inquiry extended to the etymology of the language. The Chinese, as we have seen, were well aware of the
existence both of other languages and of numerous variants of
their own tongue. As early as the third century B.C. interpreters
at court were "brought together every seventh year," says the
annalist, "to compare the languages and harmonize modes of
speech." Under the Han dynasty interpreters were called on
both for embassies abroad and for envoys to the Dragon Throne.
After the second century A.D. authoritative knowledge of the pronunciation became more essential than ever because of the numerous translations from the Sanskrit and the host of invaders from
the north and west. The first man to classify the four tones is
unknown, but it is evident that by the end of the fifth century
several scholars were giving it their attention. Even more important was the "spelling" of Chinese characters, a problem that
may have been solved by an Indian, but more likely a Chinese,
who used a second Chinese character to represent the palataliza-
tion and a third to represent the final (including the vowel), the

labialization, and the tone of any given word. The best description of this scheme is by Shên Yüeh (431–503) and was published in 543, but there is evidence of its use in the third century A.D. by the scholar, Sun Yen (d. 260?), and possibly even earlier. These and other sources have been brilliantly drawn upon, by recent western scholars in particular, to determine the standard pronunciation of the sixth-century Chinese language.

To the developments of this period must be added at least one in the minor arts—the pottery figurine. This art, which began during the Han period and grew steadily through the next few centuries, arose from the ancient aversion to putting animals and humans to death at the funerals of the wealthy. At first there were models of almost everything used by the deceased—houses, implements, and livestock. During the Wei dynasty in the north and the Liang in the south there were whole series of vessels, toilet boxes, flasks, dancing ladies, musicians, warriors, servants, and animals. These figurines have considerable archeological interest, although curiously enough they were scarcely known, let alone valued, until the turn of the present century when railroads cut through ancient cemeteries accidentally unearthed them. R. L. Hobson, a British authority on Chinese pottery, has said that some of these early painted figurines are executed in a style not unworthy of paintings on silk. They have no connection with Buddhism, except for the fact that a central principle of that faith was forbearance from sacrificing any form of life; it is more likely that they were used by such non-Buddhists as could afford to purchase them. The meaning of the figurines representing mythological creatures and monsters that have been found in almost every tomb has not yet been satisfactorily explained; probably they were part of the popular religion which scholars failed to record. The artisans who made these figurines were at their best during the latter half of the first millennium, although there are a few later mortuary figurines (the Royal Ontario Museum in Toronto has a Ming set). After 1000, the practice of burying them with the dead began to be replaced by the custom of burning paper representations of gold and silver ingots, etc., at funerals. Cremation, which became common about the eleventh century, may also have had a part in this.

Although documentary proof is almost wholly lacking, evidence from various sources indicates that the art of building seaworthy craft went on apace. Chinese historians tell of merchants from the Mediterranean Orient coming to Indo-China during the Liang dynasty (502–557), and Cosmas says in his *Christian Topography* that Chinese goods were transported to Ceylon and thence to other markets. Fleets of Chinese and Sino-Tonkin vessels on the coasts of Champa are reported in the years 248, 359, 407, and 431. Travel by water was hazardous not only because of storms and other perils of nature but also because of the pirates who infested the coasts of southeastern Asia. Fa-hsien mentioned them in his record of 413, and in 446 the Chinese sent a punitive expedition to Annam which quelled them, at least for a time.

Despite transportation difficulties in the fifth and sixth centuries, goods, culture, and folk tales continued to be exchanged, and some became firmly entrenched in China. Among the plants to be introduced, perhaps a little earlier, are the pomegranate, safflower, sesame, flax, coriander, chive, onion, shallot, garden pea, broad bean, and possibly the cucumber. Chinese games now included backgammon and elephant chess. The latter apparently originated in India and spread thence east and west at about the same time. It is first mentioned in the west in the *Karnamak*, a Pahlavi text whose date has been placed between 590 and 628; the Sui bibliography (*ca.* 600) includes books on chess, and a tenth-century encyclopedia mentions the game under the year 568. The kite, an object of usefulness as well as sport, originated in China about this time. The first verifiable reference is to its use at the siege of T'ai in 549, when the Liang emperor sent one aloft to inform his friends outside the city of his plight. The

enemy, noticing it, ordered their best archers to bring it down—
according to Laufer, the first case of anti-aircraft warfare.[51] The
use of kites spread to Moslem lands in the seventh century, to
Italy in 1589, and to England a few decades later.

Legends from abroad continued to enrich Chinese fiction.
One, of western origin, may be cited as an example. It tells of
an inaccessible valley whose floor was strewn with diamonds. To
secure these gems, covetous people from high up in the cliffs
threw flesh into the valley; the flesh, with the precious stones
adhering to it, was immediately picked up by vultures and
brought to the tableland. This justly famous tale, which is found
in slightly varying forms in Persian, Arabic, and other literatures, first appeared in China about 520 when a high official of
Szechuan told it to the emperor of Liang. It is first mentioned
in the west in the writing of Epiphanius, Bishop of Constantia
in Cyprus, who died in A.D. 403.[52]

[51] Laufer, *Prehistory of Aviation*, pp. 34–37.
[52] Laufer, *The Diamond*, pp. 6–9.

CHAPTER IV

A Reunited China: The Sui and the T'ang (590–906)

The Sui (590–618)

THE distinction of uniting China falls to Yang Chien (541–604), an official of the Chou dynasty and the founder of the Sui, who deposed a boy ruler in 581 and apparently slew him and fifty-nine princes of the blood. A few years later (587) he dethroned the last Later Liang emperor and in 589 he overthrew the Ch'ên; his empire now extended from the Great Wall to the Pescadores, small islands due east of the southern end of Fukien province. Annam, which had been in revolt since 541, submitted to him in 603, and his army pillaged Champa, the capital, in 605; this extended his domain even farther south. The new dynasty had a short life, but its achievements—the restoration of individual control and many innovations—were followed so closely by the T'ang, the greater dynasty that succeeded the Sui, that the two are often discussed together.

Yang Chien pressed his initial military successes in every direction, as did also his son and successor Yang Kuang (b. 569; r. 605–618). As early as 582, before he had conquered China, Yang Chien began to meddle in the affairs of central Asia. He turned against the eastern Turks (the T'u-chüeh), who were having domestic troubles over the khanate, and encouraged their one-time subordinates, the western Turks, to rebel. The latter's chief, Tardu, an extremely violent man, overcame the eastern

Turks so easily that in 585 Yang Chien broke his new alliance in order to preserve the balance of power on his frontier. He held Tardu at bay until the death of the eastern Turk khan; Tardu now subjugated the eastern Turks and made himself supreme in Mongolia. In 601 he menaced Ch'ang-an and attacked a branch of the eastern Turks in the Ordos. Fortunately for China, trouble broke out in the western Turk empire and Tardu fell from power in 603. His empire was divided, the astute Chinese agent P'ei Chü (*ca.* 548–627) cleverly supporting the western section whose capital was at Tashkent. (P'ei later gave the court an illustrated report on the western regions and developed commercial relations between China and other states.) The chief of the other part of the former empire, whose capital was at Ili, now gave up his ambition of becoming another Tardu and submitted to China. The chiefs of the eastern Turks also sought its protection and in 608 allowed the Chinese to reoccupy the strategic oasis of Hami. That same year the Chinese, led by P'ei Chü, drove the Mongol-speaking T'u-yü-hun from Kansu into Tibet.

Territorial expansion in the southeast was resumed in 607–610. The Lew Chew (and possibly Taiwan), known to the Chinese at least since the first century B.C. and penetrated by them in A.D. 230, was successfully invaded in 610 by a force from Kuangtung; several thousand prisoners, both men and women, were sent to the continent. In 607 Yang Kuang dispatched a mission to the East Indies, ostensibly to establish commercial relations; this mission, accompanied by an envoy, returned to China in 610. Territorial aggrandizement in the north was less successful. Koguryŏ, which now comprised two-thirds of Korea and a large part of south Manchuria, was invaded four times between 598 and 614, each expedition meeting with disaster. The Sui reputation for military prowess was based on its other campaigns, for the court was visited by a number of envoys from distant lands—from Japan in 600, 607, and 610, and from other parts of the continent in 609. Chinese ambassadors in their turn went to India and Turkestan, returning, we are told, with lion skins, agate goblets, asbestos, dancing girls, and Buddhist sūtras. Imperial China, which had almost vanished in the four centuries between the Han and Sui dynasties, was clearly emerging once more.

Although both the founder of the Sui and his son were none too securely enthroned (both men died unnatural deaths), the domestic measures they introduced distinguish the dynasty in spite of its brief life. The internal administration was improved, four state granaries were constructed near the western capital at Ch'ang-an and two near the eastern capital at Loyang, and the northern borders were fortified along the Great Wall at a prodigal cost of human life.[1] Buddhism, which had been persecuted in the north since 574, again received official favor. The officers of the Sui were especially recommended for service, as during the Han, but apparently examinations were not used in selecting them; this practice was not inaugurated until some time after 618. The Sui emperors' love of grandeur required not only the rebuilding of the two capitals near the Yellow River— with parks and palaces—but also the construction of a third at Yangchow, the inland port on the Yangtze estuary. Communication between the capitals and, more important, between the center and northwest (the major area of political control) and the lower Yangtze (the source of the greatest food supply) was established by the continuation of the canal system of eastern China. Into this effort both rulers, especially Yang Kuang, flung their man power with apparent disregard for consequences. There is no question but that some of these activities were dictated by the desire for pomp and by other selfish considerations.

---

[1] Bingham reports that one million men worked for ten days during the summer of 607 and half of them died. *The Fall of Sui and the Rise of T'ang*, p. 20. One wonders if many did not simply drift out of sight of their taskmasters and so should be counted missing rather than dead.

It is also true, however, that if the entire country was to be brought under one ruler, if the chief defense problem was the northwest, and if some useful service was to be found for the large number of military adventurers, the dispersed remnants of the earlier armies and their camp followers that are always a serious problem to a new dynasty, the extension of the canals to the neighborhood of Shensi was called for. A Chinese administrator, who wrote about 1600, said justly that the second Sui emperor "shortened the life of his dynasty by a number of years, but benefited posterity unto ten thousand generations. He ruled without benevolence, but his rule is to be credited with enduring accomplishments."[2]

Canal building began in 584 and did not really end until the eighth century. By 618, however, communications had been established north and south between the Hai River and Hangchow, and east and west between Ch'ang-an and Yangchow. A Sung historian of the period described one section as follows: "From Shanyang to the Yangtze River, the water surface of the canal was forty paces wide. Roads were constructed along both banks of the canal and planted with elms and willows. For over 2000 *li* from the eastern capital (modern Loyang) to Chiang-tu (modern Yangchow), shadows of trees overlapped each other. An imperial resting place was built between every two post stations, and from the capital in Ch'ang-an to Chiang-tu there were more than forty such pavilions."[3] An account of one portion of canal building that has survived relates that every man from fifteen to fifty was impressed into service. The punishment for evasion was decapitation. Three million six hundred thousand laborers were thus assembled. To feed and assist them each family in the neighborhood was required to contribute a child, an old man, or a woman. The final total, including section

[2] Translated by Chi, *Key Economic Areas in Chinese History*, p. 122.
[3] *Ibid.*, pp. 117–118.

chiefs, numbered 5,430,000 people. Flogging and neck weights drove the laggards on.

The Sui empire had little chance to profit from this immense engineering feat. Rather, it benefited the T'ang, which produced a succession of able administrators to maintain and improve the canals, to construct granaries, and to handle the increasing volume of trade. Although statistics are inadequate it is reported that seven million tons of grain were transported in a single three-year period around 735. By the end of that century, the people of the lower Yangtze were supporting the major cost of government; they provided nine-tenths of the revenue, it is said. The dependence of the marginal territory in the northwest on the rich delta of China's greatest river amply justified the huge expenditure of human life and of great sums of money.

Popular dissatisfaction with the intolerance, cruelty, and foolish personal extravagance of their rulers had been smoldering for some time and was brought near the combustion point by the cost of military adventures and public works. The khan of the eastern Turks, seizing on the emperor's defeats in Korea to attack, laid waste a large area and bottled up Yang Kuang himself in 615 in the siege of Yen-mên in the northwest. Civil disorders immediately broke out. The insurrection of the Li, a ducal family that was related by marriage both to the house of Yang and to the Turks, spelled the doom of the Sui dynasty. In 617 Ch'ang-an fell to Li Yüan (566–635). It took a while, however, before all opposition was quelled. Even in the palace itself there was rivalry; in 626 one son, Li Shih-min (not heir apparent), had to assassinate two of his brothers to ensure his succession to the throne on his father's abdication.

THE T'ANG DYNASTY (618–906)

The T'ang dynasty founded by Li Yüan and Li Shih-min officially began on April 11, 618, with Yang Kuang's assassination at his beautiful palace in Yangchow. The three centuries of its existence are regarded by the Chinese as perhaps the most brilliant era in their country's history. The T'ang carried on and broadened the work of the Sui at home and abroad. After all the country had been pacified, the empire was divided first into ten and then (733) into fifteen provinces. In the beginning their administration was characterized by considerable centralization, but this gave way to increasing independence after 705 and especially after 756. Education was encouraged, and examinations for civil government officials were reintroduced on a broad scale. The lands which had been abandoned during the civil wars were redistributed, probably as much to assure a flow of taxes as to satisfy and stabilize the peasantry. The official religion was fostered by the erection of temples to Confucius in every department and district, but religious tolerance prevailed. Ch'ang-an, the capital, says Obata, "became not only the center of religious proselytism, but also a great cosmopolitan city where Syrians, Arabs, Persians, Tartars, Tibetans, Koreans, Japanese and Tonkinese and other peoples of widely divergent races and faiths lived side by side, presenting a remarkable contrast to the ferocious religious and racial strife then prevailing in Europe." The canal system was extended and improved, and the severe laws of the Sui were recodified;[4] the T'ang code is believed to have been published in 653, and an amplified edition appeared in 737. This code had a profound effect on the ancient lawmakers of Annam and Japan.

During the first years of the dynasty there were attempted invasions by the Turks. Successfully resisting, the T'ang finally carried the war into Mongolia itself in 630 and by alliances with the latter's enemies and a forceful campaign subdued the eastern Turks. This dangerous foe remained submissive to Ch'ang-an until 682, the Chinese emperor Li Shih-min being known as great khan of the adjacent tribes; he knew how to serve as both

[4] Cf. E. Balazs, *Le Traité Juridique du "Souei-chou,"* pp. 25–26.

emperor and khan. A Turkish inscription of the year 732, discovered in 1889 on the eastern bank of the Orkhon River about thirty miles from the ruins of the Turkish capital, reads in part: "The sons of nobles became slaves of the Chinese people, and their pure daughters serfs. The Turkish nobles abandoned their Turkish titles, and, receiving Chinese titles of dignitaries in China, submitted to the Chinese khan, and for fifty years gave him their service and their strength. Forward, towards the rising sun, they campaigned up to the domain of the powerful khan; rearward (i.e., on the west), they made expeditions up to the Gate of Iron; but to the Chinese khan they delivered their empire and their institutions."[5]

From the Orkhon Li-shih-min moved on to the destruction of the western Turks and other smaller states during 641 to 648, clearing the path for direct contact with Iran and India. Sron-bcan-sgan-po (reigned ca. 630–650), the first king of Tibet, never unified until 607, asked him for the hand of a Chinese princess in marriage. This was at first refused; but in 641, after repulsing a Tibetan invasion, Li sent the Princess Wên-ch'êng (d. 680), a young kinswoman whose name is imperishably linked with the introduction of Buddhism and Chinese civilization into that desolate land. Some of the advance work, however, had undoubtedly already been done; the king's Nepalese consort, for example, had aided in softening and civilizing the Tibetans. In 647 the emperor sent an envoy to Assam to promote diplomatic relations; on his arrival he found that a usurper was trying to seize the throne. When, during the course of the uprising the envoy lost his entire escort, he applied to both the king of Tibet and the king of Nepal for aid and, at the head of their troops, he captured the usurper in 648 and took him to Ch'ang-an.

Only in the northeast around Koguryŏ was Li Shih-min un-

5 Translated into French by Vihh Thomsen, *Inscriptions de l'Orkhon déchiffrées,* Société Finno Ougrienne, V:99 (1896).

successful. One of the oldest monuments in Peking, the Fa Yüan Ssŭ, marks the place at which his army halted to recover itself after its decisive defeat in the year 645 near Pyong-yang in northern Korea. China's armies were not to be resisted, however. Profiting by growing disunion in Korea in 660, Li's successor sided with one of the three Korean states and in the next eight years established Chinese suzerainty over not only most of Korea (Silla remained quasi-independent) but also Koguryŏ in Manchuria. He established a secondary capital first at Pyong-yang and then at Liaotung under the command of a governor general, but all other important offices were held by Koreans. In one year (669), 38,000 insurrectionists were sent to central China. This protectorate, which lasted for ninety years (until 758), made for flourishing trade and cultural relations.

Elsewhere this emperor was equally successful in military affairs. The general who was to subdue Paekche in 663 conquered the western Turks in 657 and forced them to scatter, some fleeing to India and others across Russia into Hungary. To govern this new territory two Chinese protectorates were created, one north of the T'ien shan and the other south of the mountains. This emperor also maintained diplomatic relations with the courts west of the Pamirs and gave refuge at his own court to Peroz, the last Sassanid king, and his son.

Despite all these successes, T'ang China suffered several setbacks at the hands of Tibetans, Turks, and others from about 663 to the middle of the following century. Nevertheless, its reputation remained sufficiently high for Persia to send ten embassies (two of them included a prince) between 713 and 751; they brought such gifts as an agate bed, flame-colored woolen embroideries, and troops of dancers. The Indian princes of the Indus valley likewise acknowledged Chinese suzerainty, and envoys from many other Asiatic courts thronged Ch'ang-an. In spite of the truly imperial aspects of the reign of Hsüan-tsung (712–755) there were ominous signs. The Khitan in Manchuria

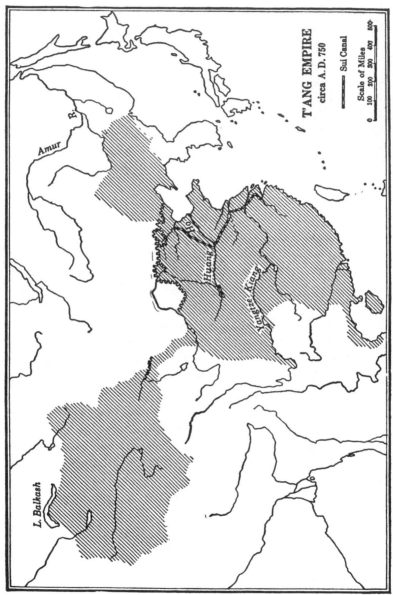

T'ANG EMPIRE
circa A.D. 750

——— Sui Canal

Scale of Miles
0   100 200 300 400 500

Amur R.

Ho

Huang

Yangtze Kiang

L. Balkash

122

were undermining Chinese influence on the Liao; Mongolia was in the hands of the Uigur Turks after 745 and was soon on terms of equality with T'ang China. The Arabs, resurgent under Moslem leadership, disputed China's dominion west of Turkestan. Even the Thai principalities in the southwest, which had been united in 730, repelled two Chinese armies between 751 and 754 and a century later challenged China on her own territory at Ch'êng-tu. Finally, the Tibetans were beginning to block intercourse between China and Iran by occupying the most important passes over the Pamirs. Hsüan-tsung ordered Kao Hsien-chih (in Korean: Ko Sŏn-ji), his viceroy and a Korean officer, to retake the passes, and the Tibetans were routed in 747 after a masterly campaign.

It looked for a time as though the Chinese had only to assert themselves in order to be victorious and to maintain their extensive but loosely held empire. But Kao Hsien-chih over-reached himself in a more than questionable move against the prince of Tashkent. The Arabs rushed to the latter's aid and defeated Kao disastrously in a great battle near the Talas River in July, 751. Not only was Turkestan promptly freed of China's authority, but the Buddhist houses, which were centered around the oases, were soon permanently displaced by western religious cults, especially Islam. Although unnoticed by European military authorities, this struggle was certainly one of the decisive battles of history. T'ang China, whose empire had been the greatest in the contemporary world for over a century, now had to face the Arabs, who were as assertive as themselves and who for a similar period of time ruled from the Kansu frontier to Spain and Morocco and usurped the Indian Ocean route as well. Nor did China have time to gather itself together, for its armies were then being defeated, as we have seen above, by the Khitan in the north and the Thai in the south. The end was swift. An internal revolt led by an adventurer of central Asiatic or Tungus origin broke out in the capital in 755; in 756 the emperor fled to Ch'êng-tu, relinquishing the throne to his son. In 757 the latter recaptured Ch'ang-an, aided by troops from the two protectorates north and south of the T'ien shan, the Uigur, and even Ferghana and Arabia. The rebellion dragged on until 763, leaving China nearly prostrate and shorn of its man power, dominion, wealth, and prestige. Not until ten centuries later did it achieve its former position in Asia, and then it was under an alien house and for a briefer span.

The next century and a half saw a gradual retreat to what may be called China's normal boundaries. Silla absorbed the other two kingdoms of Korea. The Khitan and P'o-hai divided Manchuria between them. The Uigur, on a basis of equality with the T'ang, acted as guardians of the northwest marches until 840. The Tibetans were a continued menace on China's western flank.[6] The Thai kingdom in Yünnan, at one time an ally, at another an enemy, attempted to invade China's southerly province, Tongking, during 836 to 866. The seacoast, never well defended, was ravaged by pirates; such commerce as there was seems to have been mainly in the hands of the Koreans to the north and the Persians to the south, although some Chinese merchants sailed to Japan in their own boats and others constructed a few craft for the Japanese.

Maladministration from the top down affected the entire country, resulting in a rebellion that began in Shantung in 875 and swept over all of China. The Huai basin and Honan province were pillaged in 876 to 877. In 878 the rebel leader Huang Ch'ao penetrated Fukien and there was an outbreak at the other end of the empire in Shansi. In 879 Canton was laid waste; according to an almost contemporary account by the Arab Abû Zayd (ca. 916): "With the taking of the city, its inhabitants were

---

[6] In 787 the Chinese sought the aid of the Arabs against the Tibetans. Eleven years later the celebrated Harun al-Raschid sent three envoys to China who kowtowed to the T'ang emperor and concluded a treaty of alliance against them.

put to the sword. Persons who have knowledge of the facts report that they [i.e., the rebels] slew 120,000 Mohammedans,
Jews, Christians, and Mazdeans who were established in the
town and did business there, besides numberless Chinese."[7]
Huang then turned north and sacked Loyang and Ch'ang-an;
he called himself emperor during the brief time that the fleeing
rightful emperor was near the Tibetan border in western
Szechuan. The uprising was crushed in 884, but at the price of
empire. Kiangsu fell away in 883, Szechuan in 891, and the
capital area in 906. A succession of disputes between rival commanders brought the T'ang dynasty to an end.

Religion and Culture Under the Sui and the T'ang

The religious history of this period is as rich in its diversity as
in any period except the Han. It is characterized by the growth
of Buddhism and Taoism to maturity, the penetration of several
cults from the west, and the increasing usefulness of Confucianism to the state, which had to depend on the clerically trained
for the huge bureaucracy that developed. China's religious tolerance was disrupted between 842 and 845 by the secularization
and in some cases murder of numberless priests and nuns of non-
Chinese faiths, including Buddhism, by the closing or destruction of sanctuaries, and by the public burning of canonical works.
Although this failed to exterminate Buddhism, it halted its
ascendancy, and it virtually put an end to the other religions or
forced them underground where they starved to death because
of lack of contact with the mother houses in western Asia.

During the Sui dynasty both Buddhism and Taoism enjoyed
official favor, but when the T'ang came into power it seemed as
if the Buddhists would again be suppressed. During a great de-

---

[7] Translated by Gabriel Ferrand in *Voyage du Marchand Arabe Sulaymân en Inde
et en Chine rédigé en 851 suivi de rémarques par Abû Zayd Hasan (vers 916)*, p. 76.

bate at the court of the first T'ang emperor in 624, the venerable historiographer Fu I (555–639)[8] remarked cogently:

> The priests make the people believe that Buddha is the only arbiter of life and death, of fortune and misfortune, of wealth and of poverty: as if these things did not depend on nature, on his majesty, and on every person's individual industry. They arrogate to themselves the right to educate the people, withdrawing from the emperor this right which belongs properly to him, thus diminishing his authority and prestige. . . . At present monks and nuns are more in number than a hundred thousand. They have cut beautiful silk embroideries to clothe their earthen images which bewitch and delude the ten thousand surnames (i.e., the Chinese people). I suggest that your majesty decree that every monk and nun be made to marry. This will create over a hundred thousand households, which in ten years will produce boys and girls, whom they will raise, and whom the emperor may turn into soldiers to his advantage.[9]

Thoroughly alarmed, the Buddhists repelled Fu I's attack in a special book ten chapters long that is preserved in the *Tripitaka;* but a decree of the second emperor two years later took up Fu's line of attack and cited the economic loss to the state: "Lazy and unattached individuals resort to Buddhism to evade compulsory labor service, but they still indulge in wordly passions and covet wealth. Walking about the villages, trafficking in the markets, they have amassed landed estates and goods, and live by tilling the soil, weaving and trading. Their occupation, their conduct are like those of the common people. Their behavior neither conforms to the religious commandments nor follows the laymen's code of conduct. . . ."[10] Official feeling ran very high against Buddhism, but in spite of this, it continued to flourish. It was at this time (September, 629) that the Bud-

[8] Giles (*Biographical Dictionary*, No. 589) says that he was "the originator of epitaphs," and wrote his own as follows:

> "Fu I loved the green hills and the white clouds,
> Alas! he died of drink."

[9] *Chiu T'ang shu*, chap. 79, pp. 6–7.

[10] I owe this quotation, translated from the *Chiu T'ang shu*, chap. 1, pp. 14–15, to Dr. K. A. Wittfogel, *New Light on Chinese Society*, pp. 32–33.

dhist pilgrim Hsüan-tsang (602–664) left Ch'ang-an for India. When he returned to China in April, 645, he was welcomed at the capital by a great concourse of monks, officials, and common people, and at Loyang by the emperor himself; in August, 646, the latter made appropriate gifts and wrote a letter included in the pilgrim's imperishable record of his travels to India by way of central Asia.

For the next century Buddhism received no serious check, although the official attitude, notably during the reign of the pro-Buddhist empress dowager Wu (r. 685–705), changed from time to time. In 714, for example, after a bitter attack by Yao Ch'ung (651–721), the minister of war, twelve thousand priests and nuns were secularized; the building of new temples, the setting up of new statues, and the copying of Buddhist books were banned; and no one of "good family" was permitted to have any contact with Buddhist or Taoist priests. Contemporary literature and archeology attest nevertheless to the strength and popularity of Buddhist institutions. Pilgrims still ventured to Buddhist sacred places by both land and sea; perhaps the most famous one after Hsüan-tsang was I-ching, who spent the years 671 to 690 in India, Gandhara, and Kashmir. Missionaries came to China, but their work was less important since a number of Chinese scholars now knew Sanskrit. Hsüan-tsang, who devoted himself to translating after his return from India in 645, devised a method for transcribing Sanskrit that displaced the hit-or-miss systems then in use. During 689 to 695, I-ching compiled or inspired a Sanskrit-Chinese lexicon of about a thousand words; and Li-yen (ca. 706–789), a missionary teacher from Kucha, compiled a Chinese-Sanskrit lexicon containing some twelve hundred words. At the emperor's request, the latter also translated a Sanskrit work on medicine and medicinal plants. Students, particularly from Korea and Japan, came to study under Chinese masters, and occasionally one of the latter was persuaded by his pupils to cross the China Sea and settle abroad.

The building of shrines, the decoration of halls, and the translation and copying of the scriptures went on apace all over China, the costs being borne not only by native pilgrims but by foreign travelers and merchants as well.[11] Psalmody developed, particularly in the Pure Land sect.

Astronomy and mathematics, likewise inspired by Indian teachers, made new strides. One of them composed a new calendar for the first T'ang emperor in 618. A century later I-hsing (683–747), a Chinese priest and a disciple of Subhakarasimha and Vajrabodhi, put the length of a solar year as equal to 365.-2444 days, and of a solar month as the equivalent of 29.53059 days. His reformed calendar based on these calculations was adopted by the state in 729. An elaborate study which he and another scientist made of the shadow lengths of the gnomon from one end of China to the other was carried out in the years 721–725. They set up nine stations in a line from the Great Wall to modern Hanoi, a distance of some 3500 kilometers, and—with standard 8 feet gnomons—recorded simultaneously the shadow lengths during the summer and winter solstices. This, writes Needham,[11a] "must surely be regarded as the most remarkable piece of organized research carried out anywhere in the early Middle Ages." Medicine played a conspicuous part in Buddhist proselytism, as it does today in Christian missionary activities. Buddhist temples commonly had dispensaries, and sometimes specially selected young monks were sent to study medicine at Ch'ang-an.

In so large an institution as the Buddhist church there were bound to be corruption, the unwise exercise of political influence, and the protection of the unworthy. Taoists, who at times had

---

[11] The Japanese pilgrim Ennin wrote that he was approached while in Yangchow in 839 for aid to repair a temple balcony. The solicitor said that ten million cash was needed, and that the minister of state and the Persian contingent in the city had each contributed one million, while 200,000 had been donated by a man from Champa. He asked if the group from Japan, being "few in numbers," would give 50,000.

[11a] *Science and Civilization in China* III (1959), p. 293.

great power at court, were quick to notice and report such conditions. But even more important in the end was the realization by the leaders of the huge bureaucracy that here, in the Buddhist orders, was an empire within an empire that must be made subordinate to the state if the latter was not to be supplanted. This feeling reached such proportions that the court finally took action and ordered a census of all the Buddhist clergy and their property. In the fourth moon of 845, when this census was taken, it was estimated, says the annalist, "that there were approximately 4600 temples, 40,000 shrines, and 260,500 monks and nuns." Three months later all Buddhist properties throughout China were confiscated by imperial edict. The cabinet, however, submitted the following memorial: "In accordance with ordained customs, officials in prefectural cities have been wont to offer sacrifice in the Buddhist temples on days consecrated for the commemoration of the departed emperors. In view of this, we beg to submit the following requests: that one Buddhist temple should be left intact in every prefectural city; that the images of the holy and venerable countenances should be transferred to the interior of said temples; that the Buddhist temples in every city below the rank of prefecture should be forthwith destroyed; and, finally, that, in the grand thoroughfares of the two capitals (Ch'ang-an and Loyang) ten temples should be preserved with ten monks in each." The emperor replied: "Should any temple in a prefectural city be an edifice of beauty and art, let it be preserved; otherwise, let it be destroyed. Henceforth, on days of commemorations, let the officials offer the accustomed sacrifice in Taoist temples. . . ." Thereupon the cabinet submitted another memorial: "Out of disestablished temples, let the bronze images be given into the charge of the superintendent of salt and iron who shall smelt them for the minting of coins; let the iron images be given into the charge of the prefectural magistrates to be cast into agricultural implements; let images made of gold, silver, jade and other kindred precious materials be handed over to the board of treasury; let the period of one month be granted to the people of wealth and standing during which to hand over to the authorities images of every description in their possession; let defaulters receive the same punishment as is usually meted out by the superintendent of salt and iron to those who are found in unlawful possession of bronze; and finally let images made of clay, wood, and stone be left intact in their respective temples." Finally, in the eighth moon, the emperor decreed: "We therefore ordain the destruction of 4600 temples, the secularization of 260,500 monks and nuns who henceforth shall pay the semi-annual taxes, the destruction of some 40,000 shrines, the confiscation of millions of acres of arable land, the manumission of 150,000 slaves, both male and female, who shall henceforth pay the semi-annual taxes. The monks and nuns shall be under the control of the bureau for foreign affairs in order to make it obvious that this is a foreign religion. As to the Nestorians and Zoroastrians, they shall be compelled to return to secular life lest they contaminate any longer the customs of China."[12]

The state had won. Although these decrees virtually put an end to the other foreign cults, Buddhism by now was Chinese and could not perish, but it never again had such spiritual and intellectual prestige. Nor, for that matter, did China ever have to undergo the cruelties of government by a state church, for as a rule secular power remained supreme. Some temples were rebuilt almost immediately after 845, one of them at the capital the very next year, another at the great pilgrim center of Wu-t'ai shan in Shansi in 857, but China ceased to be, for nearby countries, the Buddhist "Light of the East" that it had been for two and a half centuries.

Of the foreign cults that entered China during this period, Zoroastrianism (or Mazdaism) is the first one mentioned in

---

[12] Recent investigations by Chinese scholars indicate that Buddhist shrines in areas remote from the capital, such as Szechuan, were not affected by this order.

Chinese texts. It seems to have come in via the central Asiatic trade routes early in the sixth century, to have received imperial patronage during the third decade of that century, and to have come under government control about 550. Several rulers of the Northern Ch'i and Northern Chou dynasties participated in the cult and in its ritual dancing, partly, it is said, in order to gain the favor of the people of the west (presumably, Persia). In 621 the T'ang reestablished the bureau which controlled the cult's affairs. Records for 632 give us the name of one of its priests who came to China that year, and shrines are known to have been established in the two capitals and in three other cities in the northwest. Foreigners living in China were permitted to worship with the cult, but this was forbidden to the Chinese. The Zoroastrians apparently made little effort at evangelism, a fact that may help to explain why none of their original documents has been found in China or central Asia. The prohibition of 845 nearly ended the existence of the cult, but it is known to have survived in Chinkiang and Kaifeng until about the twelfth century.

Next to enter China was probably the Nestorian branch of the Christian church, which the Chinese after 745 called the Luminous Religion. The first missionary of whom we know came from Syria (or Persia) and settled at the capital in 635.[13] There years later the court gave this cult its blessing: ". . . The meaning of the teaching has been carefully examined: it is mysterious, wonderful, calm; it fixes the essentials of life and perfection; it is the salvation of living beings; it is the wealth of man. It is right that it should spread through the empire. Therefore let the local officials build a monastery in the I-ning quarter with twenty-one regular monks."[14] The cult undoubtedly spread beyond the capital, for it is referred to in Loyang, Ch'êng-tu, and Canton,

13 P. Y. Saeki (*The Nestorian Documents and Relics in China*, p. 86) points out, however, that a Nestorian family immigrated to Kansu in 578.

14 Translated by A. C. Moule, *Christians in China Before the Year 1550*, p. 65.

among other places, but whether it was taken up by any except the Syrian and Persian traders in the commercial centers is questionable. Despite some difficulties during 698–699 and in 713, and undoubted hardships during the rebellion of 755–762 when support from western Asia was cut off, one of the churches was rich enough in 781 to erect a beautiful stele with inscriptions in Syriac and Chinese, which fortunately still survives. Another record of first importance (Saeki discusses seven others) is the Hymn to the Holy Trinity, dating from about 800, which was recovered early in the present century from an ancient walled-in library near Tun-huang, an outpost of the Great Wall. The cult was so rigidly suppressed in 845 that little has been discovered to suggest survival in the eleventh and twelfth centuries.[15]

Third chronologically is Manicheism, the eclectic faith propounded by Mani of Babylon (216–277, or 274). It seems to have been introduced in China by Persians and others in 694, but it had a difficult existence until after the conversion of the Uigur kaghan, an ally of the Chinese state. In 763, the year after he recaptured Loyang from the rebels, he proclaimed it to be the official religion of his people, whereupon the patriarch at Babylon sent monks and nuns to propagate the doctrine throughout Mongolia. The support of the Uigur enabled the cult to spread beyond the two T'ang capitals to cities in the Yangtze valley and elsewhere. Missionary work was actively pursued, especially after the Abbasid persecutions in Persia (785–809); the lesser monks were replaced with new recruits, and connections with the houses in central and western Asia were constantly maintained. When the Uigur state lost its status of equality with T'ang China, however, Manichean influence withered with it. The monasteries in the Yangtze valley were closed in 842, and Manicheism was universally proscribed in 843, when a Chinese

---

[15] There were, however, some Nestorian Christians in the empire of the Liao at this time. See Ryuzo Torii, *Sculptured Stones of the Liao Dynasty*, pp. 60–61; also R. Grousset, *L'empire Mongole*, p. 490.

army defeated the Uigur kaghan. As a force in religious life the cult died with the proscription, although there are echoes of it, mainly as a secret society, until early in the seventeenth century. Its most interesting contributions seem to have been made by its astronomer-priests. A record of 764 attests to the fact that Sogdian Manicheans established the planetary or seven-day week; it gives in Sogdian, Persian, Indian, and Chinese the names of the seven planets in order of the week days. The Manichean name for Sunday, the principal fast day, even penetrated Fujiwara Japan and, a curious survival, has been used in provincial calendars in Fukien province until recently.

The two other cults, Judaism and Islam, are of little significance in this era. The Jews, who are known to have been in Canton before the slaughter of 879, doubtless came there by sea via India. Eighth-century Judeo-Persian documents that have been found on the central Asian trade routes and at their eastern terminus at Tun-huang also indicate a Jewish migration, but no Jewish activity in China seems to have gained the attention of Chinese historians. The Arabs, as we have seen, had long conducted trade by sea with the Chinese, and it was doubtless from these trading communities that Islam penetrated China. That the Moslems entered western China as envoys and campaigners but not as missionaries is established by the Arab travelers who visited the capital. It is assumed that Moslems were among those who sacked and burned the city of Canton in 758, and they were certainly the greatest sufferers in the Huang Ch'ao rebellion of 879. Not until the Sung and Yüan dynasties, however, were there genuine Jewish and Moslem communities in China that were able to withstand anti-foreign hostility or the overthrow of a dynasty. That the Chinese had some knowledge of both religions is made clear by passages in the T'ang annals and Arab journals.[16]

<hr>

[16] See *Hsin T'ang shu*, chap. 221 B; J. Sauvaget, *Relation de la Chine et de l'Inde, redigée en 851*, p. xxxviii; and G. Ferrand, *op. cit.*, pp. 85–92.

For all our interest in these non-Chinese cults in China, we must not forget that Taoism and Confucianism were incomparably more popular than any other religion except Buddhism. The Li dynasty had sentimental reasons for supporting Taoism; but most of its long line of rulers wisely capitulated to the official religion and actively encouraged scholastic training in order to develop the great body of state officials required for the loyal performance of administrative functions, large and small, throughout the empire. These officials were men on whom the emperor could rely for counsel and support, for they had no military or hereditary power. Their greatest disservice lay in their conservatism, in their perpetuation of outworn ideas and practices, and in their connection with the propertied class who generally despised and oppressed the poor. As was said earlier, in most cases only long training and severe application could enable one to pass the literary tests[17] requisite to holding office, and only the sons of the well-to-do could afford the time and expense necessary for that training. The long line of civil servants active in T'ang and later China thus constituted a class group that sprang from the leisured families who lived on rents from land. As long as other groups could obtain a hearing at the capital, all went well, for in a sense there was a balance of power. Only when one group became dominant or all-powerful did the system cease to function.

The second emperor's reign is an example of institutionalism at its best. Personally disposed toward Taoism, that ruler graciously honored Buddhism in 645 and was most active in the reestablishment of Confucianism. After examinations were again made a prerequisite to holding office, he founded a library and various colleges at the capital and encouraged the establishment

---

[17] After 681, the final examination for the highest degree, conducted 262 times during the T'ang, included: (1) five essays on current events, (2) essays on the Confucian classics and history, (3) an original poem and a composition in rhythmic prose, and (4) special tests covering such topics as mathematics and law. Cf. Arthur W. Hummel in *Report of the Libarian of Congress, 1938*, p. 222.

of schools in the provinces.[18] In 630 he decreed that temples to
Confucius should be erected everywhere and sacrifices offered
by government officials and ten years later he himself sacrificed
to the sage. In 647 he ordered tablets commemorating the
twenty-two most famous men in the Confucian hierarchy to be
placed in these temples. This practice rewarded not literary attainment alone but a virtuous life with a place in the hall of
fame, and was sufficiently popular to be continued until modern
times. The spring and autumn Confucian celebrations that were
conducted a century later (in 740) have continued almost without a break until recently. Just before the fall of the emperor
Hsüan-tsung in 754, there was founded an academy of letters,
the Hanlin, which did much to strengthen the official faith until
the nineteenth century. This academy, at which were assembled
some of the most competent scholars of the day, had charge of
all the court's literary activities, such as the writing of edicts and
other state papers and the inditing of sacrificial prayers, etc.
Still functioning well ten centuries later, it was held up as an
example to the much newer academies in Europe.

During this period Confucianism strengthened its hold on
China and naturally penetrated other countries in the Chinese
cultural orbit, such as Korea (after 700) and Japan. The Nara
University curriculum, which included the *Rites*, the *Tso Chronicle*, the *Odes*, the *Book of History*, the *Book of Changes*, the
Analects, and *Filial Piety*, was almost like the course of study
for any Chinese student of the time. The only difference lay in
the fact that the Japanese admitted none of the Taoist canon.
Although the Chinese sometimes included *The Lao-tzŭ* (or
Tao-tê-ching) and *The Chuang-tzŭ*, the Taoist were excluded
when the twelve classics of the day, their texts having been
normalized by imperial order in 744, were cut on stone slabs and
set up at the university at Ch'ang-an between 836 and 841.

---

[18] According to a T'ang encyclopedia, the National Academy at Ch'ang-an had
3260 Chinese students around the year 631. Later it attracted students from Korea,
Japan, Tibet, and central Asia, and boasted 8000 altogether.

Some of the Taoist advisers at court were very powerful. Many leaders of the period, especially the military who were so largely drawn from the half-Chinese and half-Turkic border chieftains, had a healthy amount of superstition and they encouraged the alchemists in their search for the elixir of immortality, a craze that brought about the death of several emperors. This brought sharp rebukes from Confucian officials. Indeed, the formal literature which is extant is so unkind to Taoism that it is difficult to present it in a just light. Most of the Taoist rebuttals of Buddhist and Confucian arguments that survived to the thirteenth century were lost in the proscriptions of 1258 and 1281. It can hardly be denied, however, that Taoism, with its mystic other-worldly character and its love of nature, gave special inspiration to painters and poets.[19] Taoism gave people a dream world in which to live; it gladdened and elevated their spirits, and even gave some assurance of the hereafter. Its greatest activity was in the period of imperial affluence. Although the Taoists were not active in proselytizing abroad, word of the Tao reached the prince of Assam, who requested Li Shih-min to send him a Sanskrit translation of *The Lao-tzŭ*, a request which the second emperor ordered the great Buddhist pilgrim Hsüan-tsang, of all people, to fulfill!

An era of expansion often has a profoundly productive effect on a people. So it was in T'ang China. China's foreign trade created a demand for luxury goods so heavy that by Hsüan-tsung's reign such merchandise clogged the imperial roads from Canton, Ch'üan-chou, and Yangchow to the western capital. It raised the domestic production of pottery and porcelain ware to heights never known before. According to an Arab reporter of 851: "The Chinese have pottery of excellent quality of which they fashion bowls as thin as flasks of glass; one may see the glint of water through them, although they are made of clay."[20]

---

[19] Cf. B. Belpaire, "Le Taoisme et Li T'ai Po," *Mélanges chinois et bouddhiques,* I:1–14 (1931–1932).

[20] Cf. translation by J. Sauvaget, *op. cit.,* p. 16.

The more romantic Lu Kuei-mêng (d. *ca.* 881) tells us that the Yüeh ware (made in modern Chekiang province near Shaohsing) "despoiled the thousand peaks of their colors." Chinese pottery was famous over a wide area, for shards of a lovely quality have recently been found in ninth-century sites from Brahminabad in India to Ctesiphon, Tarsus, Jerusalem, and Cairo. True porcelain with a high felspathic glaze was undoubtedly exported to the caliphate. This trade evolved new forms, for T'ang potters followed certain Persian, Indian, and Greek models.

Sculpture reached new peaks in some of the deathless examples of this art that were produced at the end of the sixth and the beginning of the seventh century; after this, however, it declined gradually as the religious spirit waned and became less inspiring. If we may judge from certain examples and from the words of later Chinese critics, China also had a high place in paintings, especially figure painting, although the representation of landscapes was progressing steadily. The greatest artist of this period was Wu Tao-hsüan (d. 792), whose over three hundred Buddhist frescoes and many drawings on silk (none of which survives) had a profound influence on the world of his time. One of the minor arts, printing textiles from wood blocks, also came into existence. The earliest example extant is a blue print dating from the ninth century and is in the British Museum. Much of our exact knowledge about architecture we owe to the careful copies made by the Koreans and Japanese. This art, particularly religious and court architecture, was characterized by magnificence and lavishness, if not invention. The capital city of Ch'ang-an was carefully laid out, in an area approximately six by five miles, to care for imperial requirements and for its huge population, estimated (742) for the whole prefecture at 1,960,188. (The total population for this year is calculated at 52 million.) The Japanese adopted this model for their new city, Nara. A stone bridge in southern Hopei, which dates from about 600 and is still standing, indicates how far the Chinese had progressed in bridge building. "It was constructed . . . by the master-builder Li Ch'un on a principle which, in a very modern manner, modifies the construction of the compound Roman aqueduct. A single segmental arch with a span of 37.47 meters carries on either side . . . two small arches; it is a combination that receives with ease and security the slightly convex bridgeway."[21]

In the art of letters poetry probably holds the foremost place, for this was China's golden age of poetry. "Whoever was a man was a poet," said a critic.[22] An anthology of the poems extant in 1705 contains over 48,900 by 2200 poets. One of them, Po Chü-i (772–846), became so popular during his lifetime that his fame reached Korea and Japan and he became the hero of a No play. His poetry may have the further distinction of being the first ever to be printed (in 800–810, according to Têng Ssŭ-yü).[23] Some of the work of such poets as Li Po (701/5–762), Tu Fu (712–770), Wang Wei (699–759/60), and Wei Ying-wu (ca. 740–830) has been translated, but the writings of the great monk-poets are not yet represented in European renderings. In addition to their literary contribution, the poems of these courtiers, soldiers, painters, and priests give a picture of the time not commonly presented by the essayists and historians. Some, furthermore, are written in what approximates the vernacular, and hence afford a clue to the contemporary speech and mind. Po Chü-i, for example, is said, according to eleventh-century tradition, never to have considered one of his poems complete until an old countrywoman could understand it.

In prose and scholarly works a high standard was reached. The Sui is distinguished for two excellent works on the Chinese language, one edited in 601 by Lu Tz'ŭ of the Hsien-pi, and the

---

[21] G. Ecke, in *Monumenta Serica*, II:2, 468 (1937).

[22] Quoted in S. Obata, *The Works of Li Po, the Chinese Poet*, p. 1.

[23] Waley puts it a decade or so later. *The Life and Times of Po Chü-i*, p. 160. The evidence for printing is inconclusive.

other by Lu Yüan-lang (*ca.* 564–*ca.* 630); these are now of fundamental importance to the study of Chinese linguistics and phonology. Han history was expertly edited by Yen Shih-ku (581–645), and seven histories were written by a large corps of scholars who ransacked the court archives for material on the turbulent eras just concluded. Two encyclopedias, whose subject matter ranged from government policy to crafts and medicine, were compiled during these years, largely to aid students in the civil examinations; these works must have had signal influence on the knowledge and writing of the educated youth of the day. The *T'ung Tien*, completed by Tu Yu (735–812) in 801 after 36 years' study of a wide variety of sources, is a similar work of even greater magnitude. In addition to extensive material on China, it contains contemporary material on the Arabs at Kufa, the first Abbasid capital, written by a close relative of the author. Standards for the essay style were set by another distinguished statesman and author, Han Yü (768–824), whose turbulent life included several periods of political disgrace and two of exile. Much of his writing that has survived bears the mark of intimacy, apparently freed of all artistic consciousness, and his influence on the style of his successors was tremendous. Han Yü, like others remembered chiefly by the Chinese, was a staunch Confucian and he initiated the thought that was to flower in the twelfth and thirteenth centuries. The Buddhist translators and preachers, among them Hsüan-tsang, I-ching, and others of their collaborators and successors, likewise worked diligently, translating hundreds of Sanskrit texts into Chinese with affectionate care and zeal. The story of the wanderings of Hsüan-tsang had such great appeal to the imagination of romanticists and playwrights that legends based on it have been told and acted countless times. At the hands of Buddhists and Taoists, the short story, heretofore concerned solely with fairies and magic, began to deal with everyday life and even with love, and many of them were written in the vernacular. In the field of drama, the earlier short plays performed by court fools developed into plays of some length, a development that may have had a central Asiatic origin.[24] Drama did not achieve significance as literature until later, although paid entertainment played an important role in the seventh to ninth centuries.

The literary arts of the Sui and T'ang and the demand for copies of current works—calendars, lexicons, Buddhist sūtras, Taoist charms, or the sentiments and calligraphy of Confucian masters—gave rise to an invention of world-wide importance. The early story of block printing may never be known, but the process seems to have been discovered somewhere around 700 and by the tenth century to have been gradually accepted by all literary groups not only in China but also in Korea and Japan. The time was ripe for such an invention. The Chinese had long used paper and ink; they knew how to make seals out of metals, stone, or clay; it was usual for them to take rubbings of prized inscriptions on bronze and stone. There was, furthermore, the demand—textbooks were required by the thousands after the civil examination system was instituted, and charms for prayer formulas and for warding off evils and disease were desired in Buddhist and Taoist circles. In a period of resurgence like the one under discussion, the discovery of a method of easy reproduction was inevitable. There is scattered evidence of the use of block printing as early as the eighth century, and from the ninth century on there is considerable evidence in eastern and central Asia. The earliest datable examples of block printing that have survived come from Japan (although Korea boasts one of possibly earlier date); they were small charms ordered in 764. The "world's oldest extant printed book" is the Diamond Sūtra of 868 which was found at Tun-huang. In spite of ample opportunity, block printing was not used in India during these centuries.

---

[24] The mimes that are carved on the stone pillars of the T'ang are apparently of Indian origin.

PLATE I. — Digging for
the remains of Paleolithic
man, near Peking. (Cour-
tesy, Rockefeller Foun-
dation.)

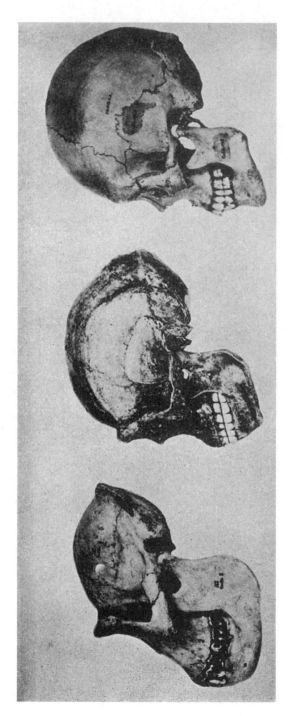

PLATE II.—From left to right: gorilla; Peking man; modern Chinese. (Courtesy, The Rockefeller Foundation.)

PLATES III and IV.—Prehistoric painted pot from Kansu. Museum of Far Eastern Antiquities, at Stockholm. (Courtesy, The University Prints, Boston.)

PLATE V.—Early bronze vessel, *ca.* 1300-900 B.C. Cernuschi Museum, Paris. (Courtesy, The University Prints, Boston.)

PLATE VI.—White pottery vessel, *ca.* 12th century B.C. (Courtesy, The Freer Gallery of Art, Washington, D. C.)

PLATE VII.—Earliest known form of Chinese writing, incised on a bone fragment, *ca.* 12th century B.C. (Courtesy, Professor Ernest K. Smith, Yenching University.)

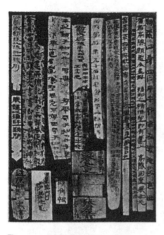

PLATE VIII.—Documents on wood of Han date. (From Stein, *On Ancient Central Asian Tracks*, Fig. 47.)

PLATE IX.—Sundial, with a reconstruction of the suggested form of gnomon in place. (Courtesy, Royal Ontario Museum, Toronto.)

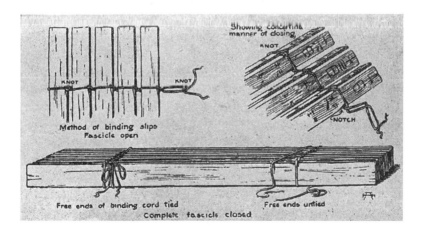

PLATE X.—How an ancient Chinese book was assembled. (From Stein, *Serindia*, II, p. 766; by permission of the High Commissioner for India.)

PLATE XI.—House model (painted pottery), of Han dynasty (202
B.C.-A.D. 220). (Courtesy, Nelson Gallery, Kansas City.)

PLATE XII.—Section of painting attributed to Ku K'ai-chih (fl. 350-400 A.D.). British Museum, London. (Courtesy, The University Prints, Boston.)

PLATE XIII.—Avalokitesvara, Northern Wei dynasty (386-535 A.D.). (Courtesy, Museum of Fine Arts, Boston.)

Plate XIV.—Detail, band of celestial musicians, from a stela, A.D. 551. (Courtesy, The University Museum, Philadelphia.)

Plate XV.—Front of a stüpa, 7th century A.D. (Courtesy, Nelson Gallery, Kansas City.)

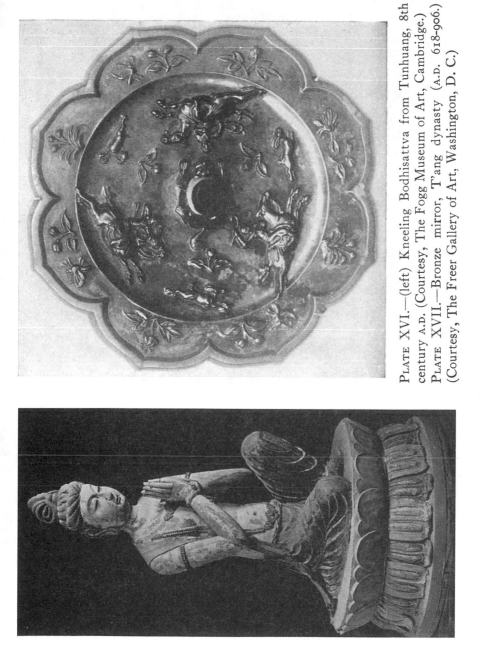

PLATE XVI.—(left) Kneeling Bodhisattva from Tunhuang, 8th century A.D. (Courtesy, The Fogg Museum of Art, Cambridge.)
PLATE XVII.—Bronze mirror, T'ang dynasty (A.D. 618-906.) (Courtesy, The Freer Gallery of Art, Washington, D. C.)

PLATE XVIII.—Wall painting: The fight for Buddha's relics, T'ang dynasty (A.D. 618-906). Photograph by Professor Paul Pelliot. (Courtesy, The University Prints, Boston.)

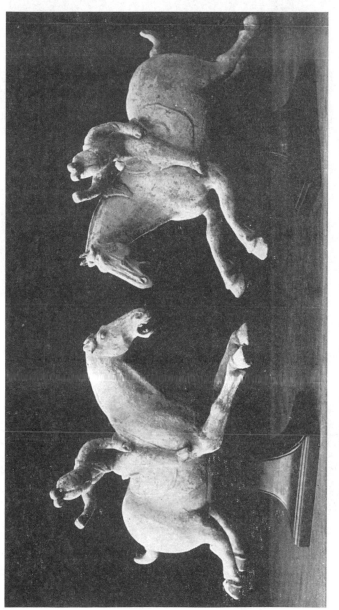

PLATE XIX.—Pottery figurines: Ladies playing polo, T'ang dynasty (A.D. 618-906). (Courtesy, Mr. C. T. Loo, New York.)

PLATE XX.—Part of oldest extant printed book: The Diamond
Sūtra scroll, A.D. 868. (The British Museum.)

PLATE XXI.—Bowl, Ting ware, Sung dynasty (A.D. 960-1279).
(Courtesy, The Museum of Fine Arts, Boston.)

PLATE XXII.—Painting: Bare willows and distant mountains, by Ma Yüan (*ca.* A.D. 1200). (Courtesy, The Museum of Fine Arts, Boston.)

PLATE XXIII.—A mountain scene in China. Photograph by Hedda Hammer, Peking.

PLATE XXIV.—The imperial palace library, Ch'ien-lung period (1736-1795 A.D.), Peking. (Courtesy, the Palace Museum, Peking.)

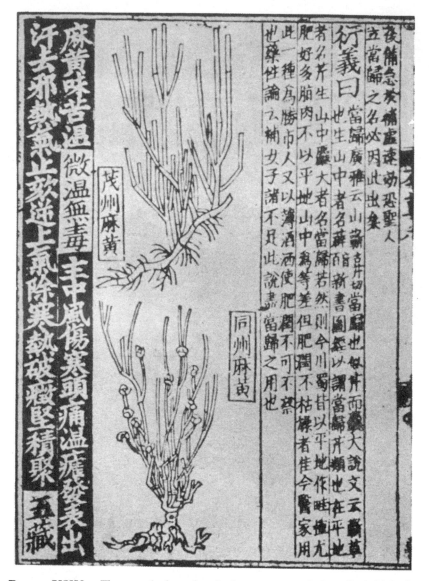

PLATE XXV.—Two varieties of ephedra, source of the alkaloid ephedrine; from an herbal printed in 1249.

The Sui-T'ang era was a period of rejuvenation for China when the energies of the various states, long dissipated by internecine strife, were united to carry the empire forward. The foreign influence at court (one ninth-century Chinese complained that all the recent cabinet ministers were barbarians) and the constant stream of traders, travelers, priests, and envoys brought to many fields numberless innovations that would not be expected in a less progressive age. In music, for example, transposition which had been long forgotten was applied to the creation of eighty-four scales based on each of the seven intervals. Such foods as pepper, sugar beet, date, lettuce, almond, fig, spinach, and possibly lemons and olives, were introduced, and croton oil, saffron, and jasmine were used as medicines. Polo was played at every military camp as well as at court, where some palace ladies also took part. Art motifs, astronomical knowledge, armor, costumes, and the like were all affected. The need for knowledge about China's wide domain resulted in a noteworthy achievement in cartography, the map made by Chia Tan (730–805) in 801; drawn to a scale of 100 *li* to an inch, it measured approximately 30 by 33 feet and covered an area of about 10,000 by 11,000 miles. It also treated seven great trade routes, both by land and sea, from China to the then known Asiatic world.

Feudalism still menaced, and the expense of government had to be met. To this end the government tried several schemes. Although the nobles and high officials had to remain at court and had no provincial authority, the size of their landholdings increased at the expense of the actual tillers of the soil. The peasants had for long borne the chief burden of taxation, but reforms were adopted in 766 and 780 which transferred part of it to the wealthy. These measures, however, were in the hands of local governors and their maladministration augmented the growing discontent which finally brought the government to ruin. Both at court and in the provinces eunuchs, too, fastened their evil hold; by 820 there were actually 4618 holding office, and even the highest ministers could approach the emperor only through them as intermediaries.[25] Unquestionably the house of T'ang by the end of the ninth century had "lost the mandate of heaven." It was great as long as it could expand and depend on the produce of distant markets, but it had not learned how to administer its own territory and hence collapsed when forced back within its own walls.

[25] Although the historian sees signs of disintegration it is interesting that north China seemed relatively well administered to Ennin from 838 to 847. *Ennin's Diary*, trans. E. O. Reischauer.

CHAPTER V

Disunion; the Sung and the Partition of the North and Northwest

THE FIVE DYNASTIES AND THE TEN INDEPENDENT STATES

THE collapse of the T'ang dynasty was followed by political chaos. Secessionist movements were successful in various parts of China; several adventures, three of them foreign (belonging to a Turkic tribe, called by the Chinese Sha-t'o), succeeded in exercising imperial power in part of the north from 907 to 960; and Manchuria and Mongolia in the extreme north were overrun between 907 and 1125 by the Khitan, a Mongol horde who constantly increased their territory at China's expense. A glance at an historical atlas shows the extent of the disunity. Chinese historians call these years the period of five dynasties and ten independent states and characterize them as some of the darkest in the history of the empire. "No wonder," says Wang I-t'ung, "that Ou-yang Hsiu [1007–1072, historian of this period] should habitually begin his 'historical essay' with the word 'Alas!' for the picture of facts and conditions of life of this time would move anyone to pity and terror. The military governors and powerful magistrates had made themselves 'princes,' 'kings,' or even 'emperors' over great or small pieces of territory, and ruled as licentious tyrants. Organized bandits counted into the millions ran over the country, pillaging, burning, killing, sacking cities, and indulging in all forms of cruelty and extortion."[1]

[1] *Historical Annual,* II:3 (November, 1936); abstracted by M. Hsitien Lin in *China Institute Bulletin,* II:4, 95 (January, 1938).

The life of luxury led by the wealthy despotic landholders gave rise to one form of sensual satisfaction, the binding of women's feet, which first appeared about 950. No one knows exactly how the practice originated, but it is believed to have begun among the dancing or ballet girls who were so popular in this age that at least a million of them were held in bondage during the T'ang period. Perhaps the style of shoe in the tenth century required excessively small feet, and the dancers' solution of the problem was rapidly and widely adopted by other women. However this may be, the practice became so deeply imbedded in Chinese mores that it persisted some time after 1912, in spite of preaching and ridicule for more than a century and government disapproval during recent decades. It is worth noting that the practice was not adopted among certain small segments of Chinese society such as the boat women of Kuang-tung and the aboriginal peoples of the southwest, or by China's neighbors and one-time conquerors, the Jurchen, Mongols, and Manchus; but in China, rich and poor alike submitted to it.

This period is marked by one great advance—printing came into its own. Instead of serving merely as an occasional substitute for copying, it now became necessary for all the literate groups in the empire. That it penetrated Korea is made clear both by material evidence and by evidence from contemporary literature. It was also taken up by the Tangut of Kansu, the Khitan and Jurchen of north China, and the Uigur of central Asia. In addition to the Diamond Sūtra of 868, there are printed calendars for 877 and 882, and three other roll books dating from about 900; one is a fragmentary dictionary and the other two are Buddhist. In the summer of 883 a Chinese official at Ch'êng-tu mentions printed works on "divination . . . and various (other) themes of the *yin-yang* (school); there were also dictionaries and (other books) of lexicography . . ."[2] As

[2] Cf. Carter and Goodrich, *The Invention of Printing in China and Its Spread Westward*, p. 60.

a matter of fact, this city in the western province of Szechuan seems to have been the printing center of the time, enjoying the patronage of a statesman with a princely purse. Here, for example, paper money was first printed (*ca.* 995), and nine of the classics were published. In 925 the imperial house at Loyang extended its sway over Szechuan and held it for nearly nine years, thus becoming aware of the activity in printing. The authentication of the Confucian text being the prerogative of empire, the imperial officials promptly (932) ordered a printed canon and commentary based on a portion of the stone inscriptions at Ch'ang-an. Despite political difficulties, the National Academy completed this sizable task (there were 130 volumes) in twenty-one years. Buddhist printing went on too, as finds during recent decades prove. The *Tripitaka,* consisting of 5048 volumes, was printed in Szechuan between 972 and 983, and copies were transported to Korea in 991 and to Japan in 985. The Taoist canon was also prepared and its 466 cases containing 4565 rolls presented to the throne in 1019, but not printed until 1116/7. Other works might be mentioned, but the above are sufficient to show that printing had attained its majority in the land of its birth and was beginning to affect neighboring cultures.

No account of cultural progress should blind one to the hard social conditions of the time. Warfare and bloodshed were general; laws were harsh and often inhumanly administered; corruption was the rule, rather than the exception, among officials; there were widespread levies on men and horses for both military service and labor; the decentralization of power so debased the coinage that barter became general; and floods, famine, and the breakdown of trade followed when the road, canal, and waterworks systems in north China were allowed to deteriorate because of lack of care and upkeep. The removal of most of the restraints and controls brought anarchy to a great part of the country.

Possibly because it was the one school capable of some resistance to autocracy, Buddhism, long a refuge for the heartsick of all classes, had to contend with another sharp attack, at least in northern China. Although the proscription was not complete, the annals of the central government record that the decree in the summer of 955 spared only 2694 monasteries; 30,336 were destroyed. But Buddhism had some strong supporters even during this period. The princes of Wu-Yüeh, who ruled at Hangchow, built numerous temples and stūpas, erected statues, had 84,000 miniature bronze stūpas struck off in 955, engaged parts of the canon on stone, and encouraged relations with the Buddhist houses in Japan. The rulers in Canton also supported the church in princely fashion.

The period was one of several critical points in China's history. If the country was not to disintegrate into a group of separate states, as in the centuries before the Ch'in and the Sui, some effort to reestablish national unity was called for. The Chinese chose the latter course, perhaps because they had a strong recollection of union (a concept foreign to the people of Europe) which they associated with order, prosperity, and possibly glory. No swashbuckler of the tenth century, however ignorant, could forget the Han and the T'ang, nor could he fail to appreciate the importance of defense for an empire that had fallen into fragments.

THE SUNG (960–1279)

When the emperor died in 959, Chao K'uang-yin (927–976), a member of a well-known family and a man who had seen both civil and military service under the empire at Loyang, became regent because the emperor's son had not yet attained his majority. After a campaign against the Khitan in the north, Chao seized absolute power in 960 and during the next sixteen years crushed all but two of the secessionist states. These two—

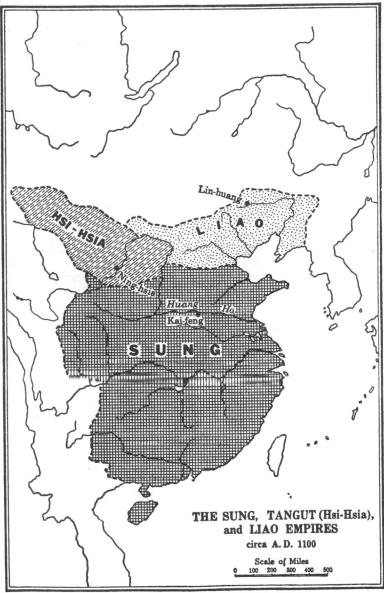

THE SUNG, TANGUT (Hsi-Hsia),
and LIAO EMPIRES
circa A.D. 1100

Scale of Miles
0   100   200   300   400   500

the Wu-Yüeh in Chekiang and the northern Han in Shansi—
did not fall until 978 and 979 respectively. Meanwhile Annam
seceded in 965, the kingdom of Nan Chao in Yünnan successfully upheld its independence, and the powerful Khitan, who
had established the kingdom of Liao beyond the Yellow River
in 947, menaced Chao's northern flank.

The Sung dynasty which Chao established continued in existence, except for one almost disastrous break (1126–1135), from
960 until 1279. Unlike the Han and T'ang, this dynasty was
not notable for additions to China's domain. Although its
troops fought heroically often, they never succeeded in breaking
the iron ring forged around the imperial boundaries by the
Khitan (until 1125), the Jurchen Tungus (until 1234), and
the Mongols in the north; by the Tangut, a Tibetan people (*ca.*
990–1227), and the Mongols in the northwest; and by Annam
and Nan Chao in the southwest and south. One reason for the
failure of the Sung in this respect was their lack of sufficient
breeding grounds and pasturage for horses, which made it impossible to wage offensive war against their more mobile and
usually hardier neighbors. Eventually the state adopted a policy
of deception and intrigue to achieve what could not be gained
by force. This raised vitally important fiscal problems, for such
a policy was expensive; furthermore, the border kingdoms
continued to exact extremely heavy tribute.[3]

In 1126–1127 the Jurchen made a successful raid on the
Sung capital and captured the emperor, his father, and most of
the courtiers (3000 in all). A young prince and the remaining
officials fled across the Yangtze River, and the prince eventually

---

[3] In 1004 the Liao penetrated Sung territory as far as a point near the capital at
Pien-liang (modern Kaifeng) and exacted an annual tribute amounting to 100,000
ounces of silver and 200,000 pieces of silk; the first payment was made in 1005. In
1041–1042, after the Sung had received help from the Liao in resisting the Tangut,
the tribute was increased to 200,000 ounces of silver and 300,000 pieces of silk. In
1043 the Sung purchased peace from the Tangut at a price of an annual tribute of
1,000,000 strings of cash, 100,000 pieces of silk, and 30,000 catties of tea.

established at Lin-an (modern Hangchow) what his people were pleased to call a temporary capital. Here the descendants of the Chao royal family maintained their hold on an even more constricted Sung empire. The Sung dynasty was overthrown by the Mongols, who in 1273, after prolonged sieges, had broken through the fortified cities on the Han River in modern Hupeh, then crossed the Yangtze, and overrun the entire coast line from Hangchow to Canton between 1276 and 1277. In 1279, at an island near Macao, they shattered the fleet bearing the last of the imperial house.

In the arts of civilization the Sung broke new ground:

The T'ang Dynasty had been a time of rapidly extending frontiers, and of contact with the lands of the West, a period of freshness and youth, an era of lyric poetry and religious faith. The Sung Dynasty, shut out from the West by the steadily encroaching nomads, was a time of ripe maturity. Lyric poetry gave way to learned prose—great compendiums of history, works on natural science and political economy, of a character and quality such as neither China nor the West, except for a short period in Greece, had ever dreamed of. Religious faith gave way to philosophic speculation, and the great systems of thought were produced that have dominated China to this day. In art the lofty tradition of the earlier period was carried on and brought to fruition, so that the greatest and best Chinese paintings that are now extant come from the period of the Sungs. In invention, what the T'ang period conceived, the Sung era put to practical use.[4]

Several new cities were founded, and city walls were built. By 1100 at least 5 cities had populations of a million or more. There was a marked increase in such public works as waterways and flood control, especially in the coastal provinces of Kiangsu, Chekiang, and Fukien; 496 projects were undertaken by the Sung, as against 91 during the T'ang period. One great engineering feat was a sea wall, begun in 910, that ran north from Hangchow for some 180 miles. Dwelling houses had higher roofs and stone floors. Whereas as late as the T'ang the lower

[4] Reprinted from Carter, *The Invention of Printing in China*, 1st ed., by permission of Columbia University Press.

classes had sat upon the floor and the upper classes on raised platforms, chairs now came into general use; sedan chairs were widely used for transportation. Gardens, once enjoyed only by princes, became the fashion for the well-to-do, particularly after the luxuriant subtropical regions south of the Yangtze were cultivated. That tea was the common beverage for north and south is indicated by the taxes in 780 and 793 and the tribute demanded in 1043 by the Tangut. The ceramic tradition of the T'ang was developed to a point which some authorities believe has never been surpassed. Sung porcelain was widely prized and was exported to Japan, the Philippines, Indo-China, India, and Syria. Some of it went even to parts of Africa; "the whole coast from Kishmayu to Zanzibar is littered with Chinese pottery,"[5] much of it dating from this time. The folding fan was introduced from Japan in 988. Playing cards and dominoes appeared, both of them apparently Chinese inventions. Cotton had been sent as tribute by Java, India, and Malaysia as early as the fifth and sixth centuries, but not until its value and uses were appreciated by the Sung did it become an object of commerce; drought resistant rice from Champa and green lentils from India were also introduced by imperial command in the eleventh century.[6]

Overseas commerce expanded, owing in part doubtless to the increased concentration of the population and moneyed interests on the south China coast. And now for the first time since their defeat by the Chin (in 1127), the Chinese established a navy which functioned as an independent force. Between 1130 and 1237 their navy grew from 11 squadrons with 3000 men to 20 squadrons with nearly 52,000 men. As a result, naval architecture really came into its own under the Sung; by the end of that dynasty the Chinese seem to have captured the coastwise lanes and the transoceanic stretches to India and beyond from the Arabs.

[5] E. H. L. Schwarz, "The Chinese Connections with Africa," *Journal of the Royal Asiatic Society of Bengal*, IV:175–193 (1938).

[6] Ho Ping-ti, *Economic History Review*, IX:200–218 (1956).

Chou Ch'ü-fei described Chinese boats as follows in 1178: "The ships which sail the Southern Sea and south of it are like houses. When their sails are spread they are like great clouds in the sky. Their rudders are several tens of feet long. A single ship carries several hundred men. It has stored on board a year's supply of grain."[7] In addition to sails, both cloth and mat, and balanced rudder, seagoing vessels had eight or ten oars, each one manned by at least four oarsmen; freshwater craft had paddle wheels. Two anchor stones were fastened at the prow of each ship by means of rattan ropes, and were lowered and raised by a pulley. Soundings were taken by a deep-sea lead, sometimes hooked, which brought up a sample of the sea floor. Hitherto Chinese mariners had checked their course by the polestar, but by the eleventh century the magnetic needle, long used by geomancers, was applied to navigation. In 1119 Chu Yü described the procedure: "The captain ascertains the ship's position, at night by looking at the stars, in the day time by looking at the sun; in dark weather he looks at the south-pointing needle."[8]

Overseas trade brought with it an increased use of imported articles, probably greater wealth to both private citizens and the government, although there was a heavy drainage of the Chinese currency, and wider contacts with foreign peoples, especially the Arabs and Jews from India and Iran. Among the imports and exports recorded in the Sung annals for 999 or thereabouts are the following: Chinese gold, silver, copper cash, lead, piece goods of all colors, and porcelain were exchanged for incense, medicine, rhinoceros horns, ivory, cornelian, coral, amber, rock crystal, strings of pearls, steel, tortoise shell, cockle (?) shell, ebony, sapan wood, and cotton stuffs. From 971 on, the government endeavored to regulate and to profit from this commerce. An edict promulgated in 995 forbade officials to

---

[7] From *Ling wai tai ta*; translated by Hirth and Rockhill, *Chau Ju-kua*, p. 33.

[8] *P'ing chou k'o t'an*, translated by Kuwabara, *Memoirs of the Toyo Bunko*, II. p. 68 (1928). There are also two earlier descriptions, one by Shên Kua (1021–1085), and the other by K'ou Tsung-shih (*ca.* 1116).

engage in foreign trade through agents, but apparently it had little effect. Some merchants, both Chinese and foreign, grew rich; one Persian trader of the eleventh century left an estate of several million strings of cash on his death in Canton. Chinese pirates as well as island "barbarians" also cut heavily into the government's profits from commerce at this time. Nevertheless, the state's income from this attempted monopoly is said to have risen from half a million strings of cash at the end of the tenth century to as much as 65,000,000 strings in 1189. This income was unquestionably important in offsetting the costs of military defense and the tribute exacted by the northern invaders. Unfortunately, however, during these years Chinese currency was taking flight abroad—to Japan, the Philippines, Singapore, Java, south India, and the east coast of Africa—in such quantities that there was a "cash famine" at home, according to a late Sung historian. One measure taken to relieve the government's financial plight from 1024 on was the issuance of paper money, but confidence in this dwindled as the state treasury's receipts fell off. A perfumed mixture of silk and paper was even resorted to to give the money wider appeal, but to no avail; inflation and depreciation followed to an extent rivaling conditions in Germany and Russia after the First World War.[9]

Another major development of this era is the application of explosive powder to war. "In China," wrote Laufer some years ago, "we can trace a rational development of gunpowder from the humble firecracker (known in the sixth century of our era), which was originally employed in religious ceremonies, to the launching of fiery projectiles in warfare as early as the twelfth century and the full development of fire weapons under the Mongols in the thirteenth and fourteenth centuries."[10] According to Chinese historians, the process of making explosive powder is first fully described in a military handbook issued in 1044.

[9] Cf. Carter and Goodrich, *The Invention of Printing in China*, p. 106.
[10] *American Anthropologist*, XIX:74 (1917).

By that date the Chinese had been acquainted with sulphur and saltpeter—the main ingredients—for a thousand years; also with paper, charcoal, *t'ung* oil, and other necessary substances. The first secure reference to military weapons using this mixture dates from the year 1000, a time when the Sung were fighting a losing war against the Liao. These may have been primitive bombs or grenades flung against the enemy by hand or by a trebuchet. During the next century, particularly in the struggles against the invading Jurchen in 1126–1127 and in 1161–1162, the Chinese utilized explosive weapons both on land and water. The Jurchen were not slow to adopt the new and gradually improving devices, using them against the Mongols when the latter began to lay siege to the walled cities of the north. One weapon may even have been a proto firearm, consisting of a long bamboo tube from which bullets were ejected by touching off the powder. Certainly this and other weapons were given full play by the Chinese in 1259 and 1272 as they vainly endeavored to halt the advancing Mongols. By this time, however, the enemy were fully as well equipped. At the end of 1272 the attackers (actually an international force made up of fighters and technicians from many parts of Asia) moved up two new weapons to the siege of the walled cities of Fan ch'êng and Hsiang-yang, which had resisted for over four years; one was an improved catapult capable of flinging large rocks, and the other was a field piece called a mangonel (*hui-hui p'ao* in Chinese), constructed to order by two Moslems. These breached the walls and ended the siege. Ironically enough, the man in charge of the *p'ao* was a Chinese; in the next two years he successfully stormed other Sung cities for the Mongol commander. It seems clear from these and other data[11] that whoever may have invented the cannon and smaller pieces the Chinese and their immediate neighbors played a significant part in the early stages of their

[11] Cf. Goodrich and Fêng, "The early development of firearms in China," *Isis* 36:114–123, 250 (1946).

development; the Chinese alone originated the firecracker and allied fireworks.[12]

That the intellectual development of the age was not high in country villages and the frontier areas is implied by such romances as the picaresque *Shui hu chuan* (The Water Marshes). In the great cities, however—from Loyang, Kaifeng, and Ch'êng-tu on the north and west, to Yangchow, Hangchow, Ningpo, Ch'üan-chou and Canton on the coast—it reached a stage never before attained. Undoubtedly there were several distinguishing intellectual groups in the various little courts during the fifth to third centuries B.C. The ebullience, virility, and diverse interests of the T'ang sowed the seed of the renaissance in all the arts (except sculpture) that flowered under the Sung. Nearly every past and contemporary literary work that was considered worthy of preservation was printed by means of wood blocks and metal plates or—a distinctly Chinese innovation—by means of movable type made successively of earthenware, tin, wood, and copper. The great increase in printed books, together with more leisure and general prosperity, at least at certain times and in certain places in the climatically favored central and southern sections, undoubtedly led to more reading and study.

The general level of education, whether in the monastery, the academy, or government offices, was indisputedly higher under the Sung. The system of competitive examinations reinaugurated by the T'ang was developed and modified, especially during the reform eras at the end of the eleventh and the beginning of the twelfth centuries. There was dissatisfaction with the strictly classical studies required of candidates for office, and with the emphasis on memorizing. The illustrious prime minister Wang An-shih (1021–1086) used his influence to promote more practical training; he urged that candidates be "conversant with ancient and modern laws and regulations, the principles of astronomy, and

[12] Wang Ling, "Invention and use of gunpowder and firearms in China." *Isis* 37: 160–178 (1947).

their bearing on the affairs of the State. They would have some idea of political economy, and know how to initiate necessary reforms."[13] In 1071 he said in a letter to the emperor: "It is admitted that the present examination system has produced a number of good men, but that is because it is the sole avenue to official preferment. But I deny that the system is a good one. For any system which compels a man in the robust strength of his youth, when he ought to be studying the fundamental principles of philosophy and government, to shut himself up in his room and devote all his time and energies to the making of poetry and the composition of rhyming couplets is of necessity utterly injurious. For such a man entering upon the duties of official life will have been denied all chance of gaining that knowledge which would be of practical value to him in that work."[14] To make his point, he himself drafted some of the questions for the final tests, and at the same time he instituted improvements in the colleges of law, medicine, and military affairs at the capital. He was instrumental in establishing public schools in every prefecture and subprefecture in the empire, these schools being supported, at least partly, by the income from land set aside for the purpose.

Private education flourished even more during this period. Scholars—Buddhist, Taoist, and Confucian—offered their services as tutors. At least 124 academies were developed under private initiative; outstanding scholars were employed as teachers, and promising students were admitted even though unable to pay the fees. Located in sylvan and mountain retreats where reflection and concentration were possible, and equipped with libraries and printing establishments, these academies promoted research and philosophic utterances untrammeled by government interference.

The extant bibliographies of private libraries of this period

---

[13] Translated by H. R. Williamson, *Wang An Shih,* I, p. 330.
[14] *Ibid.,* p. 338.

indicate the literary resources of a number of the larger centers of population. Prose and poetry streamed from them, as well as from temples and, by court decree, from the capital itself. Although the literature may lack the vitality and freshness characteristic of the work of Li Po, Han Yü, and their peers, the Sung was not without writers of note. Beset by rules and formulas, few poets achieved the literary level of their predecessors. There is, however, one exception—Su Shih (1037–1101), art critic, builder of a causeway at West Lake in Hangchow, and erstwhile court favorite, who whiled away his exile in the unhealthy damps of Hainan by writing poems about his native province.

It is in prose that the most renowned writers of this period are found. The best essayists seem to have been particularly successful in achieving high office. Ou-yang Hsiu (1007–1072), the president of the Board of War, described the sound of autumn and the pavilion of a drunken old man; the essay on the Red Cliff written by Su Shih is known to every Chinese schoolboy; and their contemporary, Wang An-shih the prime minister, wrote the most forceful state documents of the period. History is represented by Ssŭ-ma Kuang (1019–1086), whose breadth of conception is rivaled only by that of his distinguished Han predecessor of the same surname. His great work, the *Tzŭ chih t'ung chien*, on which he and three principal collaborators worked for twenty years, covered the history of China from 403 B.C. to A.D.959. Thirty of its 354 chapters constitute an appendix containing the author's comments on variations in facts as reported in the 322 books used as sources. His passion for accuracy and comprehensiveness was enriched by a style that was both simple and easy to understand. An equally critical and comprehensive historian of the next century was Chêng Ch'iao (1104–1162), an amateur natural scientist. His *T'ung chih* included monographs on such diverse subjects as the family and clan, philology, phonetics, political subdivisions, flowers and insects, library cataloguing, and archeology. Perhaps because he expressed such scorn of traditional views of scholars who failed to make first-hand investigations of their subjects, his book was long neglected, but these sections of it are highly esteemed today.

Another group of important writers were the encyclopedists, in whose work has been preserved much that would otherwise have been lost. The most outstanding men in this field were Li Fang (925–996), the president of an editorial board that produced two large compendiums of general knowledge and fiction —the *T'ai-p'ing yü lan* (1000 chapters) and the *T'ai-ping kuang chi* (500 chapters); Yüeh Shih (930–1007), who edited the *T'ai-p'ing huan yü chi*, a geography of the eastern world in 200 chapters; and Ma Tuan-lin (*ca.* 1250–1319), whose *Wên hsien t'ung k'ao* (348 chapters) brought down to 1254 the work of Tu Yu and Chêng Ch'iao, mentioned above.

More colorful were the works, all abundantly illustrated, on such antiquarian subjects as ancient bronzes, inscriptions, stone tablets, wooden slips of the Han dynasty, household utensils and furniture, clothes, and buildings. Connoisseurs in these fields had appeared at least as early as the sixth century, but collecting did not become fashionable until the eleventh, when many tombs were opened and canonical literature was searched for the ritual connected with the furniture they contained. Wang Fu wrote about the imperial collection around 1123–1125 just before it was plundered by the invading Jurchen. His description with its pictures of 527 bells, tripods, and sacrificial cups and its forty-five seals is perhaps more valuable than any; but it lacks the infectious enthusiasm of the catalogue of 2000 inscriptions by Chao Ming-ch'êng (1081–1129) and his wife, the poetess Li Ch'ing-chao (1081–1140), whom Dr. Hu Shih has called the foremost literary woman in Chinese history. They began their collection in a modest way on their marriage in 1101 and continued it as a hobby the rest of their lives. Their catalogue appeared in 1132, three years after the husband's death.

Other prose writers of the Sung period treated such subjects as architecture, horticulture, travel, and foreign commerce. The basic work on Chinese architecture is the *Ying tsao fa shih*, by Li Chieh (d. 1110), who for years was actively engaged in the construction of temples and public offices in the imperial capital at Kaifeng. His book contains specific rules for building all kinds of stone, wood, tile, and brick structures, mainly monumental. The last six chapters are profusely illustrated but not in the detail desired by modern students of medieval architecture; however, the Sung buildings that have been unearthed in Honan and nearby regions have given clues for the solution of many doubtful points. The earliest known scientific work on fruit culture is the *Li-chih p'u* of Ts'ai Hsiang (1011–1066); and the *Chü lu* of Han Yĕn-chih, a prefect in Chekiang in 1178, is the first known scientific treatise on citrus fruits in any language. A botanical encyclopedia was compiled by Ch'ên Ching-i in the thirteenth century; half of its 58 chapters deal with flowers. In 1159 four writers brought out an herbal illustrated with woodcuts "far better than most European herbals of the fifteenth and sixteenth centuries."[15] Many of the Sung envoys described their travels; one such book about Korea, dating from 1124, which contains 40 chapters, discusses its topography, history, religion, government, laws, manners, customs, and industries. Of even greater interest are the records of Chinese commerce with southern and western Asia and even Africa. The most important of these records were left by Chou Ch'ü-fei (1178) and Chao Ju-kua (13th century); they have provided us with a wealth of precise information about the inhabitants, products, and trade of Indonesia, Ceylon, south India, Arabia, Somaliland, and Sicily. Fiction was in the ascendancy, particularly after the flight of the court south from Kaifeng. The invasion of north China by the barbarian horde and the pell mell migration to the south provided tale after tale. The tellers of stories were not interested in literary qualities. They were professionals concerned only with entertaining their hearers

---

[15] Swingle, *Report of the Librarian of Congress, 1926–1927*, p. 256.

with yarns about heroes, lovers, Buddhist figures, magic, and crime. Historical anecdotes were also popular, as were witticisms at the expense of well-known statesmen and courtiers.

Scientific progress was evident. In mathematics, Ch'in Chiu-shao (fl. 1247) was among the first to use the zero invented by the Indians. Algebra, known since the first century B.C., made distinct advances in the twelfth and thirteenth centuries. In medicine, an important advance was the introduction of inoculation against smallpox. The first treatise in the world on legal medicine appeared in 1247, and at least three valuable pharmacopeia between 973 and 1116. Of one of these Joseph Needham writes: "it contains precious information on subjects such as iron and steel metallurgy or the use of drugs such as ephedrine." The author of the herbal was Su Sung (1020–1101), an all-round scholar and civil servant noted as well for his contribution to the art of clock manufacture. He not only described and illustrated in detail the construction of the device but also saw to the building of a very large one in the imperial palace.[16]

In the fine arts, the Sung is known chiefly for its painters—painters of insects, birds, and fish, both real and imaginary animals, flowers and bamboos, cottages and palaces, figures of men, arhats, and saints, and above all, landscapes. It may well be that no other people ever depicted such landscapes. The diverse topography of the country—the mountain cliffs and turbulent streams in the north and west, and the broad rivers and mist-covered hills in the east—provided an irresistible stimulus to artists. Both Buddhism, particularly the Ch'an meditative sect, and Taoism, with its love of nature and freedom, contributed to awakening in the artistic mind a love for solitude clothed in magnificent scenery. Binyon calls it a "cosmic inspiration; a feeling of affinity between the human spirit and the energies of the elements—the winds, the mists, the soaring peaks, the plunging tor-

---

[16] *Science and Civilization in China* IV, pt. 2 (1965), 446, and Needham, Wang & Price, *Heavenly Clockwork* (Cambridge 1960).

rents." The luckless emperor Hui-tsung, who died in captivity in 1135, tried to give special encouragement to the artists but with only moderate success. The court painters produced a few master-pieces, it is true, but a far greater number were painted in the religious houses on the walls, on silk rolls, and in albums modest in size but of transcendent beauty.

In religion and philosophy the Sung is notable for some fusion of Buddhist and Confucian thought and for Buddhism's gradual subsidence from its high place as the most inspiring influence in Chinese life, a process which had begun in the eighth and ninth centuries. Although Buddhism had by no means entirely lost its hold, several events conspired to loosen its grasp irrevocably. In the first place, the triumph of Islam made India no longer either a source of Buddhist missionaries or the goal of Chinese pilgrims. Some thirty-one Indian missionaries served the Liao and Sung as translators of Sanskrit texts during the period 972 to 1053, but they were the last, except for Dhyanabhadra (d. 1363), and Pandita (d. 1381), who came in Mongol times. The last sizable pilgrimage was made in the decade after 966, when a group of Chinese and Uigur monks (their number is variously put be-tween 300 and 157) went to Gandhara, Magadha, and Nepal via central Asia; but subsequent pilgrimages fell off in both number and frequency until they ceased entirely by 1050. In the second place, thinking Chinese, whose forefathers had hoped that Buddhism would impart knowledge and who had been swept off their feet by the amplitude and splendor of its gifts, now began to realize that it afforded only emotional satisfaction. They therefore culled from it and from Taoism what they wished to accept and what Confucianism had never provided, and discarded everything else. In other words, their ethical beliefs were now broadened to include the doctrine of the universality of all existence and other alien ideas. These were unwittingly forged into a new school of thought, which modern historians call Neo-Confucianism. Buddhism did not die a sudden death,

but its own records indicate that its vitality was ebbing percep-
tibly.[17] In spite of the persuasive teaching of several great Ch'an
masters and the greater availability of printed books (the tenth-
century *Tripitaka* was reprinted with supplements several times
in the following three centuries), the more attractive new philosophy lessened the influence of Buddhism, but without resort-
ing to persecution.

Neo-Confucianism emerged during a thoughtful period in
China's existence. Education was becoming general, and in addition the energetic minister Wang An-shih initiated an era of reform that stirred every thoughtful individual to a consideration
of the public policy in finance, law, the army, and government,
as well as education. In his travels to Szechuan, to Kuangtung, to
the capital, and elsewhere, Wang had the insight to discern the
rottenness in official life, the discrimination against the common
people, and the defenseless condition of the country; he had,
furthermore, the courage to express himself boldly in memorial
after memorial to the emperor Shên-tsung (1068–1085). His
proposals were not new, but they were revolutionary for those
times, and they affected every phase of life—at court, on the
farm, on the waterways, and in the counting house. Wang presented them not only to the officials, usurers, landlords, and grain
merchants, but also to the scholars and the rising generation of
students. To this end he instituted the educational reforms already discussed, and he issued a complete revision and commentary of three of the canonical works, the *Chou li*, the *History*,
and the *Odes*. In spite of the emperor's support, his program at
times collapsed, partly because of the pressure from such con-

---

[17] Cf. the *Fo tsu t'ung chi*, an encyclopedia published in 1269–1271. During the
two and one-half centuries after 1037, only twenty works (in 115 chapters) were
translated from the sacred texts of India, whereas in the earlier period 982–1011,
under imperial patronage, a translation bureau headed by three Indians published 201
works in 384 chapters. Buddhist statistics, moreover, show a steady decline in the
number of clerical functionaries, from the 397,615 monks and 61,240 nuns in 1021
to 220,660 and 34,030 respectively in 1068.

servatives as the historian Ssŭ-ma Kuang, the philosopher Shao
Yung, and the poet Su Shih, and partly because the bureaucratic
machine was either unwilling or unable to enforce his measures.
Parts of it, however, were salvaged during the years 1093–1126
but not soon enough to save China from losing the northern part
of her empire. The reform program nevertheless had one important by-product; it roused some of the people from their complacency and made them face problems in a realistic way. Although
Wang's name was muddied by the court historians of his time,
research has made it clear that he must be included in any discussion of Chinese thought and political action.

From its beginnings in the ninth century, Neo-Confucianism
took form in the period from 1050 to 1200. Its active partisans
were men with a wide variety of training and experience; some
held high positions and had great influence, but all belonged to
the conservative party of Ssŭ-ma Kuang. Like their political
adversary Wang An-shih, they insinuated their ideas into their
interpretations of the Confucian texts. Their restatement of Confucianism, based on the religious attitudes of medieval China,
emphasized the idea of universal reason. An understanding of
this reason, said Ch'êng I (1033–1107), was to be gained only
by investigating everything and eventually correlating these investigations. This idea kindled the enthusiasm of Chu Hsi, the
last and greatest teacher and scholar of them all. A brilliant
student in his youth, and deeply affected by Buddhist and Taoist
teachings during his formative years, after 1158 he devoted himself largely to developing the thought of his predecessors in vol-
uminous writings that became required reading for every literate
Chinese after the fourteenth century. "In every human mind,"
he wrote, "there is the knowing faculty; and in everything, there
is its reason. The incompleteness of our knowledge is due to our
insufficiency in investigating into the reason of things. The student must go to all things under heaven, beginning with the
known principles and seeking to reach the utmost. After sufficient

labor has been devoted to it, the day will come when all things will suddenly become clear and intelligible."[18] As Dr. Hu Shih points out, this sounds much like what is now called science. Unfortunately the path Chu urged on his followers could be traveled only by the most serious and spartan philosophers. His philosophy, moreover, had to combat the Ch'an idea of meditation and insight which was being promoted by his evangelistic contemporary Lu Chiu-yüan (1139–1193); the *Mencius* gave Lu's teachings some scriptual authority. Although Chu Hsi made distinguished contributions to thought and criticism, he and his disciples did not hesitate to distort historical facts to make them conform to "the moral law," as is evident from their immensely influential rewriting and condensing of Ssŭ-ma Kuang's history, the *T'ung chien kang mu*, which they completed around 1190. The new Confucianism was an advance over earlier philosophies, but it was inaugurated by a man who twisted the truth in his efforts to formulate a manual of applied morality, and it embodied elements that could never be fused. Its impact was not felt at once, but when it came to full flower in the fifteenth century, its influence extended into Korea and Japan.

In concluding this brief summary, we must not overlook the fact that China's civilization of the eleventh and twelfth centuries probably outdistanced that of the rest of the world. Her people might rightfully agree with Shao Yung, who is alleged to have said: "I am happy because I am a human and not an animal; a male, and not a female; a Chinese, and not a barbarian; and because I live in Loyang, the most wonderful city in all the world."[19] The complacency of such an attitude as this, however, engendered the stagnation and defeat for which China later paid dearly.

[18] Translated by Hu Shih, "Religion and Philosophy in Chinese History," *Symposium on Chinese Culture*, p. 56.

[19] Similar remarks have been attributed to Jung Ch'i-ch'i (a contemporary of Confucius), to Plato, and to Socrates.

The Khitan, Tangut, and Jurchen

Of primary importance for an understanding of the history of eastern Asia in the tenth to thirteenth centuries is some consideration of China's conquerors in the north and west. The level of their civilization was so far below that of China proper that their own was radically influenced by contact, exchange, and intermarriage with the Chinese people. Nevertheless they left their imprint on the territories they overran, and they were so powerful that both near and distant lands paid them tribute and homage.

The first of these conquerors were the Khitan or Ch'i-tan, to spell the name in the less familiar way,[20] whom we have encountered as the Hsien-pi of the mid-fourth century. A pre-Mongol people who spoke a Mongol dialect, the Khitan swarmed out of southeastern Mongolia early in the tenth century, overcame the P'o-hai king in Liaotung in 926, and shortly thereafter began to deal with the Chinese emperors on terms of equality. The Later Chin Dynasty (936–946) owed its existence to Khitan support but later foolishly defied the horde. Thereupon the capital at modern Kaifeng was invaded, and the entire court, together with "artisans, maps and registers, astronomical charts, classics cut in stone, bronze statues, water clocks, musical treatises and instruments, armor, and so forth," was taken to the chief capital in eastern Mongolia, and the dynasty came to an end.[21] Another Chinese house, in its attempts to repel the Khitan, sent Chao K'uang-yin as commander-in-chief; as was said earlier, he seized the power for himself and founded the Sung dynasty. But the Khitan state of Liao remained unconquered; the long

[20] From this word is derived the Mongol Kitat, the Arabian Hitai, the Russian Kitai, and the English Cathay, which stems from the report written by William of Rubruck in 1253.

[21] *Liao History*, chap. 4. For a great fund of information about the Khitan see the *History of Chinese Society, Liao (907–1125)*, by K. A. Wittfogel and Fêng Chia-shêng.

and costly war that broke out in 986 was brought to an end in
1005 when the Sung purchased peace by payment of heavy
tribute.

The early Khitan were a pastoral people largely dependent
on their herds of cattle and horses and on hunting and fishing.
Their tribal organization was complex, and their laws and religious customs were primitive; writing was unknown. Their
move to the plains of north China brought inevitable adjust-
ments for them. They permitted their Chinese subjects to continue farming, and eventually they themselves used agricultural
products. They developed two forms of writing, one of which
was based on the Uigur alphabet; in the other elements of
Chinese characters were used. The latter type has been preserved in a few inscriptions on stone and some frescoes, but it is
practically undecipherable. The Khitan encouraged the circulation of such standard Chinese texts as the *Historical Memoirs*
and the *Han History,* but discouraged private publication after
1064. Buddhism and Taoism made some inroads; the influence
of a few monasteries that grew immensely wealthy was probably
more political than religious. In selecting officials for their Chinese subjects the Khitan continued the T'ang examination system
but refused to permit any Khitan to compete; the subjects em
phasized were poetry, classical exegesis, and law.

For a time the Khitan state of Liao was extremely powerful.
Besides exacting tribute from the Sung, the Khitan also treated
the neighboring peoples—the P'o-hai, Jurchen, Tangut, and
Koreans—as vassals; they defeated the Tatars on the Orkhon
River, and maintained relations with Japan and Arabia, the
latter once asking them for the hand of a noble lady in marriage
to an Arab prince. The Liao empire at its height extended from
the Gulf of Peichihli to the T'ien shan ranges in central Asia.
But it was ringed with hostile states and shot through with
enemies within its boundaries. The imperial Khitan family was
continually at odds; in 1102 one prince openly led the band of

brigands which defied the last emperor. A more serious problem was the series of natural catastrophes—floods and droughts and pests of locusts—that dogged the empire during its later years. Such problems are not insuperable when China's ruling class is well in hand and public works engage the attention of every minor official from Kansu to the Shantung peninsula,[22] for then there are no great breaks in the dams, the roads and canals carry freight, and famine is mitigated by the grain depots. It is in periods when the system fails, as at the end of the 11th century, that every imaginable curse descends on the people, and banditry, cannibalism, and other deplorable conditions are rife.

The most dangerous enemy of the Liao empire were the Jurchen, who had been sharpening their teeth on the flanks of the Khitan for over a century. They intensified their attacks in 1114 and in 1124–1125 subdued or drove out the last of the Khitan who had never been truly absorbed by the Chinese. The only important Liao prince to escape was Ye-lü Ta-shih (1087–1143), who represented the eighth generation of the descendants of the founder of the house. Fleeing west in 1124, he and his small band of companions and a vast herd of horses were welcomed in central Asia by the Uigur, former Khitan vassals. Together they conquered various Turkic states in quick succession and in 1141 established a new empire called Kara-Khitaï (i.e., Black Khitaï or western Liao), which extended to both sides of the Pamirs. Ye-lü and his successors assumed the imposing title of Khan of Khans—in spite of the fact that the empire had been founded by a beaten horde! They brought a certain

---

[22] P'an Chi-hsün (1521–1595), director general of the Yellow River and Grand Canal for twenty-nine years, wrote in 1590: "Great benefit to the Grand Canal transport system can be gained by proper care of the Yellow River. Since the transport of grain tribute cannot be stopped for a single year, the Yellow River should not be neglected for a single year. To attain two ends by one act, the control of the Yellow River is indeed important. Thus, before the Sung and Yüan dynasties, the Yellow River changed its course often suddenly to the north and suddenly to the south, without a single year of peace. But under the present regime, it has not yet changed its course during more than two hundred years. This is due to the care it has been getting as a sector of the Grand Canal." Translated by Chi Ch'aoting, *Key Economic Areas in Chinese History*, p. 142.

amount of Chinese civilization into Kashgar and Samarkand, welcomed Buddhism and even a Christian bishop, and were generally a thorn in the flesh of the Moslems on their western flank. The empire came to a sudden end in 1211, when Jenghis rose to power.

Second to conquer northern China were the Tangut, a Tibetan people, half nomad, half sedentary (Lattimore calls them "semi-oasis"), whom the Khitan court recognized in 990 as the rightful rulers of a region in Kansu near the end of the Great Wall. They took the name of Hsia, made Ning-hsia their capital, and in 1032 called their state an empire which they maintained successfully against the Uigur in central Asia, the Khitan in north China, and the Chinese in the Yellow River delta. In 1043, as we have seen, the Tangut were persuaded to make peace with the Sung for a heavy price, and the next year they attempted to invade Khitan territory.

In contrast to the few Khitan texts which have survived, thousands of pieces of Tangut writing are extant, among them dictionaries dated 1132 and 1190, and two bilingual texts. The complete *Tripitaka* was translated into Tangut and printed; there are also translations of other Buddhist works, and of Tao ist texts, works attributed to Confucius, books on military strat egy, collections of proverbs and sayings of famous men, law codes, and poetry. Their script, which is extremely complicated, was derived from the Chinese through the Khitan. Buddhism was the state religion and, according to the finds made in 1908 by a Russian expedition to Karakhoto, exercised considerable influence, at least in the imperial house. But Confucianism also had a place, especially in the schools, which were patterned on Chinese models and were established in every market town. An academy of learning was established in 1154; one professor who lectured there on Tangut and Chinese literature translated the *Analects* into Tangut and appended his own extensive commentary in thirty volumes.

The Tangut included in their midst an indeterminate number

of Chinese, Tibetans, Tatars, and other peoples, and by the beginning of the thirteenth century were on the way to becoming as civilized as the Sung. Unfortunately, however, their territory lay athwart the path of the Mongols. Jenghis attacked them in 1205–1207 and again in 1209; in the second campaign he altered the course of the Yellow River in order to subdue their capital. The Tangut won a short respite when their emperor promised fealty and presented one of his daughters to the conqueror. But in 1227 a Tangut envoy refused to aid Jenghis in his campaign against distant Kharizm, whereupon the infuriated chieftain turned east and laid most of the Hsia territory waste; the capital, Ning-hsia, was on the point of falling when the conqueror himself was slain. Many of the Tangut were sacrificed at his funeral rites, but a few were spared to serve his widow. Before his death, one of his generals had proposed that the entire population be put to the sword and their land be converted into pasture for horses and camels, but this was rejected in favor of taxation wisely suggested by a Khitan adviser.

Third among the conquerors of the north were the Jurchen, a Tungusic people who lived around the Amur in the far north. First known to the Chinese in the seventh century both as agile hunters who could lure a stag within striking distance by imitating its cry and as breeders of fine horses, they succeeded the Khitan as overlords of north China; in their conquest of China four centuries later under the leadership of Nurhachi's clan, they overthrew the Ming dynasty. They differed from the Khitan in that they knew and preferred the forests and rivers of their own mountainous country, whereas the Khitan preferred the steppes. Curiously enough, however, the Jurchen ventured farther south than the Khitan did, and their empire at its height included less of the north. Except for an occasional raid, the Khitan made the Yellow River their southern frontier; the Jurchen went on down to the Huai and the Yangtze.

The Jurchen were victorious over the Khitan partly because

of the latter's growing decadence and disintegration, and partly because of the help received from the Chinese; this campaign lasted from 1114 to 1125. Their dynasty, the Chin (or Kin, gold), ended officially in 1234. The first few years were devoted to invasions of Sung territory, one of which (1130) went as far south as Ningpo; the Jurchen burned many Chinese cities, including the temporary capital at Hangchow, as well as an entire fleet of war junks on the Yangtze. In the uneasy peace concluded in 1142, the Chinese recognized themselves as vassals and paid a heavy tribute every year thereafter. But they continued to resist invasion of their shrunken empire; in 1161 the Chin attempt to cross the Yangtze was nullified when their fleet of six hundred vessels was destroyed by explosive weapons of the Sung defenders.

The Jurchen rulers made considerable effort to preserve their own civilization and government organization. The latter, however, was transformed during 1115 to 1132 when the Jurchen took over the government of the provinces in north China. The Khitan, P'o-hai, and Chinese populations were kept in check by companies of 1000 men each that infiltrated all the conquered areas. After 1132 the superior administration became more and more Chinese. The Jurchen script was created in 1120 by a member of the royal house, who was a military officer and a shaman; it was based on both the Khitan and the Chinese, and was simplified in 1138 by the emperor himself. The main body of the Chinese classics was translated into Jurchen. The language was studied in the College of Interpreters down through the period of the Ming dynasty, but it died out in the seventeenth century. The people, originally shamanists, had become acquainted with Buddhism as early as the eighth century; halls in honor of Confucius were also erected in the northern capital and in all the important towns; even Nestorian Christianity played some part. But the Jurchen, although eclectic, apparently did not take strongly to the higher forms of religion. In 1187 the emperor urged his subjects not to adopt Chinese ways indiscriminately, and forbade them to assume Chinese names and dress; but his efforts to preserve his people's culture were unavailing, especially on the Chinese plain where life was beginning to assume its normal Chinese pattern. The construction of dikes and dams and the rebuilding of canals were instituted to repair the damages inflicted during the Liao period and to make agriculture and commerce possible. The theater attained great popularity, 690 plays being reported during the time the north was a vassal state. Scholars, too, were active; progress in mathematics was no less brilliant in the north than in south China. According to a modern writer,[23] the northerner Li Yeh, who published two works in this field in 1248 and 1259, and the southerner Ch'in Chiu-shao, who flourished at the same time, far surpass any others in the long roll of Chinese mathematicians. In 1260 Li was accorded the honor of being summoned to court by Kubilai. Two important dictionaries were compiled; one of them contains an analysis of 53,525 characters, or more than are included in the last standard dictionary compiled in 1716.

[23] Van Hée, *T'oung Pao*, XV:182 (1914).

CHAPTER VI

The Mongols
(The Yüan Dynasty, 1260–1368)

THE Mongols resembled the Khitan and Jurchen, but were far more significant in world history. At first pastoral, they became nomadic when they acquired the horse. Their religion was based on animism. The many little tribes into which they were divided had to be welded into one unit loyal to one leader before they could present any formidable opposition to their neighbors. The man who accomplished this had had only a handful of hard-riding nomads under his command before he was thirty years old; when he died, half the world was in his grasp. Such was Temujin, in 1206 proclaimed Emperor of the Seas—Jenghis (Chinghiz, Chingghis) Khan (1167?–1227).[1]

By the end of the twelfth century three groups of Mongols were struggling among themselves for supremacy. Jenghis emerged master of all Mongolia in 1204, his sovereignty being confirmed by a great diet that met at Karakorum in 1206. In 1205 he moved against the Tangut and four years later against the Jurchen. Though he drew to his support all the disaffected northern peoples and made several successful forays into Manchuria and the Yellow River plain, he himself never subdued the Chin. His mobile horsemen had no trouble in open combat;

---

[1] Little is known of his early life; even the date of his birth is not known definitely. Persians historians place it between 1155 and 1156; official Chinese annalists, in 1162; and unofficial Chinese sources in 1167. Cf. Pelliot, *Notes on Marco Polo* I (Paris 1959), 281–88.

they overran the Great Wall and the north-south wall of the Chin and even shattered the defenses of such a provincial center as Tsinan in Shantung; but they were impotent against several walled cities. In 1215 Peking (then Yenching), enfeebled by certain Jurchen traitors, finally submitted to him. Even then noted for its palatial architecture, its wealth and culture—it was the center of Chinese drama—the Chin capital was looted and burned and its inhabitants were put to the sword. The Chin emperor, however, fled to Kaifeng.

At this point Jenghis, alarmed by events in Turkestan, left half of his army with an able lieutenant in north China and moved westward. This officer overran the north for eight years, pillaging and destroying it as he went, but he failed to overcome the people's resistance. Meanwhile two other Mongol officers penetrated Korea; they fought in Iran and the Crimea before returning to Mongolia. After 1223 there was a lull in the fighting in the east, but in 1227 Jenghis returned to settle his accounts with the Tangut, a campaign in which he lost his life. Ogodai, his successor, reopened hostilities in 1231. He directed one pincer which reached down the Yellow River; his brother Tului led another that pierced the Sung province of Szechuan in an immense encircling movement and then pointed toward southern Honan. Fresh from conquests in Persia and Russia, Subotai, the most brilliant tactician in the Mongol army, took Kaifeng in 1233, in the face of hand grenades and other explosive weapons, after a siege that lasted for months. In 1234 a combination of Chinese and Mongol forces finally overcame the Chin emperor, who had fled east.

This might have marked the end of Mongol conquest in eastern Asia had it not been for the stupidity of certain Sung advisers. Instead of adopting a policy of peaceful acquiescence, the Chinese were urged to attack the Mongols. This was political suicide, but it took a bitter war to prove it; hostilities lasted for forty-five years and involved China's southeastern coast, the center, and southwest flank. Unquestionably in the Chinese the Mongols encountered more stubborn opposition and better defense than any of their other opponents in Europe and Asia had shown. They needed every military artifice known at that time, for they had to fight in terrain that was difficult for their horses, in regions infested with diseases fatal to large numbers of their forces, and in boats to which they were not accustomed. Their success was probably due to their use of the ingenuity of every prisoner of war and every ally who had some special skill. From Mesopotamia they brought technicians to the east to dislodge the Chinese. From the Caucasus they brought the Alans—by 1342, some 30,000 in all—who became the guardsmen of a succession of Mongol khans. In the campaigns waged in western Asia (1253–1258) by Jenghis' grandson Hulagu, "a thousand engineers from China had to get themselves ready to serve the catapults, and to be able to cast inflammable substances." One of Hulagu's principal generals in his successful attack against the caliphate of Baghdad was Chinese.[2]

In 1227 the Mongols recognized the need of pacifying their conquered territory and of making it pay the costs both of government and of military campaigns. Almost the last act of Jenghis was to direct his Khitan adviser, Ye-lü Ch'u ts'ai (1190–1244), to collect taxes from the Tangut. When the conquered parts of China were divided into ten departments in 1230, Ye-lü was put in charge of them. Realizing that there were too few Mongol officials and Chinese bureaucrats for administrative purposes, he established several schools in north China and held a great examination; the 4030 who passed were absorbed into government service. In 1231 the Mongols overran Korea and made it a protectorate under seventy-two Mongol resident supervisors. An unexpected rebellion, in which every supervisor

---

[2] Cf. E. Bretschneider, *Mediaeval Researches*, I, p. 113. Yüan Shih-k'ai, the late president of China, and a military man himself, included both this general, Kuo K'an, and Hulagu in his list of the twenty-six military heroes of China.

was killed, broke out in 1232, but this was crushed and the administration promptly restored. The supreme government of all the conquered lands was of course Mongol, but there were Chinese, Tangut, Persian, and Uigur divisions. Since the Uigur was the principal division, the Uigur alphabet, derived from the Phoenician through several intervening Asiatic scripts, was used for the Mongol language.[3]

Of great importance was a system of imperial highways that connected China, Persia, and Russia. The first one, running to western Asia, was built in 1219 by Jenghis; his successors continued and expanded this work and established military and post stations, with the necessary grain stores and pasture lands, at frequent intervals along the roads. The roads were thronged, as probably never before or since, with couriers, caravans, and envoys, many of them en route to or from the great camp at Karakorum. Thither went booty from every land, princes from Russia, skilled craftsmen from Paris, Damascus, and Peking, and ambassadors and ecclesiastical dignitaries from Lhasa, Rome, and Little Armenia. To standardize the currency throughout Asia, the Mongols adopted the paper money of China. At first Ye-lü Ch'u-ts'ai tried to hold the amount issued to 100,000 ounces of silver, but in view of the expansion of the empire and the enormous booty and tribute paper money soon was being printed and distributed freely. As a result, treasury reserves were no longer adequate by the end of the thirteenth century and inflation set in.[4] The issuance of paper money was consequently discontinued in 1356, though the notes still circulated to some extent. Of significance to both east and west Asia is the fact

---

[3] The oldest known monument of Mongol origin is composed of five lines in the Mongol language in Uigur script. It dates approximately from 1220 to 1225.

[4] Basing his statement on C. S. Gardner's translations, Robert Blake has pointed out (*Harvard Journal of Asiatic Studies*, II:291–328 [December, 1937]) that the issue of 1260 was replaced 1 for 5 by that of 1287, and the latter 1 for 5 by the 1309 issue. Blake has failed to note that the policy followed by the treasury was dictated by western Asiatic advisers, not by Chinese.

that, to quote Blake, "huge quantities of silver were drawn off to the west" from China.

The Mongol regime was one from which China gained in some respects. Both road and water communications were reorganized and improved, and post stations with relays of 200,000 fast horses were established for official needs. Peking (Khanbaliq) was designated the winter capital in 1260 and rebuilt by a Moslem in the next thirty years. The palace grounds were dotted with halls and courts for residence, audiences, parades, and entertainment; there were artificial hills and lakes and mountains; the parks contained many kinds of fruit trees, and the broad grassy plains were stocked with the animals of the chase so dearly loved by every Mongol.[5] The city became the terminus of the Grand Canal, which was completely restored under the direction of an excellent Chinese administrator, Kuo Shou-ching (1231–1316), one of the few natives to be given major responsibility by Kubilai, grandson of Jenghis, who was khan from 1260 to 1294. The Kansu waterways, which had been damaged in numerous campaigns, were also repaired after 1264. The anti-famine policies advocated by the eleventh-century statesman Wang An-shih were reinstituted with the construction of state granaries; crops were inspected every year by imperial officials with a view to purchase in good years and free distribution in poor ones. A decree of 1260 (the year in which Kubilai proclaimed himself universal sovereign) instituted charitable relief for older literati, orphans, and the sick; and an edict of 1271 provided for the construction of houses in which the sick could be cared for. Marco Polo, who was in China from 1275 to 1292, is authority for the statement that the emperor himself distributed largesse to thirty thousand poor every day.

[5] In addition to that by Marco Polo, several foreign accounts of Peking during the Yüan dynasty have survived, as have several by Chinese. Among the latter is a formal statement by a Ming official who was a member of the commission sent to Peking soon after 1368 to make a report.

The Mongol empire was expanding. To China proper was added the important southwestern area, later known as Yünnan province, which had been the seat of the Thai kings during the T'ang period. It was invaded in 1253 or 1254 by Kubilai's general Uriangkatai, the son of the brilliant general Subotai, who had served in the expeditions to Russia and Poland before being ordered to Yünnan. The new province was administered by Mongol officers; nominal authority was in the hands of a Thai prince. Among the outstanding Mongol officials was Seyyid Edjell (or Sayyid Ajall, *ca.* 1210–1279), a Moslem descendant of a Bokhara family, who served in Yünnan from 1274 to 1279. He is known for his hydraulic projects in that province, and for the erection of the first two mosques. His sons, also Moslems, continued his administration and made Yünnan one of the strongest Islamic centers in China.

In the years 1257 to 1258 Uriangkatai invaded Annam and reduced the king to vassalage. Kubilai next turned his attention to Japan. After two attempts to bring that country to terms by means of envoys, in 1274 he sent an invasion fleet of 150 vessels largely manned by rather unenthusiastic Koreans and Chinese; this proved no more successful than his earlier efforts. (The Mongols were admittedly inferior in naval warfare. They had been successful in the naval battles involved in subjugating the Sung only because of aid received from Chinese renegades.) In 1279 Kubilai ordered four shipbuilding centers, including Yangchow and Ch'üan-chou, to provide 600 ships within two years. We have little direct information on the work this entailed; undoubtedly it was enormous. Kuwabara, a Japanese scholar, believes that the inability of these centers to build this number of vessels in this length of time contributed to the ultimate failure of the expedition. At any rate, two fleets were assembled in 1281, one in Korean harbors and the other on the southeast coast of China. The Chinese fleet arrived at the rendezvous at Hakozaki Bay behind schedule, and this fact, together with the lack

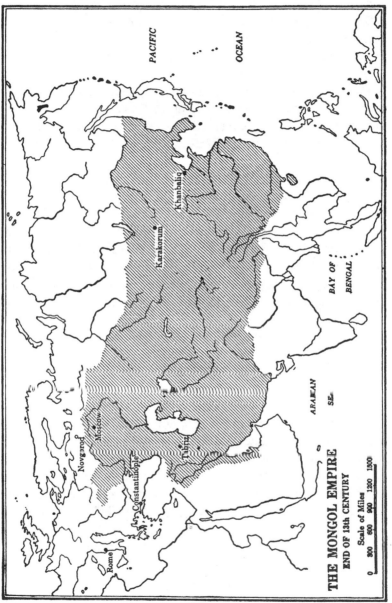

THE MONGOL EMPIRE

END OF 13th CENTURY

Scale of Miles

0   300   600   900   1200   1500

PACIFIC

OCEAN

Khanbaliq

Karakorum

BAY OF

BENGAL

ARABIAN

SEA

Moscow

Novgorod

Tabriz

Constantinople

Rome

of zeal among the Mongol vassals, the brave stand of the Japanese, and a heaven-sent typhoon, combined to rout the invaders; tens of thousands of their men were left at the mercy of the islanders.

During the next twenty years the Mongols landed in other kingdoms on the southeastern fringe of Asia, but their occupation proved only temporary. Disease, guerrilla attacks, and actual defeat forced them to withdraw from Champa, Annam, and Java, but they were temporarily successful in Burma. Certain of these states, however, acknowledged vassalage for a time and sent tribute to Peking, as for example the four elephants that Kubilai used in 1288 in his life and death struggle with the Nestorian Nayan in south Manchuria. But the kings of Annam and Champa refused to go to Peking to render homage—an interesting indication of their independence, considering the subjection of the Russian and western Asiatic provinces to the Mongol will. In 1294, after Kubilai had died and his successor Timor had proclaimed a general amnesty, the king of Annam boldly complained that the Mongol invaders had destroyed his country's libraries. Timur sent him the new copy of the Buddhist canon which he demanded.

The above paragraphs indicate how open the world had become by this time. China was no longer politically detached from western Asia and Europe; it was merely a fragment of a great dominion that extended from Korea to the Danube. While Arabs, Venetians, and Russians engaged in business in Chinese ports and entered the Mongol government—one man from north of the Black Sea took first place in the metropolitan examinations in 1321 and became a high official in Chekiang in 1341— Chinese and Mongols were gradually penetrating Persia and Europe. For example, Tabriz, the leading commercial center of western Asia, had a Chinese quarter, as did Novgorod and Moscow. As envoy of the Mongol ilkhan, Rabban Sauma, a Nestorian born in Peking about 1225, visited Byzantium and Rome in

1287–1288, saw the king of England in Gascony and Philip the Fair in Paris, and left a description of his visit to the abbey of Saint-Denis and Sainte Chapelle, among other places.

The natural interchange of ideas and culture can only be hinted at in a short account such as this. The great development of gunpowder for military purposes has already been mentioned. The Europeans may have learned about printing from the commonly used paper money that was printed not only in Peking but also in Tabriz in 1294, or from printed textiles, or even from the small amount of block printing, modeled on Chinese or central Asiatic prototypes, that was done in Egypt about the time of the Crusades.[6] "White copper," saltpeter, porcelain, and playing cards were introduced to Mediterranean peoples, apparently by the Arabs. A Chinese medical work on the pulse was translated into Persian. Chinese iconographic influences are evident in Ambrogio Lorenzetti's painting of the massacre of Franciscans at Ceuta (*ca.* 1340).[7] Chinese influence in other artistic fields is even more pronounced in Persian miniatures, architecture, ceramics, and music. That the Chinese zither was known in Prussia is evident from the picture of one, painted in the fourteenth century, that Curt Sachs discovered in the Kolberg cathedral in Pomerania.[8] Italian and central European prelates welcomed Chinese textiles enthusiastically.[9]

At least one major food crop, sorghum, was introduced to China. This plant, the original home of which was probably Abyssinia whence it came by way of India, appeared in western China in the thirteenth century and eventually competed with millet as the characteristic crop of the dry lands of north China

---

[6] The first clear occidental description of printing appears in a history of the world written by Rashid-eddin (1300–10), which was well known in European libaries. Paulus Jovius, who wrote in 1546, is the first European historian to suggest that continent's indebtedness to China for this invention.

[7] Cf. H. Goetz, *Burlington Magazine* (August, 1938), Plate VB, p. 56.

[8] *The History of Musical Instruments*, p. 186.

[9] Otto Von Falke, *Decorative Silks*, p. 30.

and Manchuria. According to contemporary Chinese books on foods and beverages, the carrot, pistachio, and grape wine appeared on Chinese tables. Distillation was first practiced in China under the Mongols, and as late as the last half of the thirteenth century men from Cairo were instructing the Chinese in the art of refining sugar. The most significant new medicine in China was probably chaulmoogra, an oil obtained from a tree native to Siam; it was first mentioned as a remedy for leprosy by Chu Chên-hêng (1281–1358). Certain western musical instruments either were introduced or became better known under the Mongol regime. The bowed zither and the three-stringed guitar began to be popular, and a remarkable organ with reeds of the single beating type was taken to Peking around 1260 by envoys from Byzantium or Baghdad. Farmer[10] lists several instruments that were brought to China from western Asia by Moslem or central Asiatic bands and that were known for a long time by ill-disguised Turkic, Persian, or Arabic names.

Chinese science was enriched by innovations from outside. The abacus, mentioned clearly in Chinese books in 1274, is a reckoning device that is still used in every shop and counting house in China, Japan, and Russia. The *pied du Roy*, a French measure of length, was used in 1345 when the gate at the Nank'ou pass in the Great Wall was built, and possibly earlier, but fell into disuse thereafter. In 1267 a Persian astronomer and geographer presented Kubilai with a new chronographical scheme that for a time superseded the Chin system, and with a Persian terrestrial globe and models of six astronomical instruments that possibly influenced Kuo Shou-ching, the noted hydraulic engineer, when he made seventeen instruments for Kubilai in 1276–1279. The knowledge of mathematics in the China of his day, however, was sufficient to make Kuo for the most part independent of foreign discoveries. There is no reason to doubt that his instruments were the finest in the world at the

[10] *Journal of the Royal Asiatic Society*, p. 332 (April, 1934).

time, as to both precision and casting. Wylie classifies several of them as inventions; two of them have survived. A gnomon, believed to have been used by Kuo in his observations, has recently been discovered. Scientists generally agree too that Kuo evolved spherical trigonometry out of the plane geometry of Shen Kua (1031–95).

Just as certain Chinese influences penetrated western art and architecture, so did Tibet, Mongolia, and the lands to the far west influence China, although the main streams of Chinese art continued to flow in their historic channels. Persian influence was evident in ceramics and in bronze work, in both shape and decoration, as pilgrim bottles, incense burners, and gourds of this age attest. Thin glass was a novelty, as was also cloisonné; the latter was made according to a process peculiar to Byzantine craftsmen but the time of its introduction is uncertain. Architecture is represented by Kubilai's famous Violet Tower, built in Mongolia probably by Moslem masons trained in Iran. Mosques were built throughout China—in the western provinces of Kansu, Szechuan, and Yünnan, in Sian, and in such important trading centers as Ch'üan-chou and Canton on the southeastern coast. Like the Buddhist monasteries before them, these mosques (the earliest dated monument is 1258) retained some of the distinctive features of the land of their origin—for instance, the seven steps to heaven, Arabic inscriptions from the Koran, and a rare minaret—but they embodied undeniable Chinese characteristics as well. Winged caryatides (of Persian inspiration?) uphold the ceiling of a famous Buddhist temple in Ch'üan-chou. The advent of the Lama church of Tibet (see below) brought with it certain artistic features. One unexplained item is the prayer cylinder which may date from this period although no authentic thirteenth-century example or literary reference has been found. Such cylinders, ubiquitous in Tibet and Mongolia, spread across China to Korea and Japan.

Religious life in the Yüan period is not marked by spiritual development though there were many faiths. As in the T'ang, every religion was free to proselytize. One important difference, however, marked the two periods. In the T'ang the court was Chinese and most of the leading officials were either Chinese or foreigners with strong Chinese tendencies. After two centuries of tolerance, the T'ang persecuted the foreign churches (except for Manicheism, which was associated with the Uigur) largely because Buddhism was either avoiding its economic responsibilities or usurping prerogatives to which it had no right; in the popular as well as in the official mind—they were all managed by a single board at the court—all foreign churches had to suffer with Buddhism. In the Yüan, a few significant figures at the capital—men like Ye-lü Ch'u-ts'ai, Kuo Shou-ching, and Chu Ssŭ-pên—were Chinese or men of Chinese education, but the great majority were not. When the empire collapsed, all foreign institutions except those solidly entrenched died with it. Rightly or wrongly, in the minds of the people the churches were associated with the invader.

Islam, Nestorian Christianity, and Roman Catholicism all penetrated China during the Yüan.[11] The last two withered away after 1368, partly because they had few adherents and partly because their land and sea connections with the supporting constituencies in Baghdad and Rome were cut. Islam, however, survived because its strongholds in central Asia and on China's western frontier were not wiped out.

Prior to the thirteenth century the Lama (Buddhist) church of Tibet had had no influence in either Mongolia or China, but with the active support of the Mongol emperors it entered Mongolia. Lamaseries were established too in certain parts of China, particularly on the western frontier and in the capital; they have

---

[11] Judaism had gained a precarious foothold during the Sung and continued to exist around the synagogue in Kaifeng; its other centers along the seacoast were wiped out at the beginning of the Ming dynasty. Manicheism, which had gone underground in 845, emerged in Fukien for a few decades during the Yüan but was rigidly proscribed by the founder of the Ming.

continued to recent times to be centers of political activity and goals mainly for Tibetan and Mongol pilgrims. The religious and political importance of Lamaism was enhanced toward the end of the Ming dynasty by the ascendancy of the reformed church of Tsong-kha-pa (1357–1419) and his successors.

Of China's primary religions—Buddhism, Confucianism, and Taoism—the last eventually suffered the hardest blow under the Mongols. This comes as a surprise to anyone who has studied the Mongolia of Jenghis' time, for the religion of the simple and superstitious-loving Chinese must have appealed strongly to the nomadic mind. Jenghis himself in 1219 honored a Taoist monk, Ch'iu Ch'u-chi (1148–1227), by summoning him from Shantung, where he was living as a recluse, to his camp by the Oxus River. On his return to China in 1224, this wise and pious man did much for Taoism at the expense of Buddhism. Not only did he have a wide knowledge of classical literature to draw on in propagating the Taoist precept, but through his efforts the authorities permitted the Taoist to occupy many of the Buddhist temples that had been laid waste during the Jurchen-Mongol wars. He also wrote two books that maligned the Buddhists. But Buddhism was not to be denied so easily. Certain of its priests were in good accord with the Mongol officers who were campaigning in China. Its hour came during the regime of Jenghis' grandsons when the Mongol leaders were no longer credulous and illiterate but fully aware of the merits of the various civilizations in Asia and eastern Europe.[12] In 1255 and 1256 two public debates were held between Buddhists and Taoists. Though the Buddhists were declared to have won, their opponents refused to give up their activities. Therefore Kubilai ordered the Taoists to return all the Buddhist properties that had been taken prior to 1227. In August, 1258, acting under his

___

[12] Mangu (or Mongka), whose mother was a Nestorian, is said to have remarked in 1254 to William of Rubruck, the envoy of Louis IX of France who was on a crusade: "As God gives us the different fingers of the hand, so he gives to men divers ways." Translated by W. W. Rockhill, *The Journey of William of Rubruck*, etc., p. 235.

elder brother's instructions, he commanded that all Taoist books be seized and burned. He issued a similar order in 1281 after his conquest of all China; only the text of the *Tao-tê-ching* and books on medicine, pharmacy, and such subjects were exempt. Three years later nine scholars of the Hanlin Academy were directed to commemorate the triumph of Buddhism in an essay engraved on stone. The burning of the Taoist books was a heavy blow, for it meant the destruction of a literature that extended back well over ten centuries. Fortunately for history, some of it was preserved surreptitiously; other fragments have been found in Japan during recent decades. Taoism itself could not be killed; instead, it lingered on as an underground movement that plagued the Mongol administration in its decadence, and it shared with other similar sects in the final overthrow of the dynasty.

Buddhism, no longer a spiritual force, wielded great political power. As it had appealed to the Wei Tatars and to subsequent northern invaders, so it aroused the interest of the third-generation Mongols. It was accorded imperial favor until the fall of the Mongol dynasty; on one occasion Kubilai received in state envoys from the rajah of Ceylon who brought him relics of the Buddha. One of Kubilai's grandsons inclined sharply toward Islam while he was governor of Shensi and Kansu, but he was slain in an abortive attempt to seize the throne in 1307. This policy of supporting the Buddhist church in China and the Lama church in Tibet and Mongolia, though debilitating for the Mongols, in all likelihood saved China from a head-on clash with Islam, for no Moslem outbreaks occurred in China proper for the next five centuries. It also made the Indian practice of cremation widespread. This custom, which had immense social and economic importance, apparently became general about the twelfth century; Marco Polo remarked it in almost every province through which he traveled. The resurgent Ming put an end to cremation in their blind desire to remove every trace of

the foreigner. The amount of land necessarily withdrawn from cultivation by the custom of burial was completely overlooked; the sole desire of later Chinese was to preserve the bodies of their ancestors in the time-honored way. Only the Buddhist clergy were permitted to continue the rite.[13]

Confucianism, which had suffered many reverses in north China during the three centuries that the Khitan and Jurchen were in control, regained some of its strength as order was restored in the mid-thirteenth century. One of its assets from this time on was a textbook that rapidly became the foundation stone of a Chinese education. Written by Wang Ying-lin (1223–1296), a scholar of south China, this "elementary guide to knowledge, . . . arranged in 356 alternately rhyming lines of three characters each and containing about 500 different characters in all,"[14] was reproduced in scores of editions during the following six centuries. The Mongol rulers made certain gestures in favor of Confucianism, as when Ogodai on the advice of the Khitan Ye-lü Ch'u-ts'ai reestablished the Kuo-tzŭ-chien, the Confucian college. A noted adherent of the Chu Hsi school was put in charge of it later by Kubilai, and a second college was sanctioned at Ch'ang-an; the latter is probably responsible for the preservation of the classics engraved on stone in the ninth century. Kubilai also ordered a temple to be constructed to Confucius in Peking; this was completed in 1306. Between 1308 and 1330 a new title was accorded to Confucius, new honors were granted to Confucian heroes, and nine Sung Confucians were accorded places in the hall of fame.

Some of the schoolmen seem eventually to have attained high places in the bureaucracy. Competitive examinations, which had been discontinued in the north in 1237 and in the south in 1274, were resumed in 1315. The triennial examinations for the high-

---

[13] For what must be almost the last account of the cremation of the common man, see the *Shui hu chuan,* translated by Pearl Buck in *All Men Are Brothers,* pp. 444–445.

[14] H. A. Giles, preface to *San Tzŭ Ching,* p. iii.

est degree were given thirteen times; the number of *chin-shih* varied from 35 (in 1360) to 108 (in 1348).[15] Most of the successful candidates were Chinese, but an occasional foreigner passed the examinations. By the decade of the 1330's the Confucians felt themselves sufficiently entrenched to protest publicly the favors shown the Tibetan lamas, but they found that their position was not as strong as it had been during earlier periods under Chinese rulers. They were given subordinate posts—in the chancelleries, provincial offices, tax bureaus, etc.—where their talents and training were needed but where their influence could be kept in check. Even the bureau of historiography, which had the responsibility of compiling the histories of the Sung, Liao, and Chin dynasties, had a Mongol as its nominal head.

A thin stream of scholarly writings continued Sung traditions during the Yüan. Many of the Chinese emissaries, travelers, and merchants of the thirteenth century wrote accounts of their journeys. The several books in this field which have survived and been translated into English parallel the journals of such travelers as John of Plano Carpini and William of Rubruck. In 1280, Kubilai, whose curiosity was apparently boundless, sent a mission to ascertain the true source of the Yellow River. Some time later Tibetan maps and books on the subject were translated into Chinese by chu Ssŭ-pên, the Chinese geographer who compiled a great atlas during 1311–1320. These two series of reports have been preserved in the annals of the dynasty.[16] Another map, whose world view seems to make it date from about 1300, took in the whole of Asia, Europe, and Africa. An imperial geography, published in 1303 in 1000 chapters, is the largest undertaking of its kind in Chinese records. A later writer, T'ao Tsung-i (*ca.* 1320–1399), a native of Chekiang province,

---

[15] See Têng Ssŭ-yü, *Chung-kuo k'ao shih*, p. 205. The *chin-shih* was the highest degree awarded under the empire; it is sometimes equated with the western degree of doctor of letters, but no original rèsearch was asked of candidates in part fulfillment of the requirements.

[16] *Yüan shih*, chap. 63.

was interested in both antiquarian and contemporary topics. His notes give us valuable information on the rising tide of resentment against the Mongols as well as on painting, pottery, lacquer, bronze, costumes, musical instruments, methods of mounting pictures, and the palatial architecture at Peking; the latter he probably learned about from the Mongol governor of his province who was at one time mayor of Peking. T'ao's notes also contain lists of plays and collections of short stories.

The age, however, was distinguished not so much for scholarship as for drama. Until the beginning of this century only 119 Yüan plays were known and they all belonged to a set edited (and tampered with) 250 years later. In 1908 fragments of another were discovered at Karakhoto by the Russian archeologist, Colonel Kozlov. A decade later thirty truncated plays were found in a box, and since then many more (36 confirmed and 17 probables) have turned up and been published. They show wide variety in theme and content, and range from serious drama to comedy. Actual performances of polished operas, thinks one student, were probably—like their Elizabethan counterparts—interrupted "with lusty farce and ribald interludes."[17] They told often of the life about them, of soldiers, priests, and scholars, and delighted especially in poking fun at practitioners of medicine. Their authors were evidently men of education, though not one gets even passing mention by the court historians. They could write both with poetic beauty and in the coarse vernacular of the times. The influence of the conquerors was passive;[18] it was their suspension of the civil examinations in north China for seventy-eight years that permitted the nascent drama to develop and flourish. The playwrights, says Yao Hsin-nung,[19] served as clerks to more or less "illiterate" Mongols or else were unemployed,

[17] James I. Crump, *The Journal of Asian Studies*, XVII:429 (May, 1958).

[18] There is evidence that there were a few Mongols in the audiences because extant plays contain a few transliterations of Mongol expressions and shifts in current pronunciation.

[19] *T'ien Hsia Monthly*, I:4, 391–392 (November, 1935).

and they naturally looked back to the days when a scholar could "leap through the Dragon's Gate" on the sheer power of his brush. The stage became a means of maintaining their traditional social influence and compensating for their waning prestige and wounded pride. On the stage, as in Elizabethan England, women's parts were usually played by men, a custom that went back to Sung times when Confucian moralists voiced their disapproval of the mingling of actors and actresses. But enterprising courtiers and professional danseuses could be seen on the stage; one authority lists the names of eighty-eight actresses of the period. The chief character often had to sing several arias, in which he was accompanied by an orchestra composed of a three-stringed guitar, flute, drum, castanets, and other instruments. The stage, props, costumes, make-up of the actors, and a part of the orchestra are shown in a large temple wall painting in Shansi.[20]

---

[20] Laurence Sickman has reproduced this in *Revue des arts asiatiques*, X:2, Plate XIX, a (1937). The painting dates from 1324.

CHAPTER VII

A Chinese House
(The Ming, 1368–1644)

THE Ming has had a bad press. Actually this period was note-worthy for reconstruction in many fields—public works, government, law, colonization, literature, and the fine arts. Only after the collapse of its successor, the Manchu dynasty in 1912, have its achievements been appraised at their true worth.

The house which succeeded the Mongol dynasty was only one of several in southern and central China that might have seized the power from the weakening Mongols. Outbreaks in that locality, as well as on the sea coast and in the river valleys, became frequent toward the middle of the fourteenth century. Nanking was captured in 1356 by Chu Yüan-chang (1328–1398), a monk of humble origin, grotesque appearance,[1] and more than ordinary brains, cruelty, and ability to lead. This insurgent immediately began to rally the other rebels to his cause; those who refused to join were slain. His army drove the Mongols out of Peking by 1368, out of China proper by 1371, and out of Yünnan by 1382.[2] One of his able generals occupied the entire northern frontier, carrying his campaign as far as the T'ien

---

[1] One portrait in the Peking palace collection depicts him as a kindly old man; another shows the snout-like face for which he was notorious in China. Incidentally, his surname, which means vermilion, lent itself to this name-calling, for it is homophonous with the common word for pig (chu).

[2] Together with Kweichow and Kuangsi, this region, although made a province, has had definite colonial features until the past few years. Cf. K. A. Wittfogel, Wirtschaft und Gesellschaft Chinas, pp. 219 ff. (1931).

shan foothills. The Mongols were even forced to give up Kara-korum, where princes and envoys from nearly all Eurasia had knelt in homage a century earlier. They also withdrew from Korea and Manchuria, and the princes of Hami, Turfan, and Ili acknowledged the suzerainty of the Chinese emperor. Not until 1404 did the Mongols in western Asia undertake a campaign against the Ming; this ended abortively, however, on the death of Timur at Otrar in 1405, after an army of 200,000 men had been on the march for a month. In the next two decades the third Ming emperor put down every effort on the part of the Mongols to regain their power, and he consolidated his conquered territory from Hami to the Sungari River basin.

The first reign was occupied with internal reorganization—the suppression of secret societies and other subversive elements (this cost many innocent people their lives), the promulgation of a new code, the reestablishment of contacts with neighboring powers, the rebuilding of the country's defenses, and the repair of irrigation systems. Quite logically Nanking, the center of Chu's strength and near the center of population and wealth, became the capital. He was succeeded by one of his grandsons. This short reign was marked by a civil war between the emperor and his uncle Chu Ti, then prince of Yen (the area around modern Peking) and an ambitious man who resented his nephew's accession to the throne. Countless lives were lost, and parts of north China, which was just beginning to recover from the campaign against the Mongols, were devastated. Chu Ti was finally victorious, and his reign, the Yung-lo (1403–1424), brought glory to Chinese annals. Peace was again restored. Scholars were put to work extracting the best in Chinese literature past and present, and compiling the opinions of 120 Sung philosophers. In 1403 eunuchs, several of whom had posts of more than ordinary responsibility, were sent on missions to Tibet, Java, Siam, and Bengal, and in 1405 and later on great expeditions to the South Seas, India, and the Persian Gulf. Three campaigns were

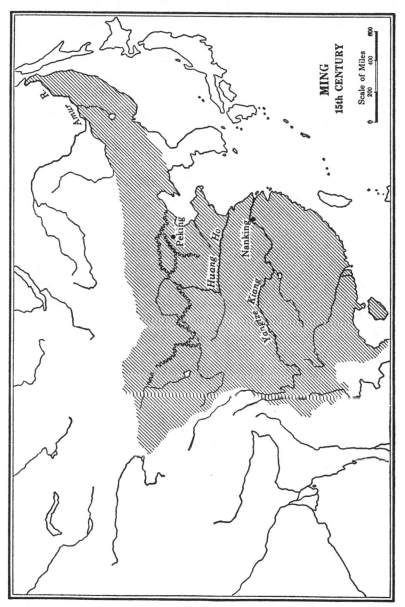

MING
15th CENTURY

Scale of Miles
0   200   400   600

Amur R.

Peking

Huang Ho

Nanking

Yangze Kiang

conducted in outer Mongolia, and in 1421 the capital was transferred to Peking. (In spite of fires, earthquakes, time, and war,
Peking is still essentially the imperial seat designed by the third
Ming emperor.) Nanking, however, continued to function as a
subordinate capital.

As soon as the routes across Asia were again open for travel,
especially after 1405, the Chinese began once more to exchange
embassies with peoples in the Tarim basin and beyond. One of
China's outstanding representatives, Ch'ên Ch'êng (d. 1455),
made three excursions to the west between 1414 and 1421, and—
following the first—submitted reports of his journeys and the
lands visited to the throne. On this initial occasion he paid
official calls on seventeen states, among them the ruler of Samarkand, Ulugh-beg, and his father Shahrukh, prince of Herat, who
in May 1417 arranged elaborate festivities in honor of the
Chinese ambassador and his suite. At the same time the heads
of states in central Asia were sending similar embassies to China.
Shahrukh dispatched one large mission in the years 1419–22,
and for this too we have an equally informing report. These
two documents taken together provide an unparalleled picture
of the situation in middle Asia in the second decade of the century. On both sides the embassies were ill disguised efforts to
spy out the land and to engage in trade.

During these same years China launched a remarkable series
of naval expeditions. Were they put to sea to gain nearby
nations as allies in order to ward off Mongol invasion by sea?
Or to develop sea trade routes, now that trade over the central
Asian routes had dwindled? Or to import horses, sulphur, copper
ores, timber, drugs, and spices on which the coastal Chinese
had come to depend? Or to assuage the emperor's pride and
vanity and enable him, when envoys and tribute streamed in
from many lands, to liken himself to the greatest of China's
rulers? Or to search out his arch enemy, his nephew, who was
reported to have escaped when the palace at Nanking was

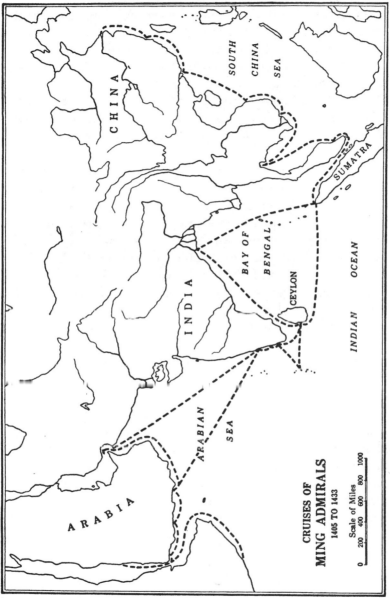

CRUISES OF
MING ADMIRALS
1405 TO 1433

Scale of Miles
0   200   400   600   800   1000

burned in 1402? All these reasons have been suggested and some actually appear in the annals; each is defensible, at least in part. In any event, though their real motive is unknown, these expeditions were commercially valuable and brought incalculable prestige to China.

The first expedition left in 1405, when Chêng Ho,[3] a eunuch in the emperor's service, assembled a fleet of junks at Soochow and set sail for the kingdoms to the south. According to Ku Ch'i-yüan (1565–1628), a later historian, "(Subaltern) officers, soldiers of the flag army, braves, civilians, buyers, and clerks numbered 27,870 men. The total number of ships was sixty-three, of which the largest were 444 [Chinese] feet long, and 180 feet wide. The middle sized ships were 370 feet long and 150 feet wide."[4] Chêng Ho captured the ruling prince of Palembang and brought him forcibly to Nanking. On his third voyage he returned with the king of Ceylon, who likewise had offered vigorous resistance. Some seven expeditions that visited Java, Sumatra, Ceylon, India, Arabia, and Africa put to sea between 1405 and 1431. In addition to ambassadors and tribute they brought back a great deal of information on sea lanes, navigation conditions, harbors, and foreign customs. Sixteen states from Malacca to Hormuz sent tribute in 1415; in 1433 the fifth emperor received in state ten or eleven foreign ambassadors who remained in Peking until 1436. Among the many curiosities that the envoys brought as gifts were ostriches, zebras, and giraffes, which, together with the embassies themselves, added much to the color and pageantry at the two capitals.

Chinese navigation and naval architecture now probably reached their peak. That Chinese navigators used the Singapore main strait, which the Portuguese probably did not discover un-

---

[3] Chêng Ho, possibly of Mongol-Arab origin, was a Mohammedan from Yünnan. It is significant that a Moslem was chosen to lead these expeditions, for Islam was the state religion in many of the places to which he went.

[4] Translated by J. J. L. Duyvendak, *T'oung Pao*, 34:357 (1939). The measurements are puzzling and have not been satisfactorily explained.

til much later, is evident from the charts that have come down to us. The Chinese junks (is this word derived from the Chinese *tsung* and the Javanese *jong?*) usually hugged the coasts but could travel at a speed of six and a quarter miles an hour in open water. They were fairly comfortable for their day, at least for officers and merchants, as is indicated by an even earlier description of Ch'üan-chou and Canton vessels by the traveler Ibn Batuta (1304–1377/8): "On each ship four decks are constructed; and there are cabins and public rooms for the merchants. Some of these cabins are provided with closets and other conveniences, and they have keys so that their tenants can lock them, and carry with them their wives or concubines. The crew in some of the cabins have their children, and they sow kitchen herbs, ginger, etc., in wooden buckets."[5]

The expeditions ceased as suddenly as they began, again for reasons only guessed at. Expensive campaigns, particularly against the Oirats on the northern frontier, starved the navy for funds; sailors and shipbuilders had to seek other occupations. A spirit of isolationism penetrated the court; the ancient policy that no Chinese ship should go outside coastal waters was revived. The result—the subjects of a China that had known all the peoples of Asia were soon forbidden to leave home or to communicate with foreigners—unquestionably changed the course of history. It left China open to raids from the nearest naval power, Japan; it lost the command of the Indian Ocean to the Arabs, and to the Portuguese seventy-five years later; it halted commerce and cut the income of the imperial customs. Worst of all, however, it isolated China just when Europeans were about to penetrate every corner of the earth.

The record of China's foreign relations from this time on is an unhappy one. Annam secured its independence in 1431 and retained it until 1788. Japanese buccaneers had been preying on the coast of China from the Shantung peninsula south since at

[5] Yule-Cordier, *Marco Polo*, II, p. 253, n. 6.

least 1350. The raids were now intensified, some of them being so severe that the inhabitants of the coast were forced to move inland. Ningpo was burned in 1523; in 1552 a flotilla moved up the Yangtze sacking cities on both its shores; in 1555 Nanking was besieged and the port of Ch'ao-chou in Fukien was plundered; in 1563 the army had to be used to eject the raiders from Fukien. Formosa was at their mercy. The raiders were no longer solely Japanese; they included freebooters from the whole coastal region. One Chinese source makes nine-tenths of them Chinese; the most famous seventeenth-century raider was the son of a Chinese father and a Japanese mother.

Tibet, which had begun to come to life again under Tsong-kha-pa (1357–1419), was almost the first power successfully to resist the emperor of the Yung-lo period. In 1413 Tsong-kha-pa refused his bidding to court. In 1449, the Mongols, probably to their own surprise, defeated a badly led Chinese army of half a million men and held the emperor captive for a year. A century later they raided north China.

European nations also showed an interest in China during the Ming dynasty. The Portuguese arrived on the China coast in 1514 but their conduct in the following decade led to their expulsion in 1522. They returned after a short period to make settlements in Macao (1553–54) and Amoy (1544); their attempted settlements in Canton, Ningpo, and certain ports in Fukien were uprooted between 1545 and 1549. After their unsuccessful attempt to gain a foothold in 1543, the Spaniards began to occupy the Philippines in 1565. From that base they established relations with China during the next decade and developed a flourishing trade which brought millions of pesos to Chinese merchants and quantities of silk, porcelain, and other Chinese goods to Mexico, Chile, and other Spanish territories. The Dutch arrived in Formosa in 1622 and also tried to oust the Portuguese from Amoy; they kept their holdings in Formosa and the Pescadores until after the end of the Ming dynasty. Five English vessels fought their way to Canton in 1637 and disposed of their cargo, but no settlement was established. The Russians, driving overland across Siberia, took tentative but unsuccessful steps to secure representation at the Ming court in 1567 and again in 1619.

China's chief external problems at the end of the sixteenth century were Japan and some Jurchen tribes in Manchuria. Japan invaded Korea, then a tributary to China, when the king of Korea refused to acknowledge the sovereignty of the new Japanese dictator. China came promptly to the aid of the Koreans and, although Seoul and Pyong-yang had already been lost, forced the Japanese back to Pusan in 1593. When subsequent negotiations failed, the Japanese reopened hostilities in 1597 but were again unsuccessful; they retired the next year. The Jurchen appeared at the turn of the century. After years of heavy fighting both north and south of the Great Wall, China lost Manchuria in 1636, when the great Ch'ing dynasty was established with its main seat at Mukden; north China in 1644, when the dynasty shifted its capital to Peking; and south China in 1659, when the last of the Ming princes was expelled from Yünnan.

China's domestic history under the Ming is one of restoration of her native culture. Defenses, paved highways, bridges, temples and shrines, stūpas, tombs, memorial arches, and rock gardens were built in profusion. Reconstruction projects were numerous; for example, 432 of the 564 city walls put up at this time (many of them faced with brick) were rebuilt walls. The Grand Canal was repaired and deepened, making it possible for large vessels to go to Peking from the mouth of the Yangtze River and thus avoid the perils of piracy and weather off the Shantung coast. In 1394 the first emperor, realizing the need for flood control and waterway repair, sent experts to all the provinces to do this work. Within a few months his Board of Works reported that a total of over 50,000 projects had been completed, 40,987 of them having to do with ponds and reservoirs, 4,162 with rivers and streams, and 5,048 with canals, dykes, and embankments. Some of the approximately sixty million people, who had recovered from the ravages of war, began to cross the old frontiers into the southwest, inner Mongolia, and Liaotung. By the end of the period thousands were seeking homes abroad—in Manila and other nearby ports; the commercial dominance which they established has been conspicuous in the history of the East Indies, Malaysia, and the Philippines during recent centuries. Cremation was abolished, and immolation of slaves and concubines—a Mongol custom which the early Ming emperors adopted—was banned by decree in the middle of the fifteenth century.

The administration of the country was reestablished along characteristic lines by the publication of a new code of law freed of most Mongol elements (this was first promulgated in 1373), by new institutes, and by examinations for civil officials and military officers. Examinations for the highest civil degree were given eighty-nine times (only in 1373–1384 was there none); an average of 280 "doctoral" candidates passed them. It is estimated that by 1469 there were more than 20,000 civil officials of all grades and over 80,000 military officers throughout the empire.[6] The tests became more and more exacting and increasingly expensive.[7] Although the system tended to make the ruling class conform to a single type, nevertheless (China's experience in this respect was not unlike that of Great Britain in the nineteenth century) it produced many excellent administrators who, de-

[6] Y. C. Chang, *Chinese Social and Political Science Review*, XXIII:2, 167 (July–September, 1939).

[7] Wang Shih-chên (1526–1590), an eminent *Chin-shih* or "doctor" of 1547, estimated that a *chü-jen* or "master" needed 600 taels of silver to take the final examinations. This of itself limited the competitors strictly to the leisured and well-to-do, and sometimes also to the well-connected.

The most harmful innovation was the requirement that each theme be treated under eight heads. This was proposed under the Yüan in 1313 but was not formally adopted until 1487; it was continued without modification until 1898.

spite emphasis on literary knowledge, were very practical. Wang Shou-jên (1472–1529), an official set over the tribes people of southern China in 1509, sent this memorial to his emperor: "The duty of the officials would be to show them how to live, how to cultivate their soil, and how to irrigate their fields. The local government should supply the natives with seeds, live-stock, and agricultural implements, which should be returned, together with one-third of the harvest. Get more farmers to plant uncultivated land; induce more merchants to come to trade; but take as low taxes as possible so the people can main-tain their accustomed worship, travel as usual, and meet all their living expenses."[8]

Two administrative abuses came to a head in the last decades of the Ming and hastened the end of that dynasty. One was the fact that the eunuchs had increased their control of affairs of state to such an extent that many good officials refused to remain in office, others were prevented from defending their country properly and some even lost their lives, and thousands were mulcted of their property through outrageous taxation. The tax rate rose repeatedly. To provide new sources of revenue in 1596, the emperor is said to have appointed eunuchs as superin-tendents of the provincial gold and silver mines and to have exacted a tax of 40 per cent on the yield; the result was that the operators of the mines were driven into bankruptcy. The owners of other land that was supposed to contain minerals were re-quired to pay an annual mining tax regardless of their actual

[8] Translated by M. J. Hagerty (?), *Report of the Librarian of Congress, Orientalia Added, 1923–1924*, p. 267.

At the age of eleven Wang went to Peking with his father, who had qualified as a *chin-shih* the preceding year. When he was twelve, the boy asked his teacher what was the most important thing in life. When the teacher answered that it was studying to become a *chin-shih*, the boy replied: "Perhaps not. Study to become a sage: that is the first and greatest occupation." In spite of a first-class mind, excellent connections, and a distinguished ancestry, Wang failed twice at the *chin-shih* examinations; not until he was twenty-eight did he pass them. Cf. F. G. Henke, *The Philosophy of Wang Yang-ming*, p. 5.

production. The court's efforts to resist its enemies further strained the country's resources and led to even higher taxes; the total for military expenditures alone in 1639 amounted to 20,000,000 taels of silver, as against a total national budget of 2,000,000 at the beginning of the dynasty. The government salt monopoly was also seriously mishandled. All these conditions made for instability throughout the country, especially in the frontier sections. The other abuse was the creation of great domains for court favorites and members of the imperial family. The prince of Fu, the second son of Chu I-chün (r. 1572–1620), for example, owned lands in Honan, Shantung, and Hukuang that totaled over 250,000 acres.[9] The peasants driven from their land in these domains formed discontented bands who lived off the country by brigandage. North and central China were overrun by dissidents, and a great many people in Szechuan were butchered. China was ripe for a change of dynasty when the Manchus appeared in 1644 and crushed the revolt led by Li Tzŭ-ch'êng, the most successful of the rebel leaders; he was slain in 1645.

Although the founder of the Ming dynasty had been a Buddhist priest, he seems not to have favored that church above the others, even though sumptuous editions of the Buddhist *Tripitaka* were brought out during his reign. The first emperor proscribed the Buddhist sects that were active in the revolt against the Mongols and might menace his own security.[10] He promoted the official faith, took great interest in the Confucian classics, forms, and sacrifices, and tried to attract scholars to his court. As an expression of his belief in Confucianism the third emperor had a hall erected in Peking in 1420 for the joint sacrifice of heaven and earth, and he made the school of thought formu-

---

[9] Maspero in his preface to the French translation of Backhouse and Bland, *Annals and Memoirs of the Court of Peking.*

[10] One leader who proclaimed the advent of Maitreya actually assumed the imperial title in 1355; he died in Nanking in 1367.

lated by the Sung philosopher Chu Hsi and his predecessors standard for all candidates for civil appointment. These teachings so dominated the scholarly class that, according to a contemporary, "Ever since the time of the philosopher Chu, the Truth has been made manifest to the world. No more writing is needed: what is left to us is practice."[11] There were some protestants, notably the above-mentioned Wang Shou-jên and a rather remarkable non-conformist named Li Chih (1527–1602), but they were in the minority. Despite the strength of the official religion in high places, Buddhism and Taoism were winning the hearts of the common people. Eunuchs gorged with money spent it lavishly on Buddhist temples in scenic spots, and places of pilgrimage were dotted with shrines. Taoism signaled its recovery from Kubilai's literary proscription by publishing its huge body of writings in 1506–1521; seventy years had been spent on the project. Its literature shows that the features, found revolting by the better elements in all classes in an earlier century, had been done away with; for example, significant festivals were no longer celebrated by sexual orgies in the phalansteries. The Taoist church also received special encouragement under the emperor of the Chia-ching period (1522–1566).

New acquisitions to the material culture during the Ming regime can scarcely be overemphasized, particularly after the era of European expansion. One item that entered a little earlier is eyeglasses. Optical lenses had been introduced into China from Greece, via the Roman Orient and India, as early as the seventh century, and crystals were used as magnifying glasses during the Sung. Eyeglasses, however, did not appear until the first years of the Ming; they came in via the Straits of Malacca from Italy, after about a century of development there and elsewhere. Eventually they were worn as a matter of course by almost everyone who could read.

Another item of special significance in the early decades of

[11] Cited by Hu Shih, *China Year Book*, p. 634 (1924).

the Ming was large-scale cotton culture and the manufacture of cotton cloth throughout the empire. Its slow penetration and tardy acceptance in the thirteenth century have been mentioned above. But when farmers were still reluctant to plant cotton on a large scale by the latter half of the next century, the government through its scientific workers proceeded to force all the farmers to include it in their crop-rotation schemes. Some of the edicts issued in this connection dwelt on methods of cultivation and the advantages of the crop; others ordered every farmer in a district that the government considered suitable for cotton to deliver a certain amount of the commodity each year in place of the poll tax. These energetic measures made China one of the great cotton-growing areas of the world by the fifteenth century.

The New World is largely responsible for the most significant innovations. The most valuable gift of the Americas was maize or Indian corn, first mentioned by a Chinese writer in 1555. The route it traveled is obscure, but one botanical historian suggests that some devout but practical Moors brought it from the Iberian peninsula to Mecca by way of north Africa, whence it was transported to west China by equally pious Chinese or central Asiatic Moslems. It seems to have appeared on the southwest frontier well before 1550. Appreciating its value more readily than contemporary Europeans, thousands of farmers, especially in north China, began to cultivate it. By the end of the Ming dynasty it was beginning to rival millet, wheat, and sorghum as a standard crop.

Along with corn came the sweet potato and peanuts, both of them probably brought by the Portuguese to their settlements on the southeast coast. Peanuts first appeared in China before 1538, and the sweet potato two or three decades later both in Fukien and independently in Yünnan (via Burma?). The Chinese promptly realized that these crops could be grown in less fertile soil than others and would add valuable items to their diet. Toward the end of the seventeenth century one Chinese wrote: "There is no place, east, west, north, and south, where the sweet potato is not grown. It thrives especially well in sandy soil and on high ground. Whether the weather is wet or dry, there is a harvest."[12] These three plants undoubtedly affected not only land use and food habits, but also population growth. Official figures are not satisfactory because they are based on the taxation of households and it was to the census-takers' interest to withhold some of the returns. Nevertheless they are suggestive; furthermore, they constitute almost the only data available on the subject. These figures show that population growth remained fairly static until the 1540's; thereafter there was a sharp rise to double the number by 1644.[13]

Tobacco dates from the beginning of the seventeenth century. It also probably reached south China, and possibly north China (via Japan, Korea, and Manchuria), indirectly through the traders at Macao and Manila. As in nearly all the civilized world at that time, it was opposed by the governing classes. Its cultivation and use were prohibited by edicts of both the Chinese and Manchu emperors in the 1630's; in spite of the severe penalties prescribed, the edicts had little effect. Another plant that may have been introduced before the end of the Ming was the cactus, used by the Portuguese and other peoples to build fences around settlements.

A new coin appeared during the Ming—the Spanish peso, which was minted to a great extent in central and South America. These dollars gradually displaced native currency from Canton to Foochow—so much so that even under the Republic

[12] Translated by L. C. Goodrich, *China Journal*, XXVII:7, 207 (October, 1937).
[13] The figures are as follows:

1290 (Yüan)	58,834,711
1393 (Ming)	60,545,812
1542	62,531,295
1644	150,000,000 (estimated)

See Ping-ti Ho, *Studies on the Population of China, 1368–1953*, Harvard 1959.

the standard Chinese unit, long since minted in China from native silver, was sometimes called a Mexican dollar.

All the New World contributions were not beneficent, however, for syphilis, the so-called *morbus americanus*, spread with appalling rapidity. It appeared in India in 1498, when Vasco da Gama arrived in the first ship to make the trip from Portugal. Somehow, no one knows exactly, it reached Canton about 1505, possibly through Arab, Indian, or Chinese sailors. Certain Chinese, who immediately recognized its characteristic symptoms as alien, began experimenting with the so-called "China root" (*smilax pseudo-China*) as a curative, but the disease must have taken a heavy toll in China during the sixteenth century as it did in Europe.

European tools and techniques were imported to China, but how many were introduced before 1644 is difficult to say. As we shall see later, the literati were greatly stimulated by the new knowledge of the scholarly Catholic missionaries in astronomy, chronography, mathematics, geography, and agriculture; but the extent to which this knowledge affected the lives of the masses of the people is not known definitely. Laufer[14] attributed the introduction of the windmill in China to Europeans of the early seventeenth century, but this is contradicted by Needham, who thinks that it derived probably from Iran; however, it embodies devices "borrowed from nautical techniques so ingeniously as to make it almost a new invention." In any event, the windmill came to be used extensively at this time in salt production.

The arts of the period showed the restorative influences of the Ming, although sculpture was an exception. New techniques of painting in water color produced novel and charming results. Landscapes and figures were used more extensively as subjects, and nature studies based on earlier models were painted. Pottery

---

[14] *Chinese Pottery of the Han Dynasty*, p. 19 n. *Science and Civilization in China* IV, pt. 2, 567.

and porcelain were enriched by celadons and blue and white ware that have never been surpassed. All the minor arts— furniture, textiles, rugs, work on ivory and semi-precious stones —give evidence of the highest technical skill. Most of the articles remained in China, but some were produced for the markets of Korea, Japan, the Philippines, Indo-China, and western Asia, which prized them highly; some of them still survive. By the end of the Ming, large quantities were exported to Europe and Spanish America; the result was that the tastes and industries of the western world were revolutionized and the quality of craftsmanship in China was lowered.

The Ming was a period of vibrant interests in countless fields, an interest which is clearly evident in the literature. Ming writers rescued and preserved the thoughts and records of earlier times, they experimented with new styles and investigated new fields, and they began to draw on the new knowledge from the west. So rich are the libraries of the modern world in books dating from the Ming that a true appraisal of the literature of the period would require at least a monograph.

The *Yung-lo ta-tien,* the great thesaurus of the Yung-lo reign, is the most notable example of a work that preserved earlier knowledge. Ordered in 1403, possibly to keep the scholars busy or to win their support for an emperor who had usurped the throne, the manuscript was completed early in 1408. Its 11,095 volumes contained 22,877 chapters, exclusive of the table of contents, and the services of at least 2180 scholars were required for the task of selection and transcription. As Swingle has said, it was "a universal compendium of all existing Chinese history, ethics, science, industry, art, geography, administration, religion, divination, in a word, of all human knowledge among the Chinese up to 1400 A.D."[15] The *Yung-lo ta-tien* was too expensive to be printed as a whole, and only one additional copy was made; these manuscripts have largely disappeared

[15] *Report of the Librarian of Congress, 1923,* p. 188.

(500 volumes are known to be in various libraries up to the present). Individual items, however, that were printed separately have survived. Other scholarly works of a similar type, albeit conceived on a less imperial scale, were produced later. These were relatively short and thus could be printed; consequently they were valuable both to students and as a means of preserving many items that otherwise might have been lost. The best examples in this field are several *ts'ung-shu* (collections), a type of compilation developed originally by twelfth-century scholars, and a number of encyclopedic works.

Ventures involving new investigations and genres include scholarly reinterpretations and studies of the canon, treatises on philology and geography, monographs on arts and sciences, criticisms of literature and art, illustrated encyclopedias, dictionaries, stories, and plays.

As we have seen, the government undertook to establish Chu Hsi as the orthodox interpreter of the Confucian classics. The statesman Wang Shou-jên, however, succeeded in converting a considerable number to a different attitude toward the canon; he argued for the dictates of "innate knowledge" rather than the "memory of a dead text." In 1543 Mei Tsu shook the conservatives of the day by claiming that parts of the *Document of History*, one of the canonical works, were spurious.

A new line of study, which Dr. Hu Shih calls "the beginning of the science of philology in China," was initiated by Ch'ên Ti (*ca.* 1541–1617). His investigation of the original pronunciation of certain words used as rhymes in the *Odes* is a landmark in technique, for it represents "a systematic application of the inductive method and a use of the very terminology we associate with that method in the west."[16]

Works on geography in the broadest sense—for the Chinese conceived this science in terms of maps, boundaries, political divisions, mountains, waterways, public buildings, monuments,

---

[16] A. W. Hummel, *Annual Report of the Librarian of Congress, 1940*, p. 170.

products, population, local customs, etc.—poured forth in an ever-widening stream. Two large authoritative works devoted to the entire empire and a few neighboring countries and prepared at the court's order appeared in 1456 and 1461. Public and semi-private enterprise was responsible for many provincial, prefectural, departmental, and district gazetteers, and for records of mountains, streams, academies and temples usually illustrated by wood blocks. Compiled generally by retired scholars of the area concerned, and financed by the government and by contributions, they show a loving care and a passionate regard for detail that make them the safest of all guides through the maze of Ming history. They are invaluable for their exact information on economic, social, industrial, and other activities. No government office was without a set of local records to aid new judges and magistrates—the law was promulgated in Nanking or Peking but it had to be interpreted in the light of local mores and practices. Hsü Hung-tsu (1585–1643), adventurer, explorer, and diarist, contributed to the knowledge of geography in another way. Unlike most well-to-do Chinese who enjoy more sedentary pursuits, Hsü chose to devote himself to exploring the principal mountains and scenic spots, keeping a day-by-day record of his observations. His most extensive journey took him into the southwest for four years, and from it resulted his principal discoveries: the true sources of the West (Hsi) and Yangtze Rivers, and the fact that the Mekong and Salween are separate streams. Matteo Ricci, who came to China in 1582 (see page 212), owed almost all his knowledge of eastern and central Asia to Chinese cartographers; we shall see later how his arrival stimulated interest in geography.

The monographic material covered almost every field. One work on music—*New Remarks on the Study of Resonant Tubes*, written by Chu Tsai-yü, a prince of the blood, and published in 1584—established, before Marsenne in 1636 and Werckmeister in 1691, that the intervals for "an equal tempered scale" are found by taking the twelfth root of two. The Chinese of the sixteenth century carried to perfection the study of ink-cakes, a minor form of art. Two books on the subject appeared about 1588 and 1594 respectively; they are models of bookmaking and together they contain over a thousand woodcuts.[17]

The *Herbal for Relief from Famine*, written by the fifth son of the founder of the Ming dynasty and a friend, and completed in 1406, was the outstanding work to appear in the field of botany. The two collaborators spent the years between 1382 and 1400 on the prince's estate near Kaifeng. Here they secured from farmers and hermits every scrap of information regarding plants that could be eaten in time of flood or drought; they set these plants out in the fields, wrote descriptions of the various stages of growth, and engaged artists to make drawings which were reproduced as small woodcuts.[18]

The field of medicine was enriched by an illustrated *materia medica* completed in 1578. Li Shih-chên, the compiler, worked for twenty-six years on it, and consulted every known publication in the medical field. According to Dr. Bernard Read,[19] 898 vegetable and around 1000 animal and mineral drugs are discussed under 62 classifications. Li's compilation also included 8160 prescriptions. Among the subjects discussed are smallpox inoculation, treatment for syphilis, and the use of kaolin, stramonium, chaulmoogra oil, ephedrine, and iodine in specific diseases. That the Chinese medical world valued this great work is evident from the fact that there were at least fourteen editions; it was also recognized as authoritative in Japan.

Of all the illustrated encyclopedias that appeared, three are

---

[17] The story of the publication of these two books—*Fang shih mo p'u* by Fang Yü-lu and *Ch'êng shih mo yüan* by Ch'êng Chün-fang—reveals a broken friendship, one which involved hundreds of artists and scholars, reached the imperial court, and ended only when one of the authors died in prison.

[18] Swingle considers this work comparable to the *Buch der Natur* (Augsburg, 1475). The herbal has recently been summarized by Read, *Famine Foods* (Shanghai, 1946); of the 414 plants described therein he has identified 358.

[19] *Chinese Medicinal Plants*, 3rd ed., 1936.

outstanding, at least in the present writer's opinion; all were compiled in the closing decades of the Ming dynasty, and all contain woodcuts. The first (appearing about 1609) is the *San ts'ai t'u hui*, the work of the scholar Wang Ch'i and his son Wang Ssŭ-i. It contains 106 chapters and is chiefly valuable for its woodcuts on such a wide variety of subjects as costumes, games, tools, architecture, botany, and animal life. A modified and expanded edition appeared in Japan a century later. The second, the *Wu pei chih*, was compiled by Mao Yüan-i and was offered to the throne in 1628. Its 240 chapters are concerned solely with offensive and defensive weapons, armor, military strategy, maps of the coast, and the like. The third, the *T'ien kung k'ai wu*, is short by comparison with the other two; it contains only eighteen chapters. This treatment of industry was compiled by Sung Ying-hsing, who failed five times in the examinations for the final degree; it appeared in 1637. It discusses such topics as grain and its grinding, clothes, dyes, the five metals (actually six), salt manufacture, sugar refining, pottery manufacture, the casting and forging of metals, the designing of ships and wheeled vehicles, coal mining, weapons of warfare (including gas explosives), inks, flour, pearl diving, and jade mining.

A dictionary and a series of vocabularies are illustrative of the interest in language. The dictionary, the *Tzŭ-hui*, was compiled by Mei Ying-tso and appeared in 1615. It contains 33,179 characters, and is significant because in it the signs of all Chinese characters were for the first time arbitrarily reduced to 214, as against the 540, 542, and 544 signs in the dictionaries of the second, sixth, and eleventh centuries respectively.[20] Since the seventeenth century both Chinese and foreign lexicographers (including Korean and Japanese) have continued to use these

---

[20] A dictionary published in 997 by a Khitan Buddhist priest reduced the signs to 242, but was apparently not accepted by the Chinese scholars south of the Sung-Liao border. Another lexicographer of the fourteenth century reduced the number to 360.

214 signs. The important fact here is that a Chinese scholar could depart so radically from the norm and that he was intelligent enough to see that this reduction would be invaluable to all future students. Mei also rearranged the radicals and characters on the basis of the number of strokes of each one; this also has been followed ever since in most handbooks and reference works. The *Tzŭ-hui*, however, is almost never referred to today, for it has been displaced by later dictionaries. The vocabularies, dated 1382, 1549, *ca.* 1620, and 1630, were compiled for the bureau of interpreters at the capital.[21] They indicate that a few scholars at court had some knowledge, albeit scanty, of the languages of Korea, Japan, Persia, Turkey, Champa, Siam, Malaysia, Annam, the Lew Chew Islands, Mongolia, and Tibet, and of Uigur and Jurchen. These vocabularies have survived, generally in manuscript form, and this fact has aided modern scholars to ferret out the secrets of two or three less familiar languages.

Just as the literary glory of the T'ang is its poetry, and of the Yüan its drama, so the glory of the Ming is its fiction. There is the *San kuo chih yen i*, a long historical story attributed to Lo Kuan-chung, a writer of the late fourteenth century, but which appeared in enlarged versions until the seventeenth. It is set early in the third century A.D. and concerns the heroes who fought in the internecine wars of the three kingdoms. There is the *Hsi yu chi* by Wu Ch'êng-ên (*ca.* 1505–1580), who appears to have been inspired by an epic poem of the Sung. The hero of this highly imaginative tale is a monkey who, converted from Taoism to Buddhism, helps Hsüan-tsang, the great seventh-century Buddhist pilgrim, on his journey not to India but to heaven. It abounds in descriptions of fabled regions and of the adventures of gods, demons, and men. There is the *Shui hu chuan*, attributed to Shih Nai-an, a late-fourteenth-century

---

[21] This bureau had functioned intermittently since the second century B.C. and was reestablished at the beginning of 1407.

writer, but supplemented two centuries later. This picaresque yarn concerns a band of twelfth-century robbers who leave their lair in the mountains of Shantung to wreak vengeance on the forces of law and order for the wrongs they have suffered at the hands of society. There is the first romance or novel, the *Chin p'ing mei*, which describes the love affairs of an erotic character of the sixteenth century. Its author is unknown; an expanded version of it appeared in 1610. Other famous works—particularly collections of short stories—have survived; but the above-mentioned books are the most popular. The numberless editions that have appeared have been read widely in spite of their generally fine print; favorite anecdotes have been quoted in tea-shops and market places; incidents have been made into plays and presented on the stage. It is not too much to say that their heroes are better known and more beloved than the most illustrious figures in Chinese history; one of them was deified in 1594.[22]

Drama also expanded and matured in this age. In addition to plots borrowed from contemporary stories, original and entirely new ones appeared. One form of theatrical that developed during the fifteenth century was called the *k'un-ch'ü* after its center near Soochow; it was particularly esteemed by the wealthy and cultured class in the lower Yangtze valley. Its essential difference from the Yüan drama was its greater freedom; it did away with the four-act pattern and the practice of assigning singing roles only to the hero or heroine. Since it was designed for less formal surroundings, its music was softer and more melodic. According to Yao Hsin-nung, "It was the sing-song girl who spread the K'un Ch'ü air over the banquet tables of officials and

[22] Chin Shêng-t'an (*ca.* 1610–1661), a scholar with a rather unconventional mind, asserted in 1640 that such imaginative works had the same type of literary merit as Confucian philosophy, poetry, and history. To substantiate this, he brought out an edition of the *Shui hu chuan* in 1641, and composed a long preface to the *San kuo chih yen i* in 1644. Li Chih, mentioned above, had earlier called these pieces of imaginative writing: "The Four Miraculous Books."

courtiers, glorified it at excursions or boating parties of poets and scholars, popularized it at tea gardens and wine houses, hummed it at hostelries and wayside taverns to tempt travelers, messengers, and merchants on trade journeys, and took it far and wide to other parts of the country."[23] But this form of drama failed to achieve widespread popularity, largely because too much emphasis was given to the literary quality and excellence of the operatic verses. It became a plaything for the literary and was supported by the court. Its popularity waned steadily during the eighteenth and nineteenth centuries; by the twentieth it was practically extinct.

The advent in the sixteenth century of the Europeans, particularly the men of culture, was bound to affect literary China. Chinese thought and civilization were not static, as we have seen; but the empire's boundaries were limited, no great arteries of communication ran through its domain, and its people were forbidden to go abroad.[24] Notwithstanding such barriers as these, the new learning in Europe managed to penetrate China, largely through the work of a few scholarly and devoted missionaries, most of whom belonged to the Society of Jesus. Not content with expounding the Gospel, these Jesuits brought the European Renaissance to China through translation, personal instruction, and original work. Broad-minded and well trained as they were, there were few better suited for the purpose. Despite some hostility at court (Moslem astronomers naturally resented the Jesuits' calm assurance in their own field), these Europeans profoundly stirred some of the most intellectual Chinese by their teachings on ethics, mathematics, astronomy, geography, physics, logic, and applied science.

The most important of these missionaries was Matteo Ricci,

---

[23] *T'ien Monthly*, II:1, 69–70 (January, 1936).

[24] The emperor who ruled during the Wan-li period wrote the Russian tsar in 1619: "By my custom, O Tsar, I neither leave my own kingdom nor allow my ambassadors or merchants to do so." Translated by Liu Hsüan-min, *Chinese Social and Political Science Review*, XXIII:4, 403, n. 31 (January–March, 1940).

who was born in Italy in 1552. Sent to Rome to study law, he instead offered himself to the Society of Jesus. After instruction in theology, mathematics, cosmology, and astronomy (under the great Clavius), he was sent to Goa, and thence to Macao in 1582. His talent in learning the Chinese language was phenomenal, and he soon gained the attention of important Chinese scholars with his discussions of mathematics and other sciences and a map of the world with textual commentary that he prepared. His map went through many editions and emendations, and left its mark on both China and Japan. From 1601 until his death in 1610 he remained at the capital, arousing the interest of the educated class in European science and technology, making converts, and reporting to the church in Rome. His own devotion, zeal, and intelligence being the best testimony of the new faith that the Chinese could have, they welcomed it, and the church was established by 1610. Some high officials were converted to Christianity; one of them, Hsü Kuang-ch'i (1562–1633), the author of a compendium on agriculture and, with Ricci, the translator of books on mathematics, hydraulics, astronomy,[25] and religion, rose to be a member of the imperial cabinet shortly before his death.

[25] Although there were thirty works on astronomy published between 1601 and 1644, revealing much of the new knowledge developing in Europe, and the memoir on astronomy in the historical work, *Ming shih kao,* was admittedly based on the writings of Ricci and of his disciples, the Jesuits were unable, because of his official condemnation by the church in 1633, to accept and spread abroad Galileo's shattering theory that the earth moved around the sun.

CHAPTER VIII

The Ch'ing, or Manchu, Dynasty
(1644-1912)

FROM a China controlled from within, we turn once more to one in the hands of an alien people, the Manchu. Descendants of the Jurchen who had harassed the Ming through the greater part of the fifteenth and sixteenth centuries, and like them stock breeders and farmers, the Manchu emerged from obscurity in the last two decades of the sixteenth century and were ready to take full advantage of the administrative weaknesses evident in China by the middle of the next century. They probably would have failed, had not China been torn by peasant rebellions, had not her armies at the front lacked leaders and supplies, had not deserters swelled the Manchu ranks, and had not the latter had less superb leaders.

The first of the Manchu[1] was Nurhachi (1559–1626), a man of good birth, unquestionable courage, and high intelligence, who knew how to use men and lead them to victory. He consolidated the lands won in Manchuria from China and his other enemies, proclaimed himself khan in 1616, and established his capital at Mukden in 1625. In 1601 he divided his troops, who included Mongols, Koreans, and Chinese as well as his own people, into four groups on the basis of the color of their banners (yellow, red, blue, and white); this was enlarged to eight in 1615 (the same colors were used, but borders were added).

[1] The use of this term here is an anachronism, for Manchu was actually not used until about the time Nurhachi died.

They were officered by Manchu nobles. Superior to the eight banners was a government fashioned along Chinese lines. He ordered two of his officials to adapt the Mongol alphabetical script to the Manchu tongue in 1599; diacritical marks and eight new letters were added a little later to make the alphabet more usable. Nurhachi called his dynasty Chin (*gold*) after that of his Jurchen predecessors, but this was changed in 1636 to Ch'ing (*clear*) to parallel the Chinese dynastic name Ming (*bright*). Thus the Manchu avoided offending the Mongols, who still recalled that the house of Chin had blocked the northward path of Jenghis, their greatest hero, and set their course of expansion southward.

By 1629 the Manchu had broken through the Great Wall and were at the gates of Peking and other cities; by 1633 they had taken Chahar from the Mongols and Liaotung from the Chinese (their success was partly due to the artillery captured from the Chinese army or produced by pro-Manchu Chinese); and by 1637 they had forced Korea into submission. In 1627 and again in 1642 the Ming were ready to sue for peace because their own internal situation was so critical and so many of their officers had joined the Manchu army. The Manchu, however, bided their time. Their great chance came in 1644 when Peking was seized by a Chinese rebel army and the Chinese officer who was defending the Great Wall asked their help. The Chinese-Manchu armies defeated the rebels under cover of a violent dust storm. Once in Peking, the Manchu refused to leave; on the contrary, they brought their emperor to the city and made it their second capital. Despite many long years of struggle and several near collapses of the Manchu power, Peking remained the main center of imperial administration until 1912.

The conquest of China was technically completed in 1659, when the last Ming prince fled the country. Actually, however, the Manchu rule was not finally established until a revolt in the southern provinces that flared up between 1674 and 1681 under the leadership of three Chinese viceroys had been put down and the naval forces led from 1645 to 1683 by four generations of the Chêng family had been demolished. One result of this fighting, which kept south China in an uproar for nearly four decades and did incalculable damage, to coastal cities in particular, was the formal incorporation of Taiwan, known to the Portuguese as Ilha Formosa, into the Manchu domain.

Except for one or two modifications, the Ch'ing dynasty took over the Ming form of government intact. Among the first few books translated into Manchu was part of the Ming statutes. In 1631 the second khan established at Mukden six ministries patterned after the Chinese; in 1634 he decreed that civil examinations be given in Manchu; and in 1636 he assumed the title of emperor. When the ministries were later moved to Peking, several of the Chinese officials consented to serve in them. In general, the principal posts were held by Manchu and Chinese in approximately an equal ratio, but between 80 and 90 per cent of the less important ones were held by Chinese. The Manchu formed eight Mongol and eight Chinese banners to raise their military strength and to absorb their new adherents. When an area was conquered, these bannermen acted as military garrisons in key defense points and in the course of time they established distinctive settlements, supported by the throne, in certain Chinese cities. At first an essential and active instrument of occupation and colonization, the bannermen gradually became objects of hatred to the Chinese and a heavy and largely unnecessary drain on the exchequer.[2] As a result, the emperor made several active efforts to settle some of them in Manchuria; and in 1803 the homeland, which had been closed up to that time, was thrown open to ordinary Chinese people. By reason of this intermingling process and the victory of China's superior civilization, the Man-

[2] According to Gibert (*Dictionnaire historique et géographique de la Mandchourie*, p. 721), in 1810 there were 220,960 men in the Manchu banners, 55,639 in the Mongol, and 143,893 in the Chinese; with their families, this totaled approximately 1,500,000 people.

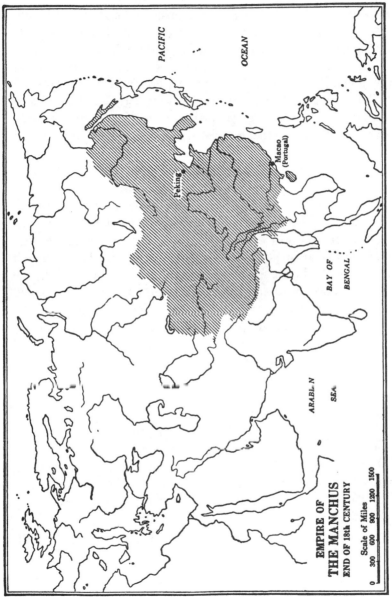

PACIFIC

OCEAN

Peking

Macao
(Portugal)

BAY OF

BENGAL

ARABIAN

SEA

EMPIRE OF
THE MANCHUS
END OF 18th CENTURY

Scale of Miles

0   300   600   900   1200   1500

chu lost touch with their own customs, language, and fighting skill to such an extent that few could call themselves truly Manchu and they lost their empire to the Chinese in 1912.

The Manchu introduced no major economic or social changes in Chinese life, except for a few that were agreed upon between the Manchu and Chinese when the invaders took Peking. These stipulations included the following: (1) No Chinese women were to be taken for the imperial seraglio. But both the first and second emperors had Chinese concubines, and the second and fourth emperors are reported to have had Chinese mothers. (2) The "first" in the civil examinations was never to be awarded to a Manchu. Between 1646 and 1905 three out of 114 "firsts" were taken by bannermen, of whom two were Chinese and the third a Mongol. (3) Chinese men were required to shave their heads and wear queues and to adopt Manchu clothes, although they could be buried in Ming costume. Curiously enough, the Koreans were not subject to this regulation and hence continued to wear Ming attire, as did also Taoist priests; but there were no other exceptions. So deeply imbedded had the custom of the shaven head and the queue become that many Chinese insisted on retaining their queues even after 1911.[3] (4) Chinese women, although not forced to adopt Manchu dress, were forbidden to bind their feet. When this regulation proved impossible to enforce, it was withdrawn (1668). Thereafter only the Chinese girls who were to enter the palace and some of the women in south China allowed their feet to remain unbound.

Unlike the Khitan and the Jurchen, the Manchu did nothing that would upset the Chinese economy. What they did do—and this was of incalculable importance—was to give the country about a century and a half of peace. After the prolonged struggle for independence was ended, a "business as before" policy was adopted. During the long period of tranquillity the Manchu

[3] In this connection, some of Lusin's short stories, translated by Chi-chen Wang as *Ah Q and Others*, are of interest.

saw to the repair, extension, and upkeep of public works; they mercilessly crushed the often legitimate uprisings of the aboriginal minorities in the south and southwest, opening these sections of the country to colonization; they assisted famine areas by remitting taxes; and they removed the threat of invasion on the whole north and west border eventually extending their control as far west as Lake Balkash and the Pamirs. These major accomplishments permitted the country to recover from several decades of warfare and internal strain and devote itself once again to the arts of civilization. The population, which had begun to grow at the end of the Ming, now increased more rapidly than ever before in the country's history.[4] This increase was due to other factors than the cessation of strife and freedom from onerous taxes.[5] Among them were the development of commerce and international trade, the reduction of new land to cultivation (this meant deforestation and soil erosion in some sections), and the widespread use of new food crops.

The commerce between the Spanish in Manila and the Chinese in Fukien and Kuangtung has already been discussed. That this became even more active is indicated by the calculations of a Spanish historian who estimates that 400,000,000 dollars in silver was imported to the Philippines from Spanish America between 1571 and 1821, about half of which went to the Chinese for silk, porcelain, and other commodities. Trade with the Japanese, Indians, Arabs, Portuguese, and Dutch, among others, became even more brisk. A greater number of ships were sailing the Indian Ocean and the nearby sea lanes than ever before; some of the vessels were Chinese—Magellan's cousin saw Chinese junks at Malacca—and Arab ships visited every port. After the Portu-

---

[4] From the approximately 150,000,000 estimated for the early decades of the 17th century, it continued to rise to *circa* 430,000,000 during the next two centuries before it was checked during the 1850's by the T'ai-p'ing and other rebellions. See p. 203 above.

[5] In 1712 the second emperor decreed that there would be no increase in the tax quotas even if the population should grow. (*Shêng-tsu shih-lu* 249, pp. 14–16).

guese wrested this commerce from the Arabs they had to defend it from the Dutch, who by 1641 had settled in Batavia and Taiwan; eventually the Portuguese were ousted from Malacca. The English began to trade with Canton in 1664; this trade continued steadily and gradually outstripped the Dutch after 1689. The volume of French trade always remained small. Direct trade with the United States, at first via the Indian Ocean and the Cape of Good Hope, began immediately after the end of the American Revolution. Meanwhile Russian trappers and adventurers were pushing their way across Siberia to the Manchu frontier, and in 1644 they penetrated the valley of the Amur. Numerous skirmishes occurred between them and the Manchu until 1689, when a boundary treaty was signed. After this, a small volume of overland commerce developed.

All of these new factors, in addition to the continuing commercial relations with Korea, Japan, Tibet, and central Asia, enlivened Chinese markets. Tea leaves pressed into bricks were shipped from central China to Mongolia and Russia. Nankeens (unbleached cotton piece goods) went from Nanking to western Europe and later to the United States. Porcelain, to its detriment, was made in every available kiln for export to western capitals. Most of the silk was produced in Chekiang and was widely prized, as were also to a lesser degree wallpaper, latticework, rugs, jewelry, fans, drugs, chairs, settees, tables, and all lacquered articles. (One French vessel, the *Amphrite,* returned in 1703 with a cargo of nothing but lacquered goods.) Voltaire once exclaimed: "People ask what becomes of all the gold and silver which is continually flowing into Spain from Peru and Mexico. It goes into the pockets of Frenchmen and Englishmen and Dutchmen, who carry on trade in Cadiz, and in return send the products of their industries to America. A large part of this money goes to the East Indies and pays for silk, spices, saltpeter, sugar-candy, tea, textiles, diamonds and curios."[6]

6 Cited by Reichwein, *China and Europe,* p. 17.

The increased use of land has not been studied extensively, but the knowledge available indicates that through the Ch'ing dynasty the Chinese encroached steadily on Manchu and Mongol territory, pushed back the aborigines of southern and southwestern China into the mountains and other infertile sections, cut away some of the centuries-old forest cover, and carved out terraces on every slope. Much of this proved to be shortsighted; as Arthur P. Chew of the United States Department of Agriculture has written, "The short life of agriculture on the hillsides ended the long life of agriculture on the plains. Every farm won from the mountainside ruined a dozen in the path of the released torrents."[7] But the individual Chinese had no other choice; he had an increasing number of mouths to feed, and the government had no conservation program.

One thing in his favor was the fact that most of the important nutritive and salable plants in the world were available to him for cultivation. Between the thirteenth and seventeenth centuries China had acquired sorghum, maize, the sweet potato, the peanut, and tobacco.[8] Other plants were introduced after 1644, but these were far less important: the pineapple, first cultivated in Taiwan, Kuangtung, Fukien, and Yünnan around 1650; the custard apple, first mentioned in south China about the same time; the "Irish" potato, which appeared in Taiwan in 1650 and reached the mainland a little later. Cayenne pepper, the cinchona tree, and possibly squash and certain varieties of bean were not known in China until the eighteenth century. Some of these could be grown in relatively poor soil; others could be planted between rows of millet or sorghum, or could be put in after the principal summer crop was harvested. They raised the

---

[7] *Atlantic Monthly*, CLIX:2, 198 (February, 1937).

[8] Snuff also appeared late in the seventeenth century and was taken up by fashionable people in Canton and Peking as it was in Paris, St. Petersburg, and London. This custom, however, has died away recently; only the Mongols still use snuff. It is remembered chiefly because of the charming snuff bottles that have been made since the mid-eighteenth century.

total acreage of arable land, enriched the diet, and increased the profits of farmer and middleman. In one or two cases imperial pressure was exerted in the cultivation of new crops. As a result of pressure of all kinds, China by 1948 held first place among all nations in the production of rice, sweet potatoes, sorghum, soybeans, broad beans, rape seed, sesame millet, and barley; possibly also of silk and tea; in corn, tobacco, peanuts, and wheat it was not far behind.[9]

One plant introduced in this period, the opium poppy, had far-reaching but exceedingly deleterious results. It despoiled great areas of land, ruined millions of homes, fattened the purses of tax collectors and shortsighted officials and landowners, and eventually led to war in 1840. Opium had been known to the Chinese for some centuries, chiefly as a medicine to be taken internally. Little was grown in China before the sixteenth century, the main source being India whence it was transported to China by Arab and Indian merchants. After 1523 the Chinese were forced to begin producing their own supply because of the pirates who infested the coasts. The Portuguese began to export opium from India to Macao at this time, and the Dutch, English, and Americans (after 1810) in turn found it a most profitable cash cargo; some of it came from India and some from Turkey. At the end of the seventeenth century—Kaempfer first mentions the practice in 1689 in Java—people began to smoke opium mixed with tobacco; later they omitted the tobacco. This practice became so widespread that the sale of opium was forbidden by imperial decree in 1729. But when this proved ineffectual, importation of the drug was prohibited in 1800. In spite of this ban, five thousand chests annually were entering Canton by 1821, most of it on British vessels but part of it on American

---

[9] Data drawn from the 1949 *Yearbook of Food and Agricultural Statistics*, published by the United Nations, pp. 31–114 (1950). All figures in this source exclude the USSR. No information on China's production of tea and silk is supplied here. In the early 1930's, China led the world in these two commodities. No adequate statistics have appeared since 1949.

and other ships. Chinese as well as foreign merchants grew rich from the illicit trade and there was a marked drainage of silver from China. But the traffic continued and by the late 1830's the annual imports amounted to thirty thousand chests. The Manchu government finally intervened and burned a huge consignment. This led to war with the British, who asserted that they had certain rights in trade and were not bound by restrictions imposed by officials at Canton. The British won the war without difficulty, and opium remained an exportable commodity until 1911, when Parliament forbade its shipment to China. Meanwhile large areas in China were being sown to the poppy and cultivation flourished, particularly in remote places and in sections where civil or military officials connived in its production for tax purposes. The results have been disastrous, as Cressey makes clear: "It was estimated in 1923 in Yunnan that poppy occupied two-thirds of the cultivated land during the winter season. The percentage in Kweichow is approximately the same. In the capital city of Yunnanfu, it is said that 90 per cent of the men and 60 per cent of the women are addicted to the habit of opium smoking. Many hsien produce from one to two million ounces and the removal of so much first-class agricultural land from useful production has induced a serious food shortage."[10] After several years of anti-opium efforts, the Nationalist government reported in 1948 to the United Nations that it was continuing its work of absolute suppression of poppy growing, opium manufacture, transport, and sale, but that its activities were hampered if not nullified because of civil strife. What is happening in areas under Communist control is as yet unknown.

By the beginning of the nineteenth century the Ch'ing dynasty was doomed. Its authority was being challenged from both within and without. Internal affairs were deteriorating rapidly; records left by contemporary writers, notably the historian Chang Hsüeh-ch'êng (1738-1801), attest to the decadence of

[10] *China's Geographic Foundations* (McGraw-Hill), p. 375.

the Manchu and to their administrative incompetence in the capital as well as in the provinces. Favorites robbed the imperial treasury and debased the probity and efficiency of the bureaucracy. The Industrial Revolution abroad was brewing a storm that swept everything before it from 1840 on and shook China as never before. Unable to see beyond their own fingertips, the court and its advisers tried to hold to a policy of isolation; Canton was made the single port of entry and a monopoly on foreign trade was given to a small association of brokers (the co-hong or hong merchants). Great Britain, first of all the western nations to try to break this monopoly, demanded Hongkong as a crown colony and the opening of five ports to trade.[11] Other western powers followed, demanding the opening of eleven other ports, extraterritorial rights for their nationals, the establishment of a maritime customs service headed by an Occidental, the opening of legations at the capital, legalization of opium imports, tolerance for Catholic and Protestant missionary activities, and formal permission to travel inland and to study the Chinese language. Russia also demanded that the empire cede certain northern lands to her.

In addition to these infringements of their sovereign rights the Manchu were faced with unrest among the Chinese people. The venality of an often corrupt officialdom, the exactions of absentee landlords, the breakdown of irrigation control systems, together with such natural calamities as earthquakes, fanned popular resentment into flames that leaped high at the first sign of revolt. Rebellions were frequent between 1774 and 1813 on the part of members of secret societies, tribespeople, and Moslems. Although they were suppressed, they left bloodshed and serious property damage in their wake. In the middle of the century, however, there were six serious revolts: one in the south

11 The greater part of this story is far from pretty reading. As an example see the objective study by Grace Fox, *British Admirals and Chinese Pirates, 1832–1869* (London, 1940).

and north by the T'ai-p'ing in 1850–1864; one in the northern and central provinces by the Nien-fei, adherents of a secret society, in 1853–1868; and four by Moslems in Yünnan, Shensi, and Kansu (1855–1873, 1862–1873) and in central Asia (1862–1876, 1866–1878). These were crushed by the imperial armies usually under Chinese officers, and in part by means of western support, but the consequences were grim. Millions of people lost their lives, several provinces were laid waste, and invaluable and irreplaceable objects were destroyed—books, manuscripts, family records, paintings, and monuments by the tens of thousands. The dynasty itself was saved for a half century longer because of the unwise leadership of the T'ai-p'ing revolt, the loyalty of countless Chinese officials who preferred even an alien dynasty to anarchy, and help from abroad. Unfortunately, however, the court and its advisers, blind to their near collapse, effected no reforms while there was still time.

There were further inroads on China's sovereignty from the 1870's on. More ports were opened; additional importations of opium were sanctioned; indemnities were exacted; and Indo-China, Burma, Taiwan, and the Pescadores were seized. Great Britain, Germany, Russia, and France all joined in the scramble for concessions; only Italy was successfully rebuffed. The United States advocated a commercial open door for everyone. Dislike for foreigners, coupled with mounting dissatisfaction with the Manchu rule, precipitated another uprising in 1900 which brought widespread death and destruction and saddled the government with a huge indemnity (amounting with interest to about $775,000,000 in terms of American currency); later, however, this was partly remitted. The court, as last realizing its danger, initiated various reforms—educational, legal, financial, and political. These failed to satisfy the revolutionists (led by Sun Yat-sen, 1867–1925) who were busy in Tokyo, London, Paris, and Canton, and they rebelled in 1911. The regime was overthrown, and China became technically a republic.

The cultural history of China under the Manchu followed the Ming traditions until the nineteenth century. Under the impetus of peace and prosperity all the minor arts flourished in a degree perhaps never surpassed. Porcelain was made in imperial kilns under strict supervision; the men who acted as supervisors between 1682 and 1749 were exceptionally able. The porcelain competed with that produced during the Ming in technique but not in originality, and has long been admired in Europe and the Americas. Painting was in vogue, but here again the freshness of certain Ming examples was lacking as the Manchu artists turned to older models for inspiration. New life was instilled into one school of painting at the capital by Brother Castiglione (1688–1766), but his influence was short-lived. Architecture also remained faithful to the older forms, in spite of the fact that a few buildings inspired by European examples were erected at the emperor's park near Peking. It is in their literature, both scholastic and romantic, that the Ch'ing were outstanding. During the long honeymoon of the K'ang-hsi reign (1662–1722), especially after 1683, and to a lesser extent during the Yung-chêng (1723–1735) and Ch'ien-lung reigns (1736–1795), scholars were exceedingly active in both public and private projects, and a few nonconformists wrote stories and novels which in some cases thinly veiled their criticisms of the thought and conditions of the day.

In spite of its poor record during its last few decades, the Ming had been strongly supported by the literati because it was native; but when the dynasty fell and the alien Manchu replaced it, hundreds of this group were set adrift. A few of them fled to the mountains with a handful of loyal students and refused to collaborate with the foreigners in any way. A few others followed one or another of the Ming princes to Fukien or Kuangtung or Yünnan. Still another handful scattered to offshore points of refuge such as Japan, where they sometimes achieved fame and whence they hoped to return to restore Chinese authority on the continent. As time passed, however, this attitude of insubordination slowly died, largely because of the enlightened policy of the second emperor and the unquestionable military prowess of the Manchu; it did not come to life again until the eighteenth century, when the repressive measures of the Yung-chêng and Ch'ien-lung reigns gave it new life. The literature produced after the advent of the Manchu is important because it differed so sharply from earlier works. Huang Tsung-hsi (1610–1695), for example, vigorously attacked monarchical rule and asserted the people's rights; Wang Fu-chih (1619–1692) sought the answers to a series of fundamental questions ("How do we know the existence of nature?" "What is the origin of knowledge?" "What knowledge is real?"); Yen Yüan (1635–1704), exploding against classical learning and "sitting in contemplation," advocated realistic living ("What I want is motion, activity, reality, utility"); and Li Kung (1659–1733) insisted on knowledge based on experience and specialization in every field of learning. A recent outstanding compilation[12] distinguishes 179 schools of thought in this dynasty and points out that the chief aim of the thinkers of the late seventeenth century was to find practical and immediate reform measures. Two works with utopian ideas appeared during the nineteenth century. The first was *Ching hua yüan*, a novel by Li Ju-chên (1763–*ca.* 1830); the other, *Ta t'ung*, a tract by K'ang Yu-wei (1858–1927). Both advocated long-overdue reforms, and the latter suggested certain changes in social control that are visionary even now. Other writers, finding speculation either unhealthy or unsuited to their tastes, launched into critical studies of China's past or into such fields as phonology. Thus Fang I-chih (*ca.* 1615–1667) suggested that a European-like alphabet be adopted for the Chinese

---

[12] *The Lives and Works of Ch'ing Scholars* (in Chinese), by ex-president Hsü Shih-ch'ang (1858–1939). For an excellent treatment of these and many other leaders in thought and action see Arthur W. Hummel (ed.), *Eminent Chinese of the Ch'ing Period*, 2 vols. (Washington, D.C., 1943–1944).

language. Ku Yen-wu (1613–1682) struck the keynote of the age when he emphasized the necessity of observation, evidence, and originality in every type of scholarly work. These principles give great value to his own studies of local customs and political and social institutions. P'u Sung-ling (*ca.* 1630–1716) was a writer in a different vein. The author of some of the most popular tales in the Chinese language—the *Liao chai chih i* includes 341 stories or anecdotes—he wrote one novel about a man and his two wives which is now regarded as fundamental for an understanding of the times.

The turn of the century brought the publication of a series of reference books, encyclopedias, and repositories of art under imperial auspices that are essential for every Chinese library. There also appeared compilations of the prose and poetry considered worthy of preservation, new commentaries on classical and historical texts, and new works on mathematics, astronomy, botany, and geography. The work of the alert and well-educated European priests at the capital influenced the production of some of these texts. The German Schall (1591–1666) and the Flemish Verbiest[13] (1623–1688) set the pace in calendrical and astronomical studies; the Frenchman Régis (1663–1738) in mapmaking. The emperor found these men congenial, highly trustworthy, and full of energy on his behalf. Only when the pope impugned his authority in 1705 did his friendship cool and the church begin to suffer.

Literary undertakings continued unabated, but with a difference, after the death of the second emperor. Freedom of thought was not tolerated to as great an extent, and prosperity favored other emphases. Philosophical speculation and discussions of po-

---

[13] The Roman Catholic church in China could hardly have been better served than by Ricci, Schall, and Verbiest. In a critical note on a biography of Schall, Professor Pelliot writes: "Schall est un des deux ou trois Européens qui ont vraiment joué un rôle, après Ricci et avant Verbiest, dans l'histoire moderne de la Chine. Il connaissait toute la science de son temps, et a beaucoup fait pour la répandre autour de lui." *T'oung Pao*, XXXI:1–2, 180 (1934).

litical and economic conditions all suffered, but historical criticism reached its zenith; and such subjects as philology, phonetics, law, local and national history, geography, mathematics, antiquities, textual criticism, and canonical exegesis were exceedingly popular. Although this type of work continued until 1912, it culminated in the eighteenth century in the exceptional classified catalogue of books assembled for the imperial library. Fifteen thousand calligraphers were engaged in making beautiful handwritten copies of these books, and 361 editors worked for nearly twenty years on the selection and rejection of titles and on a condensed description and appraisal of each of its approximately 10,000 books. Here was an undertaking that must have stirred every home with any pretension to bookishness, for every local magistrate was urged to make deliveries of rare books from his town to the capital, and the best bibliographers of the day were congregated to match wits with the Hanlin doctors and with contestants for the advanced degree. The result was worth the effort and expense not only for itself but for its effect on private publications not yet completed. Unhappily, however, the project had one unfortunate result, for the Ch'ien-lung emperor saw in the collection and appraisal of so many little-known works a chance to expunge from Chinese literature everything inimical to his own people and their Khitan, Jurchen, and Mongol predecessors, as well as anything else he considered treasonable or improper for reasons of state or prestige. He conducted the task of expurgation as vigorously as he had the compilation and editing, and in so doing destroyed the basis for an intellectual revolt against his dynasty. This explains, at least in part, why so many well-read Chinese of the mid-nineteenth century sided with the Manchu instead of with the rebel T'ai-p'ing and why many others at the beginning of the twentieth century opposed the revolutionary groups, preferring to remain under Manchu rule and to wear such a badge of servitude as the queue.

Offsetting this calculated destruction was the appearance of two imaginative works of wide popular appeal. One, the *Ju lin wai shih*, was a conscious satire of the civil service examinations that delighted the literati, who often spent most of their lives trying to satisfy petty requirements.[14] Its author, Wu Ching-tzŭ (1701–1754), a member of a good family, was a man of independent means and literary ability who refused to let his willful and independent spirit be brought to heel by the demands of an official calling. He ran through his inheritance, drinking and singing and writing bits of verse and prose; apparently he wrote his book to show his contempt for the exactions and abuses of the examination system. The series of episodes are laid in the Ming, and the book ends with the government presenting posthumous rank to all the characters who have failed or done poorly in life. The other work was the apparently autobiographical *Hung lou mêng*, by Ts'ao Hsüeh-ch'in (*ca.* 1719–1764). Descended from a family who had made money in slik for the preceding three generations, Ts'ao saw his family's wealth dissipated and himself reduced to near poverty. This story of manners and romance concerns a great family whose fortune is likewise frittered away; like the almost contemporary novels by Samuel Richardson, it has made millions weep.

Though dark shadows predominate, the landscape of the nineteenth century was not one of unremitting somberness. Native scholars, as we have seen, continued the high traditions of eighteenth-century historical and classical criticism; journalism showed its head in a few coastal centers; translations of significant European books stimulated new thought along diverse lines and suggested novel styles of writing; technical schools were opened, and selected students and missions were sent to the United States, England, France, and, especially after 1900, to

---

[14] That this applied to many people is evident from the fact that there were between 8000 and 9000 candidates at the examinations for the second degree held in a single provincial center, Wu-ch'ang, in 1870; only 61 were successful. Cf. *China Review*, II:309–314 (1873–1874).

Japan;[15] a few miles of railroads were laid, steamships launched, cables laid, and mines opened; a corps of men were trained, through the maritime customs service, for work in the ports, on the coast, on inland waterways, and in outposts; and the Protestant church began to make significant contributions to religion, thought, education, the improvement of social conditions, and public health. In their own time and in their own way, the Chinese were laboriously sifting the ideas and techniques of a new world in an effort to adapt them to their own needs. The process was expensive, but even so it was far better than the outright adoption of institutions unsuited to the Chinese mind and culture.

---

[15] 13,000 students went to Japan between 1902 and 1910. Ling Chi Hong, *Educational Review* (April, 1910), p. 8.

CHAPTER IX

The Republic (1912–)

THE Chinese Republic has not been an unqualified success. The high expectations held for it at the outset, under the leadership of such men as Sun Yat-sen, were out of place in view of the enormous problems involved. To achieve an informed public opinion required that approximately 80 per cent of the people be taught to read; in addition, the literate fringe had to be trained in democratic ways of thinking. Provincial disunity was strong; vested interests were huge; there were entanglements with foreign powers. Loyalty to individual officers split the army into small groups. Millions of the people lived below the subsistence level.[1] The almost empty state treasury could not afford the huge sums necessary to restore the rivers and canals to some measure of their earlier efficiency, to light the coasts and dredge the harbors, to build new communications, to improve agriculture, to open new mines, to modernize cities, and to provide for the public health. There was unbelievable selfishness in high places, the first president being perhaps the first to sin. He mercifully died in 1916 after failing to create a monarchy. The marvel is that republican China, confronted with problems far more staggering than any other nation has faced in modern times, has achieved so much.

[1] This assertion was sharply criticized in an anonymous review of the English edition of this book. It is therefore of some comfort to the author to note that a distinguished Chinese political scientist has recently indicated his agreement. He divided the Chinese people, according to their wealth, into three groups: the upper occupying 12% of the total, the middle 24%, and the lower 64%. The last, he writes, "are either making a bare subsistence or actually living below the subsistence line." Ch'ien Tuan-shêng, *The Government and Politics of China* (1950), p. 12.

Specifically, China's leaders, before the outbreak of war with Japan, often with foreign advice and technical and financial assistance, worked to stabilize the currency and reorganize the country's financial system; consolidated most of the semi-private armies under unified command and established small-arms arsenals and officer-training centers; developed irrigation, road-building, reforestation, and agricultural reclamation projects to help reduce the constant menace of famine from drought and flood; extended the railroads and opened air lanes; encouraged the development of commerce and industry; and trained men and women in medicine and nursing to attack the threat of plague and to cope with new problems arising in industrial centers. In addition, the government introduced reforms in the laws, worked for the unification of the country, and labored to put an end to foreign concessions. It began its fight against illiteracy, opened thousands of schools and a number of colleges, and for exceptionally able men and women instituted examinations at the capital that paralleled those of the old system; it sent the chosen few abroad for further study and training. To preserve the best in China's heritage and to promote research in modern science it created an academy (Academia Sinica) that includes institutes of history and philology, social science, psychology, climatology, astronomy, geology, botany, chemistry, physics, and engineering; the academy staff numbers outstanding scholars in every field. Both national and local governments and private societies fostered the study and preservation of ancient monuments, and a few sites were excavated under their auspices. The work in archeology initially was not as fruitful as it might have been, for much that was unearthed was lost through the depredations of grave robbers and despoilers of stone monuments. More encouraging was the record of library development and private scholarship and the extraordinary expansion of publishing activities which until 1937 made Shanghai in particular one of the greatest centers in the world. All these factors, together with Protestant and Catholic missionary aid, had a part in educating the common man and in stimulating a cultural revolution.[2]

The political history of the Republic's first years was tumultuous. The first president's abortive attempt to establish a monarchy was followed in 1917 by an unsuccessful attempt to restore the Ch'ing dynasty. The civil war that broke out shortly afterward continued through 1949, except for a few short interludes. In 1926 the Kuomintang, under Chiang Kai-shek (b. 1887), tried to seize the government; the next year it was able to establish Nanking as the capital. Chiang, the head of the new government, became the dominant figure in both the military and the political sphere, and for some two score years achieved a measure of unity, partly because he commanded the greatest loyalty from his following, partly because he had control of economically the richest areas (particularly the lower Yangtze valley), and partly because ultimately he resisted Japan, regarded (at least from 1931 to 1945) as the common enemy by all elements of the population. In addition to his early struggles with his provincial rivals, he found it expedient to work toward the elimination of the Communist group, established first in the southern provinces of Kiangsi and Fukien. In this effort he achieved less than success. It is true that he forced the Communists out of their strongholds in 1934, but, after they had endured almost unspeakable hardships and losses on a long march via Szechuan into China's northwest, they settled in the region around Yenan (in northern Shensi, Kansu, and Ning-hsia) to gather strength for another and decisive dispute with Chiang in the years following the defeat of Japan.

The Chinese have had difficulties with many foreign powers since 1912, but with no other have their relations been subjected to as much strain as with Japan. In 1915, while the attention of

---

[2] For a more leisurely exposition of China's reconstruction up to 1937, see Jean Escarra, *China Then and Now*, Part II (Peking, 1940).

most of the world was directed toward the European war, the Japanese presented a number of demands which meant the virtual surrender of Chinese sovereignty. This resulted in a series of treaties unfavorable to the mainland republic. China's independence and territorial integrity were restored as the result of a nine-power conference that met in Washington in 1922, at which time the Shantung peninsula was returned to her. After five years of conciliation, a new civil war broke out in 1927, when the Nanking government tried to take control of the northern provinces. This was followed by more serious trouble during 1931–1933, when Japan seized Manchuria, besieged and partly burned Shanghai (the fifth most important port in the world), and invaded Jehol north of Peking. This conquest was relatively so inexpensive and met with so little opposition from China and the rest of the world that it inflamed the Japanese military with ambition and lust. In 1935 Japan attempted to seize another large section of northern China but gained only northern Chahar and eastern Hopei.

In July 1937 the war of aggression began in earnest. It was launched at a moment when republican China seemed at the highest point of its career. Both economically and politically there was much to acclaim. The war leaders of Japan doubtless realized that any further delay on their part would measurably add to the cost of military operations and length of conquest. They noted achievements in reconstruction in many lines: the building of numerous motor roads; the repair, re-equipment, and extension of railroad lines; the successful floating of a number of internal bond issues and refunding of old foreign loans; the development of several air lines, with the aid of the United States and German aviation companies; improvements in such services as radio, telephone, and telegraph; partial modernization of the army under German tutelage; increase of educational facilities and in number of students enrolled in schools; development, too, of literacy movements among the masses. In some ways equally important for national morale were major gains in diplomacy. In 1929 the Chinese for the first time in many decades were able to assume direction of their own customs tariff— an act which required treaties with a dozen foreign powers, the last of which to sign was Japan. Several areas administered by foreigners were turned back to the Chinese, and even the international settlement of Shanghai came increasingly under Chinese jurisdiction. Extraterritoriality also seemed on the way out when war intervened. (The British and United States governments formally relinquished these privileges in 1943 when morale in wartime China was almost at its nadir.) Finally the Japanese expansionists doubtless noted with dismay the result of the coup engineered by a one-time Manchurian war lord on behalf of the Communists against Chiang Kai-shek. In December 1936 he was arrested at Sian and agreed to demands that he renounce his efforts to exterminate the Communists, and instead take the leadership in a campaign against the Japanese who were even then making serious inroads in north China and engaged in smuggling on a large scale.

The army launched its initial attack not far from Peiping, but soon the navy followed by invading Shanghai. Within a year and a quarter the Japanese war machine had control of the entire coast south of Canton and had seized the important inland city of Hankow. The Chinese fought back with some ability and unquestioned courage but proved no match for the foe. During these months unity was maintained to an unusual degree, a number of political and military leaders promising their loyalty to the Generalissimo. But when the heads of state found it necessary to shift their government center to Chungking in the western province of Szechuan, a real drop in morale and resistance ensued. They had lost their main ports and their principal industrial centers. Some materials seeped in through Hongkong and Indo-China, but in the main the Chinese had to depend on their own ingenuity and on a small quantity of supplies brought over-

land from the USSR (until the summer of 1941), Britain, and
the United States. There were a number of defections; chief
among them was Wang Ching-wei, who, after advising against
the war, finally deserted to the enemy and became Japan's principal Chinese representative at Nanking until an assassin laid him
low. Of greater consequence was the widening breach between
the government and the Communists. The latter remained based
on Yenan in the northwest but extended their forces, both regu-
lars and irregulars, into the areas between Japanese lines of
communication both in the north and in the lower Yangtze
valley. Their guerrilla tactics proved a constant annoyance to the
Japanese. Far from valuing this assistance, Chiang and his en-
tourage tried to muzzle it, going so far as to disband one Communist army (that in the east) and refuse supplies to the other,
surrounding it on three sides with a cordon of blockade houses.
Quite evidently Chiang realized that Communist success against
the invader would mean certain postwar competition for the
Kuomintang (the government party).

At the end of December 1941, shortly after Japan joined the
Axis, the British crown colony of Hongkong fell to the Japanese; and within a few months Indo-China, Malaya, and Burma
were overrun. Smuggling of war materials into the Chinese
hinterland virtually ceased, and the Chinese became heavily dependent on an air transport system over the mountain ranges
separating India and China. Even this was severely limited, for
China was the last stop on the immensely long route stretching
from the Americas across the South Atlantic to Africa, India, and
beyond. Inflation became serious, production fell, and serious
famines occurred, all of these sapping the strength and lowering
the morale of the people. For a time a kind of stalemate existed
in military affairs, the Japanese never succeeding in capturing the
western centers of resistance, although Chungking had the dubi-
ous reputation of being the most heavily bombed capital in the
world. When Allied help—mainly United States—began to in-

crease, however, and the Japanese leaders saw that American aviators might mount a dangerous campaign from Chinese airfields against their own industrial areas, they launched a campaign deep into the interior. But it was too late. United States bombers, winging out of west China, took their toll of mines and factories and shipbuilding centers from the China coast to Manchuria and the islands of Japan, helping to soften resistance as the United States army and navy in the Pacific leap-frogged from island to island and destroyed submarines and surface shipping. By August 14, 1945, the costliest conflict in history was over, a war of more than eight weary years for the Chinese. Countless men, women, and children had lost their lives by enemy action, by the shifting of the course of the Yellow River, and by natural causes. The losses to industry and commerce, to communication systems, to agriculture and stock raising, to cultural institutions of all sorts were immense. But with faith in their future, millions of the people trekked back to their homes or picked up where normal life had snapped in 1937, and hoped that China might resume its upward course of internal reform and economic improvement so promisingly begun in the early 1930's.

In the stock-taking of those days there were items which gave encouragement. The Chinese Republic had come of age. No longer did any limitations on its sovereignty exist. Accepted as one of the major powers, at least by Britain and the United States, at a military conference at Cairo (1943), it was welcomed by all at the conference at San Francisco (1945), and was to play its part in the United Nations thereafter. In 1945, too, the USSR and China signed a thirty-year treaty of friendship and alliance. Manchuria and Taiwan were returned as part of the spoils of victory. These, if properly managed, could prove incalculably valuable for their agricultural, mineral, and other resources. There was hope that personal freedoms, held in check for military reasons, might be restored and permitted to develop. Against these credit items the debits looked large. The USSR had occupied the Manchurian ports of Dairen and Port Arthur and swarmed into the northern half of Korea. Soon it was revealed that the Russian armies as they retired had wantonly destroyed the machinery in many plants in Manchuria and permitted quantities of unused Japanese munitions to pass into the hands of the Chinese Communist guerrillas. Taiwan, a rich prize by any standard, was overrun by Chinese (Nationalist) military looters and carpetbaggers of the worst type who brutally misused the people of the island and created hostility and a deterioration of conditions harmful both to the Taiwanese and to the Chinese of the mainland. Indications that a police state would be continued by Chiang Kai-shek were revealed as early as July 1946 with the assassination of two outspoken professors of Chinese literature at Kunming. The currency, long out of hand, continued is inflationary course. Communist and government armies faced each other in hostile poses.

To bring some succor to the harassed people the United Nations and numerous private organizations, both religious and lay, shipped in food, cotton, medical supplies, books, and technical assistance of wide variety. Others reached out and brought to Europe and America men and women students, teachers, and scientists for special training. The United States government despatched General George C. Marshall to Nanking to endeavor to bring the Nationalists and Communists together. Many vessels and a large amount of military equipment were handed over to the government, and a unit for the training of men in modern warfare was organized. In January 1947 Marshall returned to Washington criticizing both the Communists and the reactionaries in the Nationalist government and declaring that China's hope for peace lay in "the assumption of leadership by the liberals in the government and in the minority parties" under the guidance of Chiang Kai-shek. This report ended all hope that peace might come to China. Only civil war, it was clear, and the collapse of one side or the other would bring unity.

The conflict is now all but over; only Taiwan and a few small islands remain. The Communists under the leadership of Mao Tsê-tung (b. 1893) and his lieutenants drove the Nationalist forces out of Manchuria toward the end of 1948. Within another year they had broken through every barrier from Peiping to Canton and the island of Hainan, and from Shanghai to the Tibetan border. Without doubt an invasion of Taiwan was planned for the summer or autumn of 1950; it was definitely postponed by the action of President Truman (June 27) when he ordered the United States Seventh Fleet to patrol the 100-mile-wide Taiwan Strait. Parts of the invasion force were rapidly shifted to other strategic areas. In October one army plunged into Tibet against ineffective resistance and over Indian protests; in November another massive force struck across the Yalu River against Republic of Korea and United Nations armies; a third was shifted to the southern border facing north Vietnam ready to give immediate aid to fellow Communists on the other side of the line.

Throughout most of 1951 the struggle for Korea continued; it ended in an armistice on November 27, when agreement was reached on a military demarcation line approximating the 38th parallel. Other agreements regarding inspection, exchange of prisoners, and other terms were not concluded, however, until 1953. Only in 1958 did the Chinese withdraw their troops from north Korea. In 1955, after having watched with unmixed pleasure the success of the Vietminh against the French in 1953–1954, the leaders in Peking officially promised aid to the Democratic Republic of (North) Vietnam. In 1953 President Eisenhower announced the lifting of the blockade of Taiwan by the United States navy, but in 1955, following repeated attacks by the People's Republic against offshore islands held by the Chinese Nationalists, he signed a Sino-American treaty agreeing to defend Taiwan and the Pescadores (Peng-hu). The Tachen islands were evacuated but Quemoy and Matsu held. In 1962

President Kennedy, reacting to the Chinese Communist military build-up on the Fukien coast, agreed essentially with his predecessor and announced that the United States would not stand idly by if these islands were attacked.

The Communists have formally declared Peiping their capital and have changed its name back to Peking. Their government, called the People's Republic of China, with Mao Tsê-tung at the head and Chou Ên-lai (b. 1898) as premier and foreign minister (until 1958), was duly constituted on October 1, 1949, and recognized by the USSR, Great Britain, India, and a number of other nations, but their representatives have not yet displaced those of the Nationalists in the United Nations. The leaders, until 1960, maintained close relations with Moscow, but in the years since have followed an independent line, often expressing sharp criticism of their one-time ally and going so far (in 1966) as to accuse the USSR of joining with the USA in trying to encircle China and to help the latter in its war with Vietnam. Only Albania in Europe has remained a constant supporter, further exacerbating Russian feelings. In Asia the People's Republic (in 1955) made a series of agreements with Indonesia, Burma, Vietnam (North), North Korea, and Outer Mongolia, and established relations with Afghanistan and Nepal. Similar understandings with a number of the developing states in Africa and countries in Latin America followed. Peking has not hesitated to make grants and loans and supply food stuffs and technical personnel even when these were in short supply at home. Tibet was swallowed up forcefully, in 1950–51, its defense, communications, and foreign relations being taken over by Peking. In 1954 India recognized China's claim to Tibet, and relinquished certain rights acquired earlier by Great Britain, but it refused to retreat from the northern boundary of its own country drawn some fifty years before by Sir Arthur McMahon. This argument led (1959) to a serious clash when units of the Chinese army began to cross the line into Bhutan, Sikkim, Nepal, and Kashmir. Early in 1961 India formally condemned the Chinese Communists as aggressors and accused them of occupying large segments of Indian territory, particularly in Ladakh. Hostilities came to a halt at the end of the year, but an uneasy situation has remained with occasional outbursts of violence. Meanwhile both New Delhi and the Indian people became disillusioned by the repressive tactics of the Chinese in Tibet, a policy which led the Dalai Lama and thousands of his people to flee the country and seek refuge in India. The Chinese too, throughout these years, were pushing tens of thousands of settlers into Sinkiang and other border areas. These actions were not lost on neighboring countries; the record seems to show that their relations with China have generally been correct but not cordial. Pakistan in 1963 entered into agreements about frontier matters and trade, and Mongolia in 1962 signed a pact dealing with its common border of 2,500 miles. Indonesia, on the other hand, gave China its worst setback when, in 1965, it overthrew the pro-Peking Communist party there, raided the Chinese embassy in Jakarta, closed all Chinese consulates (1966) as well as its press agency, and made life difficult for people of Chinese extraction. North Vietnam doubtless receives aid of many sorts from its northern neighbor, but shows no subservience. In December 1966 riots broke out in the Portuguese colony of Macao; these were stimulated apparently by the activities of the youthful Red Guards in China proper. There was considerable bloodshed and thousands, both Portuguese and Chinese, fled to nearby Hong Kong. Unable to defend itself and receiving no support from Lisbon the colony had to submit before long to China's demands. Hong Kong became the next target of Communist agitation and rioting (1967), but the British government held firm, and stood off all efforts to bring it to heel.

In China proper the new government established its control with great rapidity. At the beginning hundreds of thousands of the youth in middle schools and colleges were hurriedly trained for bureaucratic posts, and a major part of those in office submitted to "reorientation" and were reassigned. From the reports that are available such complaints as graft, nepotism, and injustice leveled against office holders seldom apply; the new philosophy of government requiring fairness above all to peasants and workers seems to have been instilled with remarkable success. Any accused of landlordism, however, were liquidated. No one knows how many suffered the extreme penalty for this cause; the total may run into the millions. Justice is summary. Prison reform—"to cure persons who are ill and make them new members of society"—has been instituted. Intellectuals, in particular those educated abroad, have been forced to make written confessions of past errors of thought and attitude, often many times over. These have been widely publicized. When judged unsatisfactory the authors have lost their posts and been assigned to reëducation centers. In rural areas landholdings, buildings, and animals have been completely redistributed, and approximately a million collectives, or "producer co-operatives," were in operation by 1956. In spite of success in many areas all did not proceed according to plan. At a party congress in September the premier reported that natural disasters and unexpected snags encountered in collectivization made it impossible to reach the goals set for the first five year plan ending in 1957. The government nonetheless set new and larger goals for the future. The next quinquennium too was dogged by calamities of the same sort; so in 1962 at another party congress Chou Ên-lai indicated that, while economic development would be pressed in every phase of agriculture and industry, the system of people's communes launched in 1957 would be soft-pedalled, and the building of back-yard blast furnaces discontinued. In the years since targets were apparently met in industry and foreign trade, but the Chinese have produced insufficient food supply for their mounting population (reportedly 700 million), and have had to depend heavily on Australia and Canada for imports of wheat.

The cultural picture since 1950 has been mixed. Peking has

attacked illiteracy on a wide front so that after the first decade ninety million children were enrolled in primary and eight and a half million in secondary schools. Technical and teacher training too have been stressed with a reported one and a half million enrolled. Higher education, honored for two millennia and more, has had heavy going. In 1957 Mao Tse-tung emphasized the policy of "letting all flowers bloom and all schools of thought contend." Several high officials took these statements literally, as did many professors and students. Hundreds of students staged a two day anti-Communist demonstration in Hanyang in June, while the others came out boldly against Communist abuses of power, inefficiency in government, and even the appropriation by the USSR of military supplies and installations in Manchuria a dozen years earlier. A sharp crackdown followed and "rightists" were everywhere silenced. No one knows how many were affected by this muzzling. The second strike-down of the intellectuals came in 1965–66. Many of them took the occasion to criticize the government for its deviation from the line of peaceful coexistence with the West of the USSR and for its diplomatic failures in Indonesia, Africa, and Cuba. The government took prompt action to preserve "revolutionary purity and impetus." Not only were professors attacked but also writers of fiction and dramatists and old-time members of the party. Wu Han, deputy mayor of Peking and well known author of books on Ming history, was among the first to feel the lash (November 1965). Others of even greater prominence either abjectly confessed their failure to follow the teachings of Mao or disappeared from sight. By the summer of 1966 a movement to discredit all "revisionists" burst on the scene. These were Red Guards, boys and girls from secondary schools and colleges, answering to no leadership except Mao himself, who were bent on destroying everything which smacked of capitalism or of their own cultural heritage and of anyone who had in any way promoted an idea or a policy not in Mao's book.

This resulted in the dismissal of such people as the mayor of Peking and in countless diatribes against the chairman of the People's Republic (Liu Shao-ch'i) and of others of less exalted rank. For nearly two years the Red Guards had their way, storming into every city and every province from one end of China to the other, not without opposition, but nonetheless with sufficient energy to cause havoc in schools and colleges and industry and to blight all prospect for freedom of utterance in any way whatsoever. The only high official to weather the political storm was Chou En-lai. Even he has had to retreat to a spot behind Lin Piao, minister of defense, and now the Chairman's favorite.

One of the numerous casualties that might be mentioned as a result of all this turmoil is that of archeology. In the building of industrial plants and lengthening of railroad lines since 1950 the Chinese have stumbled on hundreds of sites of the greatest significance for understanding all stages of their history and prehistory, from the discovery of another skull cap of the hominid known as Peking man (1966) to the incredible riches of the tomb of the Ming emperor who reigned from 1573 to 1620 (1956). For fifteen years the government listened to the pleas of their scientists and allowed excavations to proceed for limited periods of time before road builders and construction men took over. Hundreds of students were trained in short term courses and museums sprang up in every province to house the treasures. In these years some of the reports produced were of the highest quality, and the government seemed proud of this activity. Hundreds of thousands of people yearly paraded through the museums, and China's propaganda journals trumpeted the finds. Suddenly, beginning in 1966, this has all stopped.

In two areas alone have the mainland Chinese made startling progress: in organic chemistry and in nuclear weaponry and explosives. In 1967 their scientists announced the synthesis of one of the structural components of the hormone insulin. This is regarded in the West as one of the major break-throughs of the year. In October 1964 and again in May 1965 they made their first tests of nuclear explosives, followed in 1966 by three more, all in Sinkiang province. The claim of the Chinese that their last tests involved the delivery of a nuclear warhead to a target by means of a missile they themselves had developed is nowhere doubted. Finally, on June 17, 1967, the Chinese exploded their first hydrogen bomb. This success shows advanced technology, and has had a sobering effect on world opinion.

Ever since 1950 the people on the island of Taiwan (some twelve million) of whom about nine million are native born) have continued to breathe defiance against the forces on the mainland, and their leaders continue to proclaim that they will eventually return. Taking over the industries, transport lines, and installations once in the hands of the Japanese, they have improved and extended them with United States aid. The latter amounted to over a billion U.S. dollars from 1950 to 1960 inclusive. In 1953 the government launched a four year program of development, and though the goals were not all reached the achievements in expanding industrial and agricultural production, increasing electric power and communication facilities, and bettering farm conditions were impressive. A second four year plan followed in 1957. The economic situation has improved to such an extent that the United States in 1967 discontinued its financial aid. A significant occurrence in 1954 was the election of city and county officials by 1,800,000 voters. The great majority, 4 out of 5 mayors and 15 out of 16 magistrates, were Taiwan born. Similarly, more and more native-born Taiwanese have been appointed to posts of importance in the provincial government. There was even a larger turnout of voters in 1957. Important too is the fact over 90 per cent of school-age children attend school on the island. Educational facilities at all levels (including twenty-nine colleges and universities) have been increased. Overseas Chinese are increasingly welcomed in these technical and arts colleges, now attended by over 40,000 students. Research is maintained at a high level by the Academia Sinica, Taiwan's most select group of scholars. While outwardly relations between Taiwan and the United States are cordial, latent discontent was revealed in the riots of May 24, 1957, touched off by the acquittal by a United States court-martial of an American soldier who had killed a Chinese. Rioters wrecked the United States embassy and information service center, injuring both Americans and Chinese. The Americans were accused of treating individual Chinese on a basis less than equal, but cool heads on both sides saved the situation. A shooting war still continues across the Straits, and planes based on Taiwan make frequent forays over the continent to watch for a military build-up in Fukien (90–100 miles away), and to drop leaflets and gift packages on towns and villages. A stalemate has been reached here which will be resolved only when the United States has withdrawn its shield (the U.S. navy), or when some unanticipated international event radically alters the situation in eastern Asia. An uneasy calm now prevails.

Supplementary Readings[1]

CHAPTER I

Chang, K. C., *The Archaeology of Ancient China*, New Haven, Yale University Press, 1963.

Cheng, Te-k'un, *Prehistoric China, Shang China, Chou China*, 3 vols., Cambridge, Cambridge University Press, 1959, 1960, 1963.

Watson, Burton, *Mo Tzu, Hsün Tzu, Han Fei Tzu, Chuang Tzu*, 4 vols., New York, Columbia University Press, 1963, 1964.

Hsü, Cho-yün, *Ancient China in Transition: an analysis of social mobility, 722–222 B.C.*, Stanford, Stanford University Press, 1965.

Hawkes, David, *Ch'u Tz'u, the Songs of the South*, Oxford, The University Press, 1959.

de Bary, Chan, and Watson, *Sources of Chinese Tradition*, New York, Columbia University Press, 1960.

Li Chi, *The Beginnings of Chinese Civilization*, Seattle, University of Washington Press, 1957.

Waley, Arthur, *The Book of Songs*, London, G. Allen & Unwin, Ltd., 1937.

Waley, Arthur, *The Analects of Confucius*, London, G. Allen & Unwin, Ltd., 1934.

Fung Yu-lan, *A History of Chinese Philosophy*, Princeton, Princeton University Press, 1952, vol. I.

Duyvendak, J. J. L., *The Book of Lord Shang*, London, A. Probsthain, 1928.

Walker, Richard, *The Multi-state System of Ancient China*, Hamden, Connecticut, Shoestring Press, 1953.

Creel, Herrlee Glessner, *Confucius, the Man and the Myth*, New York, John Day Co., 1949.

Needham, Joseph, and Wang Ling, *Science and Civilization in China*, Cambridge, Cambridge University Press, 1956, vol. II, pp. 216–246.

Karlgren, Bernhard, *The Chinese Language, an essay on its nature and history*, New York, The Ronald Press, 1949.

---

[1] For other suggestions, consult Charles O. Hucker, *China: a Critical Bibliography*, Tucson, The University of Arizona Press, 1962.

CHAPTER II

Lattimore, Owen, *Inner Asian Frontiers of China*, 2nd ed., New York, American Geographical Society, 1951, pp. 379–390, 399–425.

Bodde, Derk, *China's First Unifier, a Study of the Ch'in Dynasty as Seen in the Life of Li Ssŭ*, Leiden, E. J. Brill, Ltd., 1938.

Bodde, Derk, *Statesman, Patriot, and General in Ancient China*, New Haven, American Oriental Society, 1940.

Yü, Ying-shih, *Trade and Expansion in Han China*, Berkeley, University of California Press, 1967.

Dubs, Homer H., *History of the Former Han Dynasty*, 3 vols., Baltimore, Waverly Press, 1938, 1944, 1955.

Gale, Esson McDowell, *Discourses on Salt and Iron*, Leiden, E. J. Brill, Ltd., 1931.

Forke, Alfred, *Lun-hêng*, 2 parts, London, Luzac & Co., 1907–1911.

Loewe, Michael, *Everyday Life in Imperial China*, Landow, B. T. Botsford, Ltd., 1968.

Bielenstein, Hans, *The Restoration of the Han Dynasty*, 3 vols., Stockholm, 1953, 1959, 1967.

Carter, Thomas Francis, and Goodrich, L. C., *Invention of Printing in China and Its Spread Westward*, 2nd ed., New York, The Ronald Press, 1955, pp. 3–10.

Stein, Sir Mark Aurel, *On Ancient Central-Asian Tracks*, London, Macmillan & Co., Ltd., 1933, chaps. 2, 11.

Wilbur, C. Martin, *Slavery in China During the Former Han Dynasty*, Chicago, Field Museum of Natural History, 1943.

Swann, Nancy Lee, *Food and Money in Ancient China*, Princeton, Princeton University Press, 1950.

Watson, Burton, *Ssu-ma Ch'ien: Grand Historian of China*, New York, Columbia University Press, 1958.

Watson, Burton, *Records of the Grand Historian of China*, 2 vols., New York, Columbia University Press, 1960, 1961.

Sickman, Laurence, and Soper, Alexander, *The Art and Architecture of China*, Baltimore, Penguin Books, Ltd., 1956, pp. 20–40, 216–227.

Needham, Joseph, and Wang Ling, *Science and Civilization in China*, Cambridge, Cambridge University Press, 1954–1956, vol. I, pp. 109–112; vol. II, pp. 247–303.

CHAPTER III

Welch, Holmes, *The Parting of the Way: Lao Tzu and the Taoist Movement*, Boston, Beacon Press, 1957, pp. 123–143.

Waley, Arthur, *Translations from the Chinese*, New York, A. A. Knopf, 1941, pp. 59–107.

Eberhard, Wolfram, *A History of China*, London, Routledge & Kegan Paul, 1950, chap. 7.

Acker, W. R. B., *T'ao the Hermit, Sixty Poems by T'ao Ch'ien (365–427)*, London & New York, Thames & Hudson, 1952.

Gulik, R. H. van, *Hsi K'ang and his Poetical Essay on the Lute*, Tokyo, Sophia University, 1941.

Yang, Lien-sheng, *Money and Credit in China*, Cambridge, Mass., Harvard University Press, 1952, pp. 1–24.

Ch'en, Kenneth, *Buddhism in China, a Historical Survey*, Princeton, Princeton University Press, 1964, chaps. 2–7.

Wright, Arthur F., *Buddhism in Chinese History*, Stanford, Stanford University Press, 1959.

Samolin, William, *East Turkistan to the 12th Century*, The Hague, Mouton & Co., 1964, pp. 47–58.

Chapter IV

Bingham, Woodbridge, *The Founding of the T'ang Dynasty, the Fall of Sui and the Rise of T'ang*, Baltimore, Waverly Press, Inc., 1941.

FitzGerald, Charles Patrick, *Son of Heaven, a Biography of Li Shih-min*, Cambridge (Eng.), University Press, 1933.

FitzGerald, Charles Patrick, *The Empress Wu*, Melbourne, F. W. Cheshire, 1956.

Pulleyblank, E. G., *The Background of the Rebellion of An Lu-shan*, Oxford, Oxford University Press, 1955.

Chi Ch'ao-ting, *Key Economic Areas in Chinese History*, London, G. Allen & Unwin, Ltd., 1936, pp. 113–130.

Laufer, Berthold, *Sino-Iranica*, Field Museum of Natural History Pub. 201, Anthropological Series, vol. XV, no. 3, Chicago, 1919.

Carter, Thomas Francis, and Goodrich, L. C., *Invention of Printing in China and Its Spread Westward*, 2nd ed., New York, The Ronald Press, 1955, pp. 31–81.

Stein, Sir Mark Aurel, *On Ancient Central-Asian Tracks*, London, Macmillan & Co., Ltd., 1933, chaps. 12–14.

Shryock, John Knight, *The Origin and Development of the State Cult of Confucius*, New York, D. Appleton-Century Co., 1932, chap. 9.

Waley, Arthur, *The Real Tripitaka*, London, George Allen & Unwin, 1952.

Sivin, Nathan, *Chinese Alchemy:* preliminary studies, Harvard University Press, 1968.

Moule, Arthur Christopher, *Christians in China; Before the Year 1550,* London, Society for Promoting Christian Knowledge; New York, The Macmillan Company, 1930, chap. 2.

Reischauer, Edwin O., *Ennin's Travels in T'ang China* and *Ennin's Diary,* New York, The Ronald Press, 1955.

Waley, Arthur, *Translations from the Chinese,* New York, A. A. Knopf, 1941, pp. 108–298.

Hung, William, *Tu Fu, China's Greatest Poet,* Cambridge, Harvard University Press, 1952.

Giles, Lionel, *Six Centuries at Tunhuang,* London, China Society, 1944.

Waley, Arthur, *The Life and Times of Po Chü-i,* New York, The Macmillan Company, 1949.

Feifel, Eugene, *Po Chü-i as a censor,* 'S-Gravenhage, Mouton & Co., 1961.

Schafer, Edward H., *The Golden Peaches of Samarkand, a study of T'ang exotics,* Berkeley, University of California Press, 1963.

Schafer, Edward H., *The Vermilion Bird,* T'ang images of the South, Berkeley, University of California Press, 1967.

Zurcher, E., *The Buddhist Conquest of China,* 2 vols., Leiden, E. J. Brill, 1959.

Twitchett, Denis, *Financial Administration under the T'ang Dynasty,* Cambridge, Cambridge University Press, 1963.

Wang, Chi-chên, *Traditional Chinese Tales,* New York, Columbia University Press, 1944.

Edwards, Evangeline Dora, *Chinese Prose Literature of the T'ang Period,* 2 vols., London, A. Probsthain, 1937–1938.

Sirén, Osvald, *Chinese Sculpture from the Fifth to the Fourteenth Century,* New York, Charles Scribner's Sons, 1925.

CHAPTER V

Shryock, John Knight, *The Origin and Development of the State Cult of Confucius,* New York, D. Appleton-Century Co., 1932, chap. 10.

Williamson, Henry R., *Wang An Shih,* 2 vols., London, A. Probsthain, 1935–1937.

Hirth, Friedrich, and Rockhill, W. W., *Chau Ju-kua: His Work on the Chinese and Arab Trade in the 12th and 13th Centuries, Entitled Chu-fan-chi,* St. Petersburg, Printing Office of the Imperial Academy of Sciences, 1911.

Sickman, Laurence, and Soper, Alexander, *The Art and Architecture of China*, Baltimore, Penguin Books, Ltd., 1956, pp. 94–145, 255–282.

Schafer, Edward H., *The Empire of Min*, Rutland, Vermont, C. E. Tuttle, 1954.

Kracke, Edward A., *Civil Service in Early Sung China*, Cambridge, Harvard University Press, 1953.

Hobson, Robert Lockhart, *A Catalogue of Chinese Pottery and Porcelain in the Collection of Sir Percival David, Bt., FSA*, London, Stourton Press, 1934.

Bruce, Joseph Perry, *Chu Hsi and His Masters*, London, A. Probsthain, 1923.

Fung Yu-lan, *A History of Chinese Philosophy*, Princeton, Princeton University Press, 1953, vol. II.

White, William C., *Chinese Jews*, 3 parts, Toronto, University of Toronto Press, 1942.

Wittfogel, Karl A., and Fêng, Chia-shêng, *History of Chinese Society, Liao (907–1125)*, New York, The Macmillan Company, 1949.

Lin Yutang, *The Gay Genius: the Life and Times of Su Tungpo*, New York, John Day Co., 1947.

Huang Siu-chi, *Lu Hsiang-shan, a Twelfth Century Chinese Idealist Philosopher*, New Haven, American Oriental Society, 1944.

Wang Gung-wu, *The Structure of Power in North China during the Five Dynasties*, Kuala Lumpur, University of Malaya Press, 1963.

Liu, James T. C., *Reform in Sung China: Wang An-shih (1021–86) and his new policies*, Cambridge, Mass., Harvard University Press, 1959.

Watson, Burton, *Su Tung-p'o Selections from a Sung Dynasty Poet*, New York, Columbia University Press, 1965.

Yoshikawa, K., *An Introduction to Sung Poetry* (tr. by Burton Watson), Cambridge, Mass., Harvard University Press, 1967.

Gernet, Jacques, *Daily Life in China. On the eve of the Mongol Invasion, 1250–76* (tr. by Hope M. Wright), New York, The Macmillan Co., 1962.

Chapter VI

Hudson, Geoffrey Francis, *Europe and China; a Survey of Their Relations from the Earliest Times to 1800*, London, E. Arnold & Co., 1931, chap. 5.

Waley, Arthur, *The Travels of an Alchemist: the Journey of the Taoist Ch'ang-ch'un*, London, G. Routledge & Sons, Ltd., 1931.

Bretschneider, E., *Mediaeval Researches from Eastern Asiatic Sources*, London, K. Paul, Trench, Trübner & Co., Ltd., 1888, vol. I, pp. 3–34, 109–172.

Olschki, Leonardo, *Marco Polo's Precursors*, Baltimore, Johns Hopkins Press, 1943.

Martin, Henry Desmond, *The Rise of Chinghis Khan and his Conquest of North China*, Baltimore, The Johns Hopkins Press, 1950.

Schurmann, Herbert Franz, *Economic Structure of the Yüan Dynasty*, Cambridge, Harvard University Press, 1956.

Moule, Arthur Christopher, *Christians in China; Before the Year 1550*, London, Society for Promoting Christian Knowledge; New York, The Macmillan Company, 1930, chap. 4.

Moule, Arthur Christopher, and Pelliot, Paul, *Marco Polo, 1254–1323? . . . The Description of the World*, 2 vols., London, G. Routledge & Sons, Ltd., 1938.

Zucker, Adolph E., *The Chinese Theater*, Boston, Little, Brown and Co., 1925, chap. 2.

Grousset, René, *The Civilizations of the East*, New York, A. A. Knopf, 1931–1934, vol. I, pp. 291–339; vol. III, pp. 333–338.

Pelliot, Paul, *Notes on Marco Polo*, Paris, Imprimerie Nationale, 2 vols., 1959, 1963.

Ch'en Yüan, *Western and Central Asians in China under the Mongols* (tr. and annot. by Ch'ien Hsing-hai and L. C. Goodrich), Los Angeles, Monumenta Serica, 1966.

Chapter VII

Bretschneider, E., *Mediaeval Researches from Eastern Asiatic Sources*, London, K. Paul, Trench, Trübner & Co., Ltd., 1888, vol. II, pp. 157–167, 256–261.

Wang Yi-t'ung, *Official Relations Between China and Japan (1368–1549)*, Cambridge, Harvard University Press, 1953.

Tsunoda, R., and Goodrich, L. C., *Japan in the Chinese Dynastic Histories*, South Pasedena, P. D. & Ione Perkins, 1951.

Chang T'ien-tsê, *Sino-Portuguese Trade from 1514 to 1644*, Leiden, E. J. Brill, Ltd., 1933.

Schurz, William Lytle, *The Manila Galleon*, New York, E. P. Dutton & Co., Inc., 1939.

Hudson, Geoffrey Francis, *Europe and China; a Survey of Their Relations from the Earliest Times to 1800*, London, E. Arnold & Co., 1931, pp. 195–203, 232–258.

Pope, John A., *Chinese Porcelains from the Ardebil Shrine*, Washington, Freer Gallery of Art, 1956.

Irwin, Richard G., *The Evolution of a Chinese Novel: Shui-hu-chuan*, Cambridge, Harvard University Press, 1953.

Bishop, John Lyman, *The Colloquial Short Story in China*, Cambridge, Harvard University Press, 1956.

Strange, Edward Fairweather, *Chinese Lacquer*, New York, Scribner, 1926.

Sirén, Osvald, *A History of Later Chinese Painting*, London, The Medici Society, 1938.

Prip-moller, Johannes, *Chinese Buddhist Monasteries*, Copenhagen, G. E. C. Gad; London, Oxford University Press, 1937.

Pokotilov, D., *History of the Eastern Mongols during the Ming Dynasty from 1368 to 1634*, 2 parts, Chengtu, West China Union University, 1947–1949.

Boxer, C. R., *Fidalgos in the Far East, 1550–1770, Fact and Fancy in the History of Macao*, The Hague, Martinus Nijhoff, 1948.

Boxer, C. R., *South China in the Sixteenth Century*, London, Hakluyt Society, 1953.

Hsiung, S. I., *The Romance of the Western Chamber (Hsi Hsiang Chi)*, London, Methuen & Co., Ltd., 1935.

Hummel, Arthur W. (ed.), *Eminent Chinese of the Ch'ing Period*, 2 vols., Washington, U.S. Government Printing Office, 1943–1944.

Zucker, Adolph E., *The Chinese Theater*, Boston, Little, Brown & Co., 1925, chap. 3.

Brewitt-Taylor, Charles Henry, *San Kuo or Romance of the Three Kingdoms*, 2 vols., Shanghai, Kelly & Walsh, Ltd., 1925.

Egerton, Clement, *The Golden Lotus*, 4 vols., London, G. Routledge & Sons, Ltd., 1939.

Buck, Pearl S., *All Men Are Brothers (Shui Hu Chuan)*, New York, John Day Co., 1933.

Howell, E. Butts, *Inconstancy of Madam Chuang and Other Stories*, London, Laurie, 1924.

Howell, E. Butts, *The Restitution of the Bride and Other Stories from the Chinese*, London, Laurie, 1926.

Waley, Arthur, *The Monkey*, by Wu Ch'êng-ên, New York, John Day Co., 1943.

Hucker, Charles O., *The Traditional State in Ming Times (1368–1644)*, Tucson, The University of Arizona Press, 1961.

Hucker, Charles O., *The Censorial System of China*, Stanford, Stanford University Press, 1966.

Ho, Ping-ti, *Studies on the Population of China, 1368–1953*, Cambridge, Mass., Harvard University Press, 1959, chaps. I and II.

Ho, Ping-ti, *The Ladder of Success in Imperial China: Aspects of Social Mobility, 1368–1911*, New York, Columbia University Press, 1962.

Dunne, George Harold, *Generation of Giants, The Story of the Jesuits in China in the Last Decades of the Ming Dynasty*, Notre Dame, The University of Notre Dame Press, 1962.

The Arts of the Ming Dynasty, New York, Collings, 1958.

Sung, Ying-hsing, *Chinese Technology in the Seventeenth Century* (tr. by Sun, E-tu Zen and Sun, Shiou-chuan), University Park, Pennsylvania State University Press, 1966.

CHAPTER VIII

Lattimore, Owen, *Inner Asian Frontiers of China*, 2nd ed., New York, American Geographical Society, 1951, pp. 103–138.

Wang, C. C., *Dream of the Red Chamber, by Tsao Hsueh-chin*, New York, Twayne Publishers, 1958.

Giles, Herbert Allen, *Strange Stories from a Chinese Studio*, New York, Boni, 1925.

Bodde, D. and Moeris, C., *Law in Imperial China*, Harvard University Press, 1967.

Yang, Hsien-yi, and Yang, Gladys, *The Scholars, by Wu Ching-tzu*, Peking, Foreign Language Press, 1957.

Waley, Arthur, *Yüan Mei, 18th Century Chinese Poet*, London, G. Allen & Unwin, Ltd., 1956.

Swisher, Earl, *China's Management of the American Barbarians*, New Haven, Far Eastern Publications, Yale University, 1951.

Wright, Mary C., *The Last Stand of Chinese Conservatism; The T'ung-chih Restoration, 1862–1874*, Stanford, Stanford University Press, 1957.

Zucker, Adolph E., *The Chinese Theater*, Boston, Little, Brown & Co., 1925, chap. 4.

Goodrich, L. Carrington, *The Literary Inquisition of Ch'ien-lung*, Baltimore, Waverly Press, Inc., 1935.

Williams, S. Wells, *The Middle Kingdom*, New York, Charles Scribner's Sons, 1901, vol. I, pp. 519–572.

Malone, Carroll Brown, *History of the Peking Summer Palaces Under the Ch'ing Dynasty*, Urbana, University of Illinois, 1934.

Morse, Hosea Ballou, and MacNair, Henry Farnsworth, *Far Eastern Inter-*

national Relations, Boston, Houghton Mifflin Company, 1931, chaps. 4–15, 18–23.

Dennett, Tyler, *Americans in Eastern Asia*, New York, The Macmillan Company, 1922.

La Fargue, Thomas E., *China's First Hundred*, Pullman, State College of Washington, 1942.

Broomhall, Marshall, *Islam in China, a Neglected Problem*, London, Morgan & Scott, Ltd., 1910, pp. 129–163.

Hail, William James, *Tseng Kuo-fan and the Taiping Rebellion*, New Haven, Yale University Press, 1927.

Bales, William Leslie, *Tso Tsung-t'ang, Soldier and Statesman of China*, Shanghai, Kelly & Walsh, 1937.

Hughes, Ernest Richard, *The Invasion of China by the Western World*, New York, The Macmillan Company, 1938, pp. 1–132.

Reichwein, Adolph, *China and Europe*, New York, A. A. Knopf, 1925.

Gamble, Sidney David, *Peking, a Social Survey*, New York, Doubleday, Doran Co., 1921.

Burgess, John Stewart, *The Guilds of Peking*, New York, Thesis for Columbia University, 1928.

Eberhard, Wolfram, *Chinese Fairy Tales and Folk Tales*, London, Kegan Paul, Trench, Trübner & Co., Ltd., 1937.

Kulp, Daniel Harrison, *Country Life in South China*, New York, Bureau of Publications, Teachers College, Columbia University, 1925.

Fei Hsiao-tung, *Peasant Life in China*, London, G. Routledge & Sons, Ltd., 1939.

Escarra, Jean, *China Then and Now*, Peking, Vetch, 1940, pp. 1–148.

Buck, John Lossing, *Land Utilization in China*, Chicago, University of Chicago, 1937.

Wong K. Chimin and Wu Lien-teh, *History of Chinese Medicine*, 2nd ed., Shanghai, National Quarantine Service, 1936.

Hummel, Arthur W. (ed.), *Eminent Chinese of the Ch'ing Period*, 2 vols., Washington, U.S. Government Printing Office, 1943–1944.

Sirén, Osvald, *Gardens of China*, New York, The Ronald Press, 1949.

Têng Ssŭ-yü, *Chang Hsi and the Treaty of Nanking, 1842*, Chicago, University of Chicago Press, 1944.

Rosso, Sisto Antonio, *Apostolic Legations to China of the Eighteenth Century*, South Pasadena, P. D. and Ione Perkins, 1948.

Hu Hsien-chin, *The Common Descent Group in China and Its Functions*, New York, The Viking Fund, 1948.

Britton, Roswell S., The Chinese Periodical Press, 1800–1912, Shanghai, Kelly & Walsh, 1933.

Lin Yutang, *A History of the Press and Public Opinion in China*. Shanghai, published for China Institute Pacific Relations by Kelly & Walsh, 1936.

Michael, Franz, *The Origin of Manchu Rule in China*, Baltimore, Johns Hopkins Press, 1942.

Lin Mousheng, *Men and Ideas*, New York, John Day Co., 1942, chaps. 13–15.

Spence, Jonathan D., *Ts'ao Yin and the K'ang-hsi Emperor, Bondservant and Master*, New Haven, Yale University Press, 1966.

Fu, Lo-shu, *A Documentary Chronicle of Sino-Western Relations, 1644–1820*, Tucson, University of Arizona Press, 1966.

Teng and Fairbank, *China's Response to the West, 1829–1923*, Cambridge, Mass., Harvard University Press, 1954.

Boorman and Howard (eds.), *Biographical Dictionary of Republican China*, New York, Columbia University Press, Vols. I & II (to date), 1967–68.

Chapter IX

Escarra, Jean, *China Then and Now*, Peking, Vetch, 1940, pp. 149–229.

Sharman, Lyon, *Sun Yat-sen, His Life and Its Meaning, a Critical Biography*, New York, John Day Co., 1934.

Hughes, Ernest Richard, *The Invasion of China by the Western World*, New York, The Macmillan Company, 1938, pp. 132–309.

Hu Shih, *The Chinese Renaissance*, Chicago, University of Chicago Press, 1934.

Hummel, Arthur William, *Autobiography of a Chinese Historian*, Leiden, E. J. Brill, Ltd., 1931.

Wang, C. C., *Ah Q and Others, Selected Stories of Lusin*, New York, Columbia University Press, 1941.

Peake, Cyrus Henderson, *Nationalism and Education in Modern China*, New York, Columbia University Press, 1932.

Buck, John Lossing, *Chinese Farm Economy*, Chicago, University of Chicago, 1930.

Ch'ien Tuan-sheng, *The Government and Politics of China*, Cambridge, Harvard University Press, 1950.

Meijer, M. J., *The Introduction of Modern Criminal Law in China*, Batavia, De Unie, 1950.

MacNair, Harley F. (ed.), *China*, Berkeley and Los Angeles, University of California Press, 1946.

Rowe, David Nelson, *China Among the Powers*, New York, Harcourt Brace, 1945.

Fairbank, John K., *The United States and China*, Cambridge, The Harvard University Press, 1948.

Shih Kuo-hêng, *China Enters the Machine Age*, Cambridge, Harvard University Press, 1944.

Wilbur, C. M., and How, Julie, *Documents on Communism, Nationalism, and Soviet Advisers in China, 1918–1927*, New York, Columbia University Press, 1956.

Compton, Boyd, *Mao's China: Party Reform Documents, 1942–1944*, Seattle, University of Washington Press, 1952.

Schwartz, Benjamin I., *Chinese Communism and the Rise of Mao*, Cambridge, Harvard University Press, 1951.

de Francis, John, *Nationalism and Language Reform in China*, Princeton, Princeton University Press, 1950.

Scott, A. C., *The Classical Theatre of China*, London, G. Allen & Unwin, 1957.

Lang, Olga, *Chinese Family and Society*, New Haven, Yale University Press, 1946.

Löwenthal, Rudolf, *The Religious Periodical Press in China*, Peiping, The Synodal Commission in China, 1940.

Winfield, Gerald, *China: The Land and the People*, New York, William Sloane Associates, 1948.

Harrison, James P., *The Communists and Chinese Peasant Rebellion*, New York, Atheneum, 1969.

The Department of State, *United States Relations with China*, Washington, D.C., 1949.

Kirby, E. Stuart, *Introduction to the Economic History of China*, London, G. Allen & Unwin, 1954.

Riggs, Frederick W., *Formosa Under Chinese Nationalist Rule*, New York, Macmillan, 1952.

Chronological Table

The Hsia Kingdom (traditional?)	*ca.* 1994 B.C.–*ca.* 1523
The Shang (or Yin) Kingdom	*ca.* 1523 B.C.–*ca.* 1028
The Chou Kingdom	*ca.* 1027 B.C.–256
The Ch'in dynasty	221 B.C.–207
The Western (or Earlier) Han dynasty	202 B.C.–A.D. 9
The Hsin dynasty	A.D. 9–A.D. 23
The Eastern (or Later) Han dynasty	25– 220
The Three Kingdoms	220– 265
Shu, 221–264	
Wei, 220–265	
Wu, 222–280	
The Western Tsin dynasty	265– 317
The Eastern Tsin dynasty	317– 420
The Former (or Liu) Sung dynasty	420– 479
The Southern Ch'i dynasty	479– 502
The Southern Liang dynasty	502– 557
The Southern Ch'ên dynasty	557– 589
The Northern Wei dynasty	386– 535
The Eastern Wei dynasty	534– 550
The Western Wei dynasty	535– 556
The Northern Ch'i dynasty	550– 577
The Northern Chou dynasty	557– 581
The Later Liang dynasty	555– 587
The Sui dynasty	590– 618
The T'ang dynasty	618– 906
The Five dynasties	907– 960
Later Liang, 907–923	
Later T'ang, 923–936	
Later Chin, 936–947	
Later Han, 947–950	
Later Chou, 951–960	
The Liao dynasty	907– 1125
The Northern Sung dynasty	960– 1126

The Hsi-hsia dynasty	990–	1227
The Southern Sung dynasty	1127–	1279
The Chin dynasty	1115–	1234
The Yüan dynasty	1260–	1368
The Ming dynasty	1368–	1644
The Ch'ing dynasty	1644–	1912
The Republic	1912–	

CHRONOLOGICAL CHART

Christian Calendar (B.C.)	Outside World	Key Facts	Dynasties	Religion and Thought	Art	Culture	(B.C.)
2000 B.C.	Bronze Age, First Dynasty, Babylon—	Emergence from Stone Age			Black pottery	Domesticated pig and dog, Cultivated millet and wheat, Potter's wheel, Domesticated ox, goat, sheep, horse	2000 B.C.
1500	Dynasty XVIII, Egypt	Bronze Age	HSIA				1500
		Earliest writing, Urban development	SHANG	Religion animistic and orgiastic	White incised pottery, Bronze ritual vessels and weapons, Carved ivory and stone, Jades	Script, Practice of divination, Silk culture, Wheeled vehicles, Cowry shells	
	MOSES, Iron Age			Recognition of spirit world, Ancestor worship	Turquoise inlay	Brush and ink, Composite bow, Books of bamboo slips	
1000	Rigveda					Wet rice, Fowl, Water buffalo	1000
		Raids cause shift of capital, Feudalism	CHOU	The Odes		Use of rime	
	ZOROASTER						
500	BUDDHA, DARIUS	Iron Age, First law code, Canal and wall building, SHIH-HUANG-TI	CH'IN	CONFUCIUS, MO-TZŬ, CHUANG-TZŬ, LAO-TZŬ, LORD SHANG	Bronze vessels, Bronze mirrors, Lacquer, Palace architecture	Advances in astronomy, Traction plow, Crossbow, Round coins, Fighting on horseback, Trousers, boots	500
	ALEXANDER, CHANDRAGUPTA, ASOKA	Hsiung-nu raids, Expansion under WU-TI	FORMER HAN	Civil examinations, SSŬ-MA CH'IEN, Canonical research	Garden retreats, Wall painting, Sculpture	Iron sword, Mule, ass, camel introduced, Soy bean	

CHRONOLOGICAL CHART

A.D. scale: 500 — 1000 — 1500 — 1950

World Figures
- JESUS
- KANISHKA
- MARCUS AURELIUS
- MANI
- ATTILA
- MOHAMMED
- HARUN AL-RASHID
- *Magna Carta*
- The Polos
- COLUMBUS
- Magellan
- Two World Wars

Chinese Events
- WANG MANG
- Buddhism firmly established
- South China colonized
- Grand canal
- Expansion up to 751
- Block printing
- Foot binding
- WANG AN-SHIH
- JENGHIS KHAN
- Mongols expelled
- CHENG HO voyages
- Peking rebuilt
- Portuguese traders
- Spaniards take P.I.
- Japanese raids
- The Manchus
- K'ANG-HSI era
- CH'IEN-LUNG era
- Mohammedan rebellions
- T'ai-p'ing rebellion
- SUN YAT-SEN
- Japanese invasions
- Communist control

Dynasties
- LATER HAN
- 3 KINGDOMS
- TSIN
- WEI
- SUNG / CH'I / LIANG / CH'EN / CHOU
- SUI
- T'ANG
- 5 Dynasties
- No. SUNG
- LIAO
- CHIN / So. SUNG
- YÜAN
- MING
- CH'ING
- REPUBLIC

Thought and Religion
- Alchemy
- PAN KU / PAN CHAO
- Buddhist sutras translated
- Taoism
- Pilgrims to India
- T'AO CH'IEN
- Chinese nuns
- Examination system
- Alien faiths
- HSÜAN-TSANG
- HAN YÜ
- Proscription of Buddhism
- Printing of all canonical works
- Classical renaissance
- Antiquarianism
- Judaism
- Drama
- CHU HSI
- Mathematics
- Islam
- Christianity
- Lamaism
- Encyclopaedias
- Gazetteers
- WANG SHOU-JEN
- Fiction
- Jesuit influence
- Critical scholarship
- Dictionaries
- Libraries
- Literary inquisition
- Protestant Christianity
- Western education
- Mass education

Arts
- Glazed pottery
- Calligraphy
- KU K'AI-CHIH Greco-Indian influences in rock temples
- Tomb figurines
- Painting
- Porcelain
- Landscapes
- Private gardens
- Music
- Cloisonné
- Old and new styles in painting
- Colors on porcelain
- Under glaze blue and enamel
- European influences
- Archeology

Technology and Material Culture
- Football
- Paper
- Map of China
- Tea
- Water mill
- Sedan chair
- Use of coal
- Kite
- Firecracker
- Law code
- Elephant chess
- Polo game
- Block prints
- Chairs
- Paper money
- Ships for ocean travel
- Compass
- Cotton
- Gunpowder
- Sorghum
- Abacus
- Distillation of liquor—Chaulmoogra oil
- Spectacles
- Syphilis
- Maize and sweet potato
- Peanuts
- Tobacco and snuff
- Imposition of queue
- Mexican dollar
- Opium smoking
- Factories
- Steamships
- Railroads
- Motor transport
- Aviation

List of Chinese Characters

An Shih-kao	安世高	Chêng family	鄭
Chan Kuo	戰國	Ch'êng I	程頤
Ch'an sect	禪宗	*Ch'êng shih mo yüan*	程氏墨苑
Chang Hêng	張衡	*Chi chiu chang*	急就章
Chang Hsüeh-ch'êng	章學誠	Ch'i	齊
Chang Jung	張融	Ch'i, northern	北齊
Chang Lu	張魯	Ch'i, southern	南齊
Changes: I	易	Chia Tan	賈耽
Chao	趙	Ch'iang	羌
Chao, Early	前趙	Chiang Kai-shek	蔣介石
Chao, Later	後趙	Ch'ien-lung	乾隆
Chao Ju-kua	趙汝适	Ch'ih-i	鴟夷
Chao K'uang-yin	趙匡胤	Chin, state of	晉
Chao Ming-ch'êng	趙明誠	Chin dynasty	金
Ch'ên	陳	Chin, Later	後晉
Ch'ên Ching-i	陳景沂	*Chin p'ing mei*	金瓶梅
Ch'ên Shou	陳壽	Chin Shêng-t'an	金聖嘆
Ch'ên Ti	陳第	Ch'in dynasty	秦
Chêng	政	Ch'in, Early	前秦
Chêng Ch'iao	鄭樵	Ch'in Chiu-shao	秦九韶
Chêng Ho	鄭和	Ch'in-lun	秦論
Ch'êng	成	*Ching hua yüan*	鏡花緣
Ch'êng Chün-fang	程君房	Ch'ing dynasty	清朝

Ch'iu Ch'u-chi 邱處機

Chou 周

Chou, northern 北周

Chou Ch'ü-fei 周去非

Chou Ên-lai 周恩來

Chou Hsing-tz'ŭ 周興嗣

Chou li 周禮

Chu Chên-hêng 朱震亨

Chu Hsi 朱熹

Chu I-chün 朱翊鈞

Chu Ssŭ-pên 朱思本

Chu Tao-shêng 竺道生

Chu Ti 朱棣

Chu Tsai-yü 朱載堉

Chu Yüan-chang 朱元璋

Chu-ko Liang 諸葛亮

Ch'u 楚

Ch'ü lu 橘錄

Ch'ü Yüan 屈原

Chuang-tzŭ 莊子

Ch'un ch'iu 春秋

Co-hong 公行

*Commentary on the Water
   Classic* 水經注

Confucianism 儒教

Confucius 孔子

Conversion of the Barbarians, The
   化胡經

Description of South China
   南越志

Ennin 圓仁

Fa-hsien 法顯

Fa Yüan Ssŭ 法源寺

Family Sayings of Confucius
   孔子家語

Fan Chên 范鎮

Fang I-chih 方以智

Fang shih mo p'u 方氏墨譜

Fang Yü-lu 方于魯

Filial Piety, Book of 孝經

Fo-t'u-têng 佛圖澄

Fu, Prince of 福王

Fu Hsi 傅翕

Fu I 傅奕

Fu Jung 苻融

Han 漢

Han, northern 北漢

Han history 漢書

Han Kao-tsu 漢高祖

Han Yen-chih 韓彥直

Han Yü 韓愈

Han-lin 翰林

Herbal for Relief from Famine
   救荒本草

History, Document of 書

Hong 行

Hsi Han	嵇含	Hui-tsung	徽宗
Hsi K'ang	嵇康	Hui-yüan	慧遠
Hsi yu chi	西遊記	*Hung lou mêng*	紅樓夢
Hsi Wang Mu	西王母	I (tribe)	夷
Hsia	夏	*I wu chih*	異物志
Hsia (Tangut)	夏	I-ching	義淨
Hsiao T'ung	蕭統	I-hsing	一行
Hsieh Ho	謝赫	Jou-jan	柔然
Hsieh Hsüan	謝玄	*Ju lin wai shih*	儒林外史
Hsieh Shih	謝石	Juan-juan	蠕蠕
Hsien-pi	鮮卑	Jung Ch'i-ch'i	榮啓期
Hsin dynasty	新朝	K'ang-hsi	康熙
Hsiung-nu	匈奴	K'ang Yu-wei	康有爲
Hsü Hung-tsu	徐宏祖	Kao Hsien-chih	高仙芝
Hsü Kuang-ch'i	徐光啓	*Kao sêng chuan*	高僧傳
Hsüan-tsang	玄奘	Kaolin	高嶺
Hsüan-tsung	玄宗	Khitan	契丹
Hu (central Asians)	胡	Ko Hung	葛洪
Hu, Empress of Wei	魏胡人后	Ku Ch'i yüan	顧起元
Hu Shih, Dr.	胡適	Ku Hui	顧徽
Huan Wên	桓温	Ku K'ai-chih	顧愷之
Huang Ch'ao	黃巢	Ku Yen-wu	顧炎武
Huang Tsung-hsi	黃宗羲	*Kuang-chou chi*	廣州記
Huang-ti	黃帝	K'un-ch'ü	崑曲
Hui-chiao	慧皎	K'ung family	孔家
Hui-i	慧益	Kuo Hsiang	郭象
Hui-shêng	惠生	Kuo K'an	郭侃
Hui-ssŭ	慧思	Kuo Shou-ching	郭守敬

Kuo-tzŭ-chien	國子監	Liu I-ch'ing	劉義慶
Kuomintang	國民黨	Liu Ling	劉伶
Lao-tzŭ	老子	Liu Pang	劉邦
Li Chieh	李誡	Liu Sung	劉宋
Li Ch'ing-chao	李清照	Lo Kuan-chung	羅貫中
Li family	李	Lord of Shang	商君
Li Fang	李昉	Lu Chi	陸機
Li Ju-chên	李汝珍	Lu Chiu-yüan	陸九淵
Li Kung	李塨	Lu Kuei-mêng	陸龜蒙
Li Ling	李陵	Lu Tz'ŭ	陸慈
Li Po	李白	Lu Yüan-lang	陸元朗
Li Shih-chên	李時珍	Lu Yün	陸雲
Li Shih-min	李世民	Lung Hu, Mount	龍虎山
Li Ssū	李斯	Lü Kuang	呂光
Li Tao-yüan	酈道元	Ma Tuan-lin	馬端臨
Li Tzŭ-ch'êng	李自成	Mao Tsê-tung	毛澤東
Li Yeh	李冶	Mao Yüan-i	茅元儀
Li Yüan	李淵	Mei Tsu	梅鷟
Li-chih p'u	荔枝譜	Mei Ying-tso	梅膺祚
Liang	梁	Ming (dynasty)	明
Liang, later	後梁	*Ming shih kao*	明史稿
Liao dynasty	遼	Mo Ti	墨翟
Liao, western	西遼	Nan Chao	南詔
Liao chai chih i	聊齋誌異	Nan Yüeh	南越
Ling-hsien	靈憲	*Nan-fang ts'ao-mu chuang*	
Litchi nut	荔枝		南方草木狀
Liu Chi	劉季	*New Remarks on the Study*	
Liu Hsieh	劉勰	*of Resonant Tubes*	科學新說
Liu Hsin	劉歆	Nien-fei	捻匪

Nurchachi	努爾哈赤	Shên-tsung	神宗
Odes, Book of	詩	*Shih chi*	史記
Ou-yang Hsiu	歐陽修	Shih-huang-ti	始皇帝
Ou-yang Hsün	歐陽詢	Shih Hu	石虎
Pan Chao	班昭	Shih Nai-an	施耐菴
P'an Chi-hsün	潘季馴	Shu	蜀
Pan Ku	班固	Shu Han	蜀漢
Pan Piao	班彪	*Shui hu chuan*	水滸傳
P'ei Chü	裴矩	So Ching	索靖
P'ei Hsiu	裴秀	*Spring and Autumn Annals*	春秋
P'i-pa	琵琶	Ssŭ-ma Ch'ien	司馬遷
Po Chü-i	白居易	Ssŭ-ma Kuang	司馬光
P'u Sung-ling	蒲松齡	Su Shih	蘇軾
Pure Land sect	淨土宗	Sui (dynasty)	隋
Record of Central Asia	西域傳	Sun Ch'ang-chih	孫暢之
Romance of Mu, Son of Heaven		Sun Kuo-t'ing	孫過庭
	穆天子傳	Sun Yat-sen	孫逸仙
San kuo chih yen i	三國志演義	Sung (dynasty)	宋
San ts'ai t'u hui	三才圖會	Sung Ying-hsing	宋應星
San tzŭ ching	三字經	Sung Yün	宋雲
Sêng-hui	僧會	*T'ai-p'ing huan yü chi*	
"Seven Sages of the			太平寰宇記
Bamboo Grove"	竹林七賢論	*T'ai-p'ing kuang chi*	太平廣記
Sha-t'o	沙陀	*T'ai-p'ing yü lan*	太平御覽
Shang (dynasty)	商	T'ang (dynasty)	唐
Shao Yung	邵雍	Tao-an	道安
Shên (state)	申	T'ao Ch'ien	陶潛
Shên Huai-yüan	沈懷遠	*Tao-tê-ching*	道德經
Shên Yüeh	沈約	T'ao Tsung-i	陶宗儀

T'ao Yüan-ming	陶淵明	Tung Tso-pin	董作賓
Taoism	道教	*T'ung chien kang mu*	通鑑綱目
Tea classic	茶經	*T'ung chih*	通志
Têng Ssǔ-yü	鄧嗣禹	T'ung oil	桐油
Thousand Character Classic		*T'ung tien*	通典
	千字文	*Tzǔ chih t'ung chien*	資治通鑑
Ti (tribe)	狄	*Tzǔ-hui*	字彙
T'ien kung k'ai wu	天工開物	Wan-li period	萬曆
T'ien-t'ai sect	天台宗	Wang An-shih	王安石
T'o-pa	拓跋	Wang Ch'i	王圻
T'o-pa Chün	拓跋濬	Wang Ching-wei	汪精衞
T'o-pa Hung	拓跋弘	Wang Ch'ung	王充
T'o-pa Ssǔ	拓跋嗣	Wang Fu	王浮
T'o-pa Tao	拓跋燾	Wang Fu-chih	王夫之
Ts'ai Hsiang	蔡襄	Wang Hsi-chih	王羲之
Ts'ao Chih	曹植	Wang Hsien-chih	王獻之
Ts'ao Hsüeh-ch'in	曹雪芹	Wang I-t'ung	王伊同
Ts'ao Ts'ao	曹操	Wang Mang	王莽
Tsin (dynasty)	晉	Wang Pi	王弼
Tso chuan	左傳	Wang Shih-chên	王世貞
Tsu Ch'ung-chih	祖沖之	Wang Shou-jên	王守仁
Ts'ui Hao	崔浩	Wang Ssū-i	王思義
Ts'ung-shu	叢書	Wang Su	王肅
Tu Fu	杜甫	Wang Wei	王維
T'u-chüeh	突厥	Wang Ying-lin	王應麟
Tu Yu	杜佑	Wei (dynasty)	魏
T'u-yü-hun	吐谷渾	Wei Po-yang	魏伯陽
Tung Cho	董卓	Wei Shou	魏收
Tung Hu	東胡	*Wei shu*	魏書

Wei Shuo	衞鑠	Yao Hsin-nung	姚莘農
Wei Wên-hsiu	韋文秀	Ye-lü Ch'u-ts'ai	耶律楚才
Wei Ying-wu	韋應物	Ye-lü Ta-shih	耶律大石
Wên-ch'êng	文成	Yen (state)	燕
Wên hsien t'ung k'ao	文獻通考	Yen-mên	雁門
Wu (state)	吳	Yen Shih-ku	顏師古
Wu, Empress	武后	Yen Yüan	顏元
Wu Ch'êng-ên	吳承恩	Yin	殷
Wu Ching-tzŭ	吳敬梓	*Yin-li p'u*	殷曆譜
Wu pei chih	武備志	*Ying tsao fa shih*	營造法式
Wu Tao-hsüan	吳道玄	Yü Fa-k'ai	于法開
Wu Tao-tzǔ	吳道子	Yüan, Emperor	元皇帝
Wu-ti	武帝	Yüan dynasty	元朝
Yang Chien	楊堅	Yüan Shih-k'ai	袁世凱
Yang Chu	楊朱	Yüeh	越
Yang Fu	楊孚	Yüeh-chih	月氏
Yang Hsüan-chih	楊衒之	Yüeh Shih	樂史
Yang Kuang	楊廣	Yung-chêng	雍正
Yao Ch'ung	姚崇	*Yung-lo ta-tien*	永樂大典

Chia Ssu-hsieh	賈思勰
Sun Yen	孫炎
Yin-yang	陰陽

Ch'ên Ch'êng	陳誠	Shên Kua	沈括
Jurchen	女真	Wu Han	吳晗
Lin Piao	林彪	Fu Chien	符堅

Index

Abacus, 180
Abbasid, 133, 140
Aborigines, 60, 144, 219, 221
Abū Zayd, 125
Abyssinia, 179
Academia Sinica, 233, 245
Academies, 135–136, 155–156, 168
Afghanistan, 45, 49, 60, 101
Africa, 150, 152, 158, 186, 194
Agate, 117, 123
Agriculture, 4, 5, 7, 17, 23, 29, 36, 45, 55–56, 83, 110, 127, 165, 198, 201–202, 203, 213, 232–233, 238, 242
Alans, 173
Alashan, 77
Alchemy, 67, 68, 70–71, 92, 111, 136
Alexander, 60
Alfalfa, 50
Almond, 142
Alphabet, 65, 174, 215, 228
Altai Mountains, 49, 51
Amber, 151
Ambrogio Lorenzetti, 179
America, 2, 201, 203, 204, 220, 221, 223, 226
American Revolution, 220
Amidst sect, see Pure Land sect
Amitabha, 88
Amitâyus sûtra, 64
Amoy, 196
Amphrite, 220
Amur River, 168, 220
An Shih-kao, 61, 64, 91
Analects of Confucius, 51, 54, 74, 87, 136, 168
Ancestors, 13, 14, 15, 40, 185
Anchor, 151

Anhui, 62, 100
Animals, 1, 2, 4, 27, 28, 39, 50, 175, 208
    See also Domestic animals
Annals, 31, 52, 71, 72, 134, 146, 186, 192
Annam, 13, 43, 98, 109, 113, 115, 120, 146, 148, 176, 178, 195, 209
Antiquities, 157, 229
Anyang, 8, 11
Arabia, 125, 159, 166, 194
Arabic, 114
Arabs, 80, 99, 120, 123–124, 125, 134, 140, 150, 151, 159, 178, 179, 181, 195, 203, 220, 222
Arboriculture, 34
Archeological finds, 1–2, 4, 7, 8–10, 17–18, 43, 46–47, 49, 73, 168
Archeologists, 7, 49, 187
Archeology, 128, 157, 233, 243
Archers (bowmen), 28, 30, 99, 114
Architecture, 8, 49, 65, 103–104, 105, 138, 157, 158, 172, 179, 181, 187, 208, 226
    naval, 150, 194
Areca, 50
Armenia, 174
Armies, 8, 32, 36, 39, 40, 45, 83, 100, 118, 161, 196, 232, 233, 240
Armor, 17, 30, 142, 164, 208
Arrowheads, 5, 16
Arsenic, 71
Artifacts, 5, 12
Artillery, 215
Aryans, 19

Asbestos, 117
Asia, 1, 18, 27, 35, 90, 125, 173,
    174, 178, 195
  central (or middle), 16, 19, 28,
    38, 45, 47, 49, 52, 64, 73,
    76–77, 90, 95, 99, 104, 106,
    115, 128, 131–132, 134–
    135, 141, 144, 160, 166–
    167, 179, 180, 182, 192,
    207, 220, 225
  eastern, 13, 18, 43, 60, 80, 84,
    101, 110, 141, 164, 172,
    174–175, 207
  northern, 101
  western, 4, 10, 19, 38, 39, 41,
    45, 77, 104–105, 126, 132,
    133, 158, 173, 174–175,
    178, 180, 190, 204
Asoka, 60, 103
Assam, 121, 137
Assyrian, 48
Astrology, 16, 47, 52
Astronomy, 16, 27, 30, 48, 51, 64,
    89, 129, 133, 142, 155, 180,
    203, 212, 213, 228, 233
Attila, 84
Australia, 242
Avars, 84, 98, 99, 101
Aviation, 235

Babylon, 16, 133
Bacon, Roger, 71
Bactria, 38, 45, 55, 60
Baghdad, 173, 180, 182
Balkan peninsula, 101
Bamboo, 4, 10, 13, 52, 55, 56, 75,
    79, 96, 153
Banditry, 60, 82, 143, 166
Bannermen, 216, 218
Banners, 214, 216
Barium, 28
Barley, 222
Basket, 17, 49
Bas-relief, 62, 65

Batavia, 220
Battle-axe, 16
Bazin, Louis, 98
Bean, 55, 56, 113, 222
Bells, 17
Bengal, Bay of, 27, 193
Bhutan, 241
Bibliographies, 51, 156
Bielenstein, Hans, 45
Bingham, 117
Binyon, Laurence, 94, 160
Bishop, Carl, 18, 35
Black Khitaï, see Kara-Khitaï
Boat women, 144
Boats, 39, 40, 50, 56, 77, 90–91,
    96, 113, 125, 150–151, 169,
    173, 176, 192–194, 209, 220
Bodhgayā, 65
Bokhara, 176
Bomb, 153, 238
Books, 23, 26, 51–52, 75, 141,
    144–145, 153, 154, 161,
    185–186, 204, 207, 228–230
  destruction of, 34, 72, 75, 126,
    184, 225
  proscription of, 70, 128, 187,
    200, 229, 230
Botany, 79, 158, 207, 208, 228,
    233
Bow and arrow, 4, 12, 16, 30, 82,
    100
Bowmen, mounted, 82, 100
Boxer uprising, 225
Brahminabad, 137
Breast strap, 56
Brick, 50, 56, 158
Bridges, 138, 197
Brigandage, 143, 199
  See also Banditry
British Museum, 94, 138
Bronze, 5, 7, 10, 16, 17, 18, 23,
    29, 42, 50, 56, 84, 130, 141,
    146, 157, 164, 181, 187

Bronze Age, 17, 19, 27
Buch der Natur, 208
Buddha, 127
Buddhism, 61–69, 70–71, 75–77, 80, 87, 88–92, 102–106, 108–110, 112, 117, 121, 123, 126–131, 134–135, 137, 138, 140–141, 144–146, 155, 159, 160–161, 165, 167, 170, 178, 182–183, 184–185, 188, 200, 210
Burial, 5, 13, 17, 28, 48, 49, 75, 112–113, 168, 185, 218
Burma, 76, 178, 202, 225, 237
Byzantines, 99, 181
Byzantium, 101, 178, 180

Cables, 231
Cactus, 203
Cadiz, 221
Cairo, 138, 180, 238
Calendar, 15, 16, 18, 30, 47–48, 52, 129, 133–134, 141, 144, 228
Caliphate, 138
Calligraphy, 73, 93–94, 141, 229
Cambodia, 64, 76, 77
Camel, 28, 41, 168
Canada, 242
Canal, 31, 34, 95, 117, 118, 119, 120, 145, 166, 170, 175, 197, 232
Cannon, 13, 153
Canon, *see* Classics
Canton, 39, 43, 54, 125, 132, 134, 137, 146, 149, 152, 154, 181, 194, 196, 203, 220, 221, 223, 224, 226, 240
Carrot, 179
Carter, Thomas Francis, 7, 144, 149
Caryatides, 181
Castiglione, Brother, 226
Catai, 97
Catalogue, 65, 75, 88, 157, 158, 229

Catapult, 153, 173
Cathay, 80, 164
Cattle, 5, 15, 16, 17, 56, 165
Cavalry, 32, 38, 45, 99–100
Cayenne pepper, 222
Ceramics, 150, 179, 181
Ceuta, 179
Ceylon, 60, 62, 64, 77, 90, 113, 159, 184, 194, 241
Chahar, 100, 215, 235
Chair, 150, 220
Champa, 76, 113, 115, 129, 150, 178, 209
Chan Kuo, 18
Ch'an sect, 69, 89, 108–109, 159, 161, 163
Chang Hêng, 48
Chang Hsüeh-ch'eng, 224
Chang Jung, 109
Chang Lu, 67
Ch'ang-an, 43, 44, 46, 60, 76, 83, 84, 89–91, 107, 116–124, 126, 127, 129, 130, 135–136, 138, 145, 185
Changes, Canon of, 51, 73, 75, 84, 136
Chao, 25
Early, 83
Later, 87, 92, 106
Chao Ju-kua, 158
Chao K'uang-yin, 146–148, 165
Chao Ming-ch'êng, 157
Ch'ao-chou, 195
Character, 10–13, 15, 50, 54, 73, 98, 112, 165, 170, 209
Chariot, 5, 17, 19, 30, 56, 83, 99
Charms, 4, 68, 141
Charts, *see* Maps
Chaulmoogra oil, 180, 208
Chekiang, 80, 108, 137, 146, 149, 158, 178, 186, 220
Ch'ên, 98, 103, 115
Ch'ên Ching-i, 158
Ch'ên Shou, 78
Ch'ên Ti, 206
Chêng, *see* Shih-huang-ti

Chêng Ch'iao, 157
Chêng family, 216
Chêng Ho, 192, 194
Ch'êng, *see* Shu
Ch'êng Chün-fang, 207
Ch'êng I, 95, 162
Ch'êng shih mo yüan, 207
Chengchou, 8
Ch'êng-tu, 58–59, 95, 124, 132, 144, 154
Chess, 13, 113–114
Chew, Arthur P., 221
Chi chiu chang, 87
Ch'i, 98
  northern, 98, 101, 131
  southern, 103, 105, 109
Chia Ssu-hsieh, 110
Chia Tan, 142
Ch'iang (Tibetans), 41, 82
Chiang Kai-shek, 234, 236–237, 239–240
Chiang-tu (Yangchow), 118
Ch'ien-lung reign, 226, 227
Chih-i (Chih-k'ai), 108
Chih-k'ai, *see* Chih-i
Chile, 196
Chin, state of, 53, 75
Chin dynasty, 169, 171–172, 180, 186, 215
  Later, 164
Chin p'ing mei, 210
Chin Shêng-t'an, 211
Ch'in, 18, 23, 30–36, 40, 41, 51, 100, 146
  Early, 100
Ch'in Chiu-shao, 159, 170
Ch'in-lun, 76
China root, 203
Chinese-English Dictionary, 12
Chinese Turkestan, 78, 101, 117
Ching hua yüan, 227–228
Ch'ing dynasty, 197, 214–232, 234
Chinkiang, 95, 132
Ch'iu Ch'u-chi, 183
Chive, 113

Chopsticks, 29
Chou, 18–30, 31, 37, 43, 46, 50, 97, 115
  northern, 98, 131
Chou Ch'ü-fei, 150, 158
Chou Ên-lai, 241
Chou Hsing-tz'ŭ, 110
Chou li, 162
Christian Topography, 113
Christianity, 41, 132, 182, 213
Christians, 125, 129, 167, 245
Chronicles of Liang or Wei, Chin and royal houses, 75
Chronography, 15–16, 47, 180, 203
Chu Chên-hêng, 180
Chu Hsi, 162–163, 185, 200, 205
Chu I-chün, 199
Chu Ssŭ-pên, 182, 186
Chu Tao-shêng, 89
Chu Ti, 190
Chu Tsai-yü, 207
Chu Yüan-chang, 189
Chu-ko Liang, 81
Ch'u, 18, 23, 32
Chü lu, 158
Ch'ü Yüan, 29
Ch'üan-chou, 137, 154, 176, 181, 194
Chuang-tzu, 24, 29, 37, 66, 109
Chuang-tzŭ, The, 67, 74, 136
Ch'un ch'iu, 18
Chungking, 236, 238
Chinchona, 222
Cinnabar, 10
Citrus fruit, 158
City gods, 69
Civil examinations, 51, 72, 117, 120, 135, 140, 141, 154–155, 178, 187, 197, 216, 218, 230
Civil servants, 135
Classics, 23, 51, 53, 73, 87, 109, 110, 126, 135–136, 145, 164, 170, 185, 200, 205, 228
Clavijo, 189

Clavius, 212
Clenell, 63
Clocks, 159
Cloisonné, 181
Clothing, 4, 17, 28, 36, 57, 65, 83, 98, 153, 157, 187, 209, 218
Coal, 97, 209
Cochin-China, 43, 76
Codes, see Laws
Coffin, 28
Co-hong, see Hong
Coke, 97
Collecting, 157
Collections, 111, 205, 229
Collectives, 242
Colleges, 51, 135, 155, 185, 233, 241, 244–245
Colonies, 4, 39, 42, 45, 58
Colonization, 189, 216, 219
Commentary on the Water Classic, 110
Communes, 242
Communists, 224, 234, 236, 237, 239–243
Compass, 111, 151
Composite bow, 16, 30
Concessions, foreign, 225, 233
Concubines, 194, 197, 218
Confucianism, 26, 37, 42–45, 51, 63, 72–76, 87, 92, 102, 109–111, 126, 134–137, 140–141, 145, 155, 160–161, 162–163, 168, 173, 185–188, 200, 205, 211
Confucius, 24, 29, 51, 54, 72–73, 120, 135, 167, 170, 185
Conversion of the Barbarians, The, 69–70
Copper, 16, 71, 96, 151, 154, 179, 192
Coral, 151
Coriander, 113
Cornelian, 151

Cosmas, 113
Cosmetics, 49, 96
Cotton, 150, 151, 201, 220, 239, 242
Cowry, 4, 27
Creel, 13
Cremation, 113, 184–185, 197
Cressey, 223
Crimea, 51, 172
Crossbow, 30, 100
Croton oil, 142
Crusades, 179
Crystal, 41, 151, 201
Ctesiphon, 137
Cuba, 243
Cucumber, 113
Currency, see Money
Custard apple, 221
Customs tariff, 236
Cycle, 15
Cyprus, 114

Dagger axes, 10, 17
Dairen, 239
Dalai Lama, 241
Damascus, 174
Dancers, 57, 117, 123, 131, 144, 188
Danube, 101, 178
Darius, 27, 35
Dates, 142
Deccan, 90
Deforestation, 219, 221
Degrees, 135, 186, 197–198, 230
Description of South China, 110
Dharmaraksa, 91
Dhyāna, see Ch'an sect
Dhyanabhadra, 160
Dialects, 14, 54
Diamonds, 58, 114, 221
Diamond Sūtra, 141, 144
Dictionaries, 12, 54, 112, 128, 144, 167, 170, 207, 209
Dieulafoi, 65

Distillation, 180
Divination, 5, 10, 23, 34, 51, 52, 144, 205
Dog, 4, 5, 15
Dollars, 203, 219
Domestic animals, 2, 4, 15–16, 26, 28, 41, 56, 96
Dominoes, 150
Donkeys, 28, 41
Drama, 140, 170, 172, 187–188, 210, 211, 244
Drawloom, 82
Drought, 82, 166, 207, 233
Drugs, see Medicine
Dubs, 7, 30, 42, 53, 66, 71, 96
Dutch, 196, 220–221, 222
Dwellings, 2, 4, 17, 29, 149
Dyes, 71, 209

East Indies, 116, 197, 221
Ebony, 151
Education, 51, 110, 120, 127, 154–155, 161, 168, 185, 226, 231, 233–234, 236, 243
Egypt, 10, 28, 179
Eisenhower, 240
Eitel, 65
Elephant, 62, 178
Embassies, 76, 111, 123, 245
Embroidery, 50, 123, 127
Encyclopedias, 114, 135, 139, 157–158, 161, 205, 207, 208, 228
Engineering, 27, 138, 149, 233
Engineers, 173, 180
England, 12, 114, 178, 188, 196, 198, 220, 221–225, 231, 236–237, 238, 241
Ennin, 129
Envoys, 38–39, 43, 50, 60, 76, 77, 82, 111, 116, 121, 125, 134, 141, 158, 168, 174, 176, 178, 184, 189, 190, 192, 194

Ephedrine, 159, 208
Epiphanius, 14
Epitaphs, 126
Essays, 74, 110, 139–140, 143, 156, 184
Ethics, 76, 160–161, 205, 212
Eunuchs, 14, 41, 45, 142, 190, 192, 199, 200
Eurasia, 190
Europe, 2, 16, 32, 42, 47, 71, 80, 81, 84, 93, 97, 104, 120, 124, 139, 146, 158, 173, 178–179, 183, 186, 195–196, 201–204, 211–212, 220, 226, 228, 231, 235, 239, 241
Examinations, 165, 173, 185, 233
See also Civil examinations
Excavation, 233
Expeditions, 35–36, 39–40, 43, 90, 113, 116, 121, 190
See also Naval expeditions
Explosive powder, 152–153
Extraterritoriality, 224, 236
Eyeglasses, 201

Fa-hsien, 90–91, 113
Fa Yüan Ssŭ, 121
Falconry, 56
Family Sayings of Confucius, 73
Famine, 27, 48, 60, 82, 145, 166, 175, 207, 219, 233, 237
Fan Chên, 110
Fan-ch'êng, 153
Fang I-chih, 228
Fang shih mo p'u, 207
Fang Yü-lu, 207
Fans, 96, 150, 220
Farmer, 32, 40, 55, 60, 81, 93, 180, 198, 201–202, 207, 222, 243
Farming, 4, 7, 15, 34, 165
Fei (river), 100
Ferghana, 39, 77, 125

Feudalism, 14, 24, 31, 34, 37, 60, 142
Fiction, 65, 140, 156, 159, 205, 210, 226, 228
Fig, 142
Filial Piety, Book of, 73, 87, 109, 136
Fire, 1, 48
Firecracker, 152–153, 154
First Emperor, *see* Shih-huang-ti
Fishing, 1, 4, 42, 57, 165
Five dynasties, the, 143
Flax, 113
Fleets, 149, 169, 176, 195
Flood control, 36, 96, 149, 170, 197
Floods, 8, 27, 31, 48, 82, 145, 166, 207
Flowers, 158
Folklore, *see* Legends
Foochow, 203
Food, 1, 2, 4, 8, 31, 50, 113, 117, 142, 202, 239, 242
  crops, 1, 55, 175, 201, 219, 221, 222
Foot binding, 144, 218
Football, 57
Foreign relations, 76, 77, 79, 101, 116, 117, 121, 123, 174, 178, 194, 195, 196, 219–220, 225, 235–236
Formosa, 216
Fossils, 1
Fo-t'u-têng, 87, 88, 97, 106
Fowl, 27
France, 65, 180, 183, 220–221, 225, 231, 240
Franciscans, 179
Freer Gallery, 7
Frescoes, 138, 165
Fruit, 50, 55, 56, 79, 96, 158, 175
Fu, Prince of, 199

Fu Hsi, 109
Fu I, 126–127
Fu Chien, 100
Fu-nan, 76, 77
Fujiwara, 134
Fukien, 34, 115, 125, 134, 149, 182, 195, 196, 202, 219, 221, 227, 234, 245
Furniture, 29, 157, 204, 220
Furs, 16, 41, 56, 84, 117

Galileo, 42, 213
Games, 57, 208
  backgammon, 113
  chess, 13, 113–114
  dice, 96
  dominoes, 150
  football, 57
  juggling, 56, 76
  knuckle bones, 57
  pitch-pot, 57
  playing cards, 150, 179
  polo, 142
  wei-ch'i, 57
Gandhara, 55, 64, 90, 106, 108, 128, 160
Gardens, 29, 50, 149, 197
Gascony, 178
Gauchet, 181
Gazetteers, 95–96, 206
Genealogies, 86
Geography, 28, 54, 66, 77–79, 110, 157, 186, 203, 205, 206, 207, 212, 228, 229
Geomancers, 151
Germany, 152, 225, 235–236
Giles, Dr. Herbert A., 12, 93, 126, 185
Giraffe, 194
Glass, 28, 50, 137, 181, 201
Gnomon, 47, 129, 181
Goa, 212

Gobi, 2, 31, 99
Gold, 29, 39, 40, 41, 42, 70, 84, 92, 111, 113, 130, 151, 199, 221
Government, 5, 8, 10, 14–19, 21, 23, 26, 32, 35, 36, 40, 45, 55–56, 58, 60, 71, 103, 110, 119, 120, 123, 130, 134, 140, 142, 145, 155, 161, 169, 173, 176, 186, 189, 198, 206, 215
Grain, 31, 36, 38, 40, 69, 81, 96, 119, 151, 209
Granaries, 36, 117, 119, 166, 174, 175
Granet, 66
Grape, 50
  wine, 179
Great Britain, see England
Great Wall, 26, 32, 36, 37, 83, 84, 96, 98, 99, 102, 115, 117, 129, 133, 167, 171, 180, 197, 215
Greece, 13, 24, 27, 28, 42, 55, 104, 138, 149, 192, 201
Grenade, 153, 172
Guerrillas, 237, 239
Guitar, 104, 180
Gunpowder, 71, 152–153, 179

Hai River, 118
Hainan, 43, 156, 240
Hakozaki Bay, 176
Halberd, 16
Halley's comet, 30
Hami, 101, 116, 190
Han, 38, 40, 43–57, 58, 66, 73–75, 83, 87, 97, 99, 105, 109, 111–112, 117, 126, 139, 146, 148, 157
  northern, 146
  northern (early Chao), 82
Han History, 165
Han Kao-tsu, see Liu Chi

Han River, 149
Han Yěn-chih, 158
Han Yü, 140, 156
Hangchow, 4, 56, 118, 146, 148, 149, 154, 156, 159
Hanoi, 129
Hanlin, 136, 184, 229
Hanyang, 243
Harness, 17, 56, 100
Harun-al-Raschid, 125
Hemp, 4, 17
Hêng-shan, 108
Henry III of Castile, 189
Herat, 192
Herbal for Relief from Famine, 207
Herrmann, 78
Hinayana, 64, 89
Hindu, 28, 77
Historians, 16, 48, 52, 143, 192, 224
Historical criticism, 228
Historiography, bureau of, 186
History, 5, 16, 23, 52, 72, 136, 139, 149, 152, 156, 157, 162, 163, 165, 186, 229
History, Document of, 51, 72–73, 87, 136, 162, 206
Hog, see Pig
Hominid, 1–2, 244
Homo sapiens, 2
Honan, 4, 7, 8, 19, 21, 28, 32, 100, 101, 103, 125, 158, 172, 194
Hong, 224
Hongkong, 224, 237
Hopei, 103, 138, 235
Hormuz, 194
Horse, 5, 15, 16, 17, 28, 30, 41, 50, 56, 77, 99–100, 145, 148, 165, 167, 168, 171, 173, 175, 192

Horsemen, 38, 80, 83, 100—101, 171
Horticulture, 158
Hsi Han, 79
Hsi K'ang, 74
Hsi yu chi, 210
Hsi Wang Mu, *see* Mother Queen of the West
Hsia, 5, 8
Hsia (Tangut), 167, 168
Hsiang-yang, 153
Hsiao T'ung, 111
Hsieh Ho, 111
Hsieh Hsüan, 100
Hsieh Shih, 100
Hsien-pi, 77, 139, 164
Hsien-yang, 32, 36
Hsin (dynasty), 41—43
Hsiung-nu, 32, 37—41, 45, 51, 77, 78, 82, 83, 84, 101
Hsü Hung-tsu, 206—207
Hsü Kuang-ch'i, 213
Hsüan-tsang, 127—128, 137, 140, 210
Hsüan-tsung, 123, 124, 136—137
Hu (central Asiatic nomads), 41, 83
Hu, Empress, 106
Hu Shih, Dr., 63, 106, 110, 158, 163, 206
Huai, 83
Huai Basin, 125
Huai River, 95, 169
Huan River, 7
Huan Wên, 95
Huang Ch'ao, 125, 134
Huang Tsung-hsi, 227
Huang-ti, 53, 61, 66, 70
Hui-chiao, 105
Hui-i, 106
Hui-shêng, 106
Hui-ssŭ, 108

Hui-tsung, Emperor, 160
Hui-yüan, 88
Hulagu, 173
Hummel, Arthur, 97, 102, 135, 227
Hunan, 108
Hung lou mêng, 230
Hungary, 123
Huns, *see* Hsiung-nu
Hunting, 1, 4, 14, 42, 50, 57, 165, 168, 175
Hupeh, 149
Hydraulics, 176, 180, 213
Hymn to the Holy Trinity, 132

I and Ti tribes, 36
I wu chih (Record of Strange Things), 79
I-ching, 128, 140
I-hsing, 129
Iberian peninsula, 201
Ibn Batuta, 194
Ili, 116, 190
Illiteracy, 183, 233, 243
Immolation, 15, 106, 112, 197
Incense, 65, 151, 181
Indemnities, 225
India, 4, 13, 16, 19, 35, 43, 45, 48, 60, 65, 68, 69, 77, 89, 90, 91, 92, 96, 104, 106, 110, 112, 113, 117, 121, 123, 127—128, 129, 133, 137—138, 141, 150—152, 159, 160, 161, 179, 184, 192, 194, 201, 203, 210, 220, 222, 237, 241
Indian corn, *see* Maize
Indian Ocean, 39, 50, 60, 76, 77, 124, 195, 220
Indo-China, 49, 113, 149, 204, 225, 237
Indo-Iranian, 98
Indonesia, 159, 241

Inductive method, 206
Indus, 27, 123
Industrial Revolution, 224
Industry, 55–56, 71, 80, 208, 233,
    237, 238, 239, 242
Ink, 10, 29, 141, 207, 209
Inscriptions, 5, 10–11, 14, 16,
    120, 132, 141, 145, 157,
    165, 181
    rubbings of, 141
Insulin, 244
Interpreters, 111, 170, 209
Iodine, 208
Iran, 27, 43, 56, 64, 67, 88, 104,
    121, 124, 151, 172, 181
Iron, 2, 23, 29, 40, 42, 56, 71, 84,
    96, 97, 130
Irrigation, 15, 23, 31, 58, 81, 96,
    145, 178, 190, 198, 224,
    233
Islam, 124, 134, 160, 182, 184,
    192
Italy, 114, 179, 201, 212, 225
Ivory, 16, 17, 151, 204

Jade, 10, 29, 41, 49, 50, 81, 130
Jakarta, 241
Japan, 2, 13, 35, 39, 45, 47, 78,
    80, 88, 96, 105, 111, 116,
    120, 125, 128, 129, 134,
    135, 136, 138, 139, 141,
    145, 146, 150, 152, 162,
    166, 176, 180, 181, 184,
    195–196, 203, 204, 208,
    209, 212, 220, 227, 231,
    233, 234–235, 236, 237,
    238, 239
Japanese, 111, 244
Jasmine, 142
Jātaka tales, 65
Java, 64, 76, 90, 150, 152, 178,
    190, 194, 223

Jehol, 100, 235
Jenghis, 167, 168, 171–175, 183,
    215
Jerusalem, 137
Jesuits, 150, 212, 213, 228
Jesus, 24
Jewelry, 4, 5, 50, 204, 220
Jews, 125, 134, 151
Jîvaka, 91
John of Plano Carpini, 186
Jou-jan, *see* Avars
Journalism, 231
Ju lin wai shih, 230
Juan-juan, *see* Avars
Judaism, 134, 182
Jung Ch'i-ch'i, 164
Junks, *see* Boats
Jupiter, 28, 30
Jurchen, 111, 144, 148, 153, 157,
    159, 164, 166, 168–170,
    171–172, 183, 185, 196,
    210, 214–215, 218, 229

Kaempfer, 222
Kaifeng, 31, 132, 147, 148, 154,
    158, 164, 172, 182, 207
Kalgan, 99
Kalpa, 68
Kanishka, 65
Kansu, 2, 19, 21, 37, 45, 78, 90,
    100, 103, 116, 124, 132,
    144, 166, 167, 175, 181,
    184, 225, 234
K'ang-hsi reign, 226
K'ang Yu-wei, 228
Kao Hsien-chih, 124
Kao sêng chuan, 105
Kaolin, 208
Kara-Khitaï, 167
Karakhoto, 168, 187
Karakorum, 170, 174, 189–190
Karashar, 90
Karlgren, 7

Karnamak, 114
Kashgar, 89, 167
Kashmir, 64, 69, 89, 128, 241
Kennedy, President, 241
Khanbaliq, 175
Kharizm, 168
Khitan, 123–125, 143, 144, 146–
    147, 164–169, 171, 173,
    185, 209, 218, 229
Khotan, 50, 62, 64, 66, 77, 90
Khrushchev, 243–244
Kiangsi, 67, 75, 80, 92, 234
Kiangsu, 61, 62, 66, 79, 95, 126,
    149
Kin dynasty, *see* Chin dynasty
Kirghizia, 51
Kishmayu, 150
Kite, 114
Ko Hung, 92
Koguryŏ, 98, 116, 121, 123
Kokonor, 84
Kolberg cathedral, 179
Koran, 181
Korea, 13, 18, 35, 39, 45, 47, 49,
    77, 84, 88, 95, 98, 101, 111,
    116, 119, 120, 123, 125,
    128, 135, 136, 138, 139,
    141, 144–145, 158, 163,
    165, 172, 173, 176, 178,
    181, 190, 196, 203–204,
    209–210, 214–215, 218,
    220, 239, 240
Korean, 111
K'ou Ch'ien-chih, 67
Kozlov, Colonel, 187
Ku Ch'i-yüan, 192
Ku Hui, 79
Ku K'ai-chih, 94
Ku Yen-wu, 228
Kuang-chou chi, 79
Kuangsi, 34, 75, 189
Kuangtung, 34, 76, 79, 112, 144,
    160, 219, 221, 227
Kubilai 170, 175–176, 178–181,
    183–185, 186, 200

Kucha, 64, 77, 89, 92, 99, 105,
    128
Kufa, 140
Kumārajīva, 89, 90, 96
Kunming, 239
K'un-ch'ü, 211
K'ung family, 71
Kuo Hsiang, 74
Kuo K'an, 173
Kuo Shou-ching, 175, 180–182
Kuo-tzŭ-chien, 185
Kuomintang, 234, 237
Kushan, 44, 45, 61
Kuwabara, 176
Kweichow, 189, 223

Lacquer, 29, 49, 56, 187, 220
Ladakh, 241
Lake Balkash, 84, 219
Lama church, 181–182, 184, 186
Land reform, 142, 242
Landscapes, 95, 138, 159, 204
Language, 2, 14, 28, 29, 54, 61,
    65, 83, 90, 98, 105, 111–
    112, 139, 170, 174, 188,
    206, 209, 212, 228
Lao-tzŭ, 24, 26, 37, 53, 61, 66,
    69, 70, 74
Lao-tzŭ, The, 66–67, 136–137
Latin, 13, 23
Latin America, 241
Latticework, 220
Lattimore, 167
Laufer, 71, 81, 114, 152, 204
Law, 26, 35, 72, 226
Laws, 23, 32, 54, 120, 135, 145,
    155, 158, 161, 165, 167,
    187, 190, 197, 206, 212,
    229, 233
Lead, 71, 151
Leather, 17, 84
Legations, 224
Legends, 1, 23, 54, 62, 65, 91,
    106, 114, 140
Lemons, 142

Lentils, 150
Leprosy, 180
Lettuce, 142
Lew Chew Islands, 116, 209
Lexicon, 141, 144
Lhasa, 174
Li, 62, 78, 79, 141
Li Chieh, 158
Li Chih, 200, 211
Li Ch'ing-chao, 158
Li family, 119, 134
Li Fang, 157
Li Ju-chên, 228
Li Kung, 227
Li Ling, General, 78
Li Po, 139, 156
Li Shih-chên, 208
Li Shih-min, 119, 120, 121, 123, 127, 137
Li Ssŭ, 32
Li Tao-yüan, 110
Li Tzŭ-ch'êng, 200
Li-Yeh, 170
Li Yen, 128
Li Yüan, 119
Li-ch'êng, 104
Li-chih p'u, 158
Liang, 98, 105, 106, 110, 114
 later, 90, 98, 103, 110, 112, 113, 115
 state of, 75
Liang-chou, 90
Liao, western, *see* Kara-Khitaï
Liao chai chih i, 228
Liao dynasty, 148, 160, 165–166, 170, 186
Liao River, 98
Liaotung, 39, 47, 123, 164, 197, 214
Libraries, 51, 71, 72, 75, 96, 135, 156, 157, 178, 204, 228, 229, 233–234
Lin-an, 148
Lin-i, 76
Lin Piao, 244

Ling-hsien, 48
Lion, 28, 117
Litchi nut, 50
Literacy, 236
Literary criticism, 53–54, 205, 231
Literature, 23, 28, 34, 46, 51–52, 54, 65, 72–75, 79, 92–93, 108, 110–111, 114, 135, 137, 139–140, 149, 156–159, 167–168, 184, 186–188, 189, 204–210, 227–231, 244
Liu Chi, 36–38
Liu Hsieh, 111
Liu Hsin, 47
Lui I-ch'ing, 111
Liu Ling, 74
Liu Shao-ch'i, 243
Liu Sung, 98, 103
Lo (river), 21, 47, 101
Loans, 42, 235
Lo Kuan-chung, 210
Lo-lang, 39, 49
Lob-nor, 77
Loess, 2, 17, 97
Logic, 212
London, 221, 226
Lord of Chang, 24, 26, 31
Lotus sect, *see* Pure Land sect
Louis IX, 183
Loyang, 43, 46, 51, 58, 59, 60, 61, 64, 65, 72, 74, 83, 88, 92, 103, 104, 106, 110, 117, 118, 126, 127, 130, 132–133, 145–146, 150, 154, 164
Lu Chi, 97
Lu Chiu-yüan, 163
Lu Kuei-mêng, 137
Lu Tz'ŭ, 139
Lu Yüan-lang, 139
Lu Yün, 97
Lung Hu, Mount, 67
Lung-mên, 104
Lü Kuang, 90

Ma Hao, 62
Ma Tuan-lin, 157
Macao, 149, 196, 203, 212, 222
Magadha, 90, 160
Magellan, 220
Magnetic needle, 151
Mahābodhi temple, 65
Mahāyāna, 64, 89, 106
Maize, 201, 221, 222
Malacca, 194, 201, 221
Malaya, 237
Malaysia, 150, 197, 210
Manchu, 111
Manchuria, 2, 13, 18–19, 21, 37,
    45, 77, 84, 95, 100, 102,
    116, 123, 125, 143–144,
    171, 178–179, 189–190,
    196–197, 200, 203, 214–
    231, 235, 236, 238–239,
    240, 243
Mangonels, 153
Mangu, 183
Manicheism, 133, 182
Manila, 197, 203, 219
Mao Tsê-tung 240–243
Mao Yüan-i, 208
Maps, 78, 142, 164, 186, 206,
    208, 212, 229
Marco Polo, 97, 175, 184
Marcus Aurelius Antoninus, 76
Margouliès, 74
Marin of Tyre, 78
Maritime customs, 195, 224, 231
Marriage, 14, 23, 68, 70, 87, 228
Marsenne, 207
Marshall, General George C., 239
Mathematics, 28, 48, 111, 129,
    135, 159, 170, 180, 203,
    212, 213, 228, 229
Mathura, 104
Matsu, 241
Maurice, 99
Mazdaism, see Zoroastrianism

McMahon, Arthur, 241
Medicine, 34, 51, 64, 71, 91–92,
    96, 128–129, 140, 142, 151,
    155, 159, 179, 180, 184,
    192, 208, 220, 222, 233
Mediterranean, 13, 28, 50, 76,
    113, 179
Mei Tsu, 206
Mei Ying-tso, 209
Mekong River, 207
Mencius, 29
Mencius, The, 163
Mercury, 71
Mesopotamia, 173
Metals, 5, 8, 10, 209
Mexico, 196, 203, 221
Mica, 96
Military science, 28, 51, 155, 167,
    172–173, 208
Millet, 4, 8, 179, 202, 222
Minaret, 181
Mines, 199, 209, 231, 232
Ming, 113, 169–170, 182, 183,
    184, 189–213, 215–216,
    218, 219, 226–227, 230
Ming, emperor, 49
Ming shih kao, 213
Miniatures, 179
Minor arts, 112, 138, 204, 207,
    226
Mirror, bronze, 29, 49–50
Missionaries, Buddhist, 61, 62–63,
    64, 65, 87, 88, 91, 105, 109,
    128, 160
    Manichean, 133
    Nestorian, 132–133
    Protestant, 224, 234
    Roman Catholic, 203, 212–213,
    224, 234
Monasteries, 102, 108, 146, 154,
    156, 165
Mohammedans, see Moslems
Money, 4, 23, 35, 40, 42, 60,

130, 145, 151–152, 174–175, 179, 196, 203, 221, 233, 239, 242
Mongha, *see* Mangu
Mongol, 98, 111
Mongolia, 2, 13, 37, 47, 49, 51, 77, 78, 80, 82, 84, 101, 111, 116, 120, 123, 133, 143–144, 148–149, 152, 153, 160, 164, 168, 171–188, 189–190, 192, 195, 197, 200, 209, 214–215, 216, 220, 221, 229
Mongoloid race, 2, 86
Monks, 61–62, 66, 67, 75, 77, 88, 89, 91, 93, 102, 103, 105, 106, 127, 129, 130–131, 132, 133, 139, 160, 161, 183
  See also Priests
Monuments, 48, 55, 72, 96, 103, 158, 206, 225, 233
Moors, 201
Morals, 26, 63, 70, 72, 74, 163
Morocco, 124
Moscow, 178, 241, 243
Moslems, 93, 114, 124, 125, 134, 144, 167, 175–176, 180–181, 184, 192, 202, 212, 225
Mosques, 176, 181
Mother Queen of the West, 66
Mo Ti, 24, 26
Motor roads, 235, 241
Moule, A. C., 132
Mountains, 206, 207
Movable type, 154
Mukden, 197, 214, 216
Mule, 28, 41
Museums, 243
Music, 17, 28, 46, 54, 55, 56–57, 65, 104–105, 129, 141–142, 164, 179, 180, 187, 188, 207, 211, 244

Nan chao, 148
Nan Yüeh, 39
Nan-fang ts'ao-mu chuang (Flora of the Southern Regions), 79
Nankeen, 220
Nanking, 58, 59, 64, 65, 69, 76, 84, 91–92, 98, 106, 189–195, 206, 220, 234, 235, 237
Nank'ou pass, 180
Nara, 136, 138
National Academy, 135, 145
National bibliography, 86, 96
Nationalists, 223, 239–241
Naval architecture, 150
Naval expeditions, 176, 192–195
Navigation, 151, 194
Navy, 150, 195
Nayan, 178
Near East, 27, 28
Needham, Joseph, 129, 159, 204
Negritos, 86
Neo-Confucianism, 161–163
Neolithic, 4–6, 17
Nepal, 88, 121, 160
Nestorians, 131, 132, 133, 170, 178, 182, 183
New Delhi, 241
New Remarks on the Study of Resonant Tubes, 207
Newspapers, 244
Nien-fei, 225
Nine-power conference, 235
Ning-hsia, 167–168, 234
Ningpo, 154, 169, 195–196
Nomads, 19, 56, 83, 99, 167, 171, 183
North America, 2, 11
Novel, 210, 226, 228
Novgorod, 178
Nuclear Explosives, 244
Nuns, 102, 126–127, 128, 129, 130–131, 133, 161
Nurhachi, 169, 214–215
Nursing, 233

Obata, S., 120, 139
Ocarina, 17
Odes, Book of, 23, 51, 87, 136, 162, 206
Ogihara, 65
Ogodai, 172, 185
Oirats, 195
Ojibways, 10
Olive, 142
Onion, 113
Opening of ports to trade, 224–225
Opium, 222–225
Optical lenses, 201
Oranges, 50
Ordos, 100, 116
Organ with reeds, 180
Orkhon River, 102, 120–121, 165
Ostrich, 194
Otrar, 190
Ou-yang Hsiu, 143, 156
Ou-yang Hsün, 73
Oxen, *see* Cattle
Oxus River, 64, 183

Paddle wheel, 151
Paekche, 88, 98, 123
Pahlavi, 114
Painting, 29, 48–49, 94–95, 103, 111–112, 138, 149, 159–160, 179, 187, 204, 225, 226, 243
Palaces, 8, 34, 46, 49, 117, 175
Palembang, 194
Paleolithic, 1–4
Palmyra, 51
Pamirs, 28, 38, 60, 123, 124, 167, 219
Pan Chao, 53
P'an Chi-hsün, 166
Pan Ku, 53
Pan Piao, 53
Pandita, 160
Paper, 52, 141, 152

Paper money, 145, 152, 174, 179
Paris, 174, 179, 221, 226
Parliament, 223
Parthia, 28, 30, 61–62, 64
Pataliputra, 90
Paulus Jovius, 179
Pea, garden, 113
Peanut, 202, 221–222
Pearls, 39, 50, 151, 209
Peasants, 8, 87, 120, 142, 199, 214, 241
P'ei Hsiu, 78–79
Peichihli Gulf, 2, 166
P'ei Chü, 116
Peiping, *see* Peking
Peking, 121, 159, 172, 174–175, 179–180, 185, 187, 189, 190, 191, 192, 194, 197, 198, 200, 206, 215, 216, 218, 221, 226, 235, 236, 240, 241
Peking man, *see* Hominid
Pelliot, Professor, 64, 79, 96, 97, 228
People's Republic, 240–244
Pepper, 142
Peroz, 123
Persia, 16, 27, 55, 101, 114, 120, 123, 125, 129, 131, 132, 133, 138, 150, 152, 171, 172, 174, 178–181, 204, 209
Persian Gulf, 192
Peru, 221
Pescadores, 115, 196, 225, 241
Peshawar, 65, 104
Pesos, 196, 203
Phalansteries, 70, 102, 201
Philip the Fair, 178–179
Philippines, 150, 152, 196, 197, 202, 204, 219
Philology, 13, 139, 157, 205–206, 228, 229, 233
Philosophy, 109, 160, 163, 229
Phoenician alphabet, 174
Phonetics, *see* Philology

Phonology, *see* Philology
P'i-pa, 55
Pied du Roy, 180
Pien-liang, 148
Pig, 2, 5, 15, 56, 81
Pilgrimages, 65–66, 90, 105, 106–108, 127–128, 129, 131, 160, 183, 200, 210
Pineapple, 221
Piracy, 113, 125, 152, 195, 197, 222
Pistachio, 179
Plague, 233
Planes, 245
Planets, 30, 133
Plato, 164
Playing cards, 150, 179
Plow, 17, 23, 28, 29, 55–56
Plumes, 16
Po Chü-i, 139
P'o-hai, 125, 164–165, 169
Poetry, 23, 29, 51, 54, 66, 74, 93, 139, 149, 156, 165, 167, 210, 228
Poland, 176
Polo, 142
Pomegranate, 113
Pomerania, 179
Pope, 229
Population, 8, 21, 39, 40, 42, 45, 86, 138, 150, 161, 202, 206, 216, 219, 243
   transfer of, 31, 60
Porcelain, 49, 71, 80, 137–138, 150, 151, 179, 196, 203, 220, 226
Port Arthur, 239
Portugal, 194, 195, 196, 203, 220, 222, 242
Potato, 222
Potter's wheel, 4
Pottery, 2, 4, 5, 8, 9–10, 17, 49, 56, 137–138, 150, 187, 203, 209
   figurine, 112
P'oyang Lake, 92

Prayer cylinder, 181
President (of the Republic), 234
Priests, 10, 14, 15, 21, 68, 70, 103, 105, 106, 126–129, 133, 139, 141, 183, 200, 218, 228
Printing, 52, 138–139, 141, 144–145, 154, 156, 161, 167, 179, 188
Proscriptions, 109, 133, 137, 146, 200
Protestants, 231, 234
Prussia, 179
Ptolemy, 78
Pusan, 192
P'u Sung-ling, 228
Public works, 8, 15, 27, 35–36, 117, 119, 149, 166, 170, 174–175, 189, 197, 232, 233
   See also Irrigation; Roads
Publishing, 234
Puppetry, 57
Pure Land sect, 88–89, 108, 125
Pyong-yang, 39, 121, 123, 196
Pythagorean musical scale, 28

Queue, 218, 230
Quemoy, 241

Rabban Sauma, 178
Radio, 235, 244
Railroads, 231, 233, 235, 242
Rape seed, 222
Rashid-eddin, 179
Read, Dr. Bernard, 97, 208
Rebellion, 31, 36, 37, 43, 46, 103, 115, 124–125, 173, 190, 234–235
Record of Central Asia, The, 69
Red Guards, 241–243
Reference books, 228
Reforestation, 233
Reforms, 42, 161–162, 225, 226, 228, 233, 241

Régis, 228
Reichelt, 63
Reischauer, Edwin O., 129
Religion, 5, 8, 10, 14, 15, 16, 40,
    48, 60–74, 76, 83, 87–89,
    92, 102, 104, 106, 108–110,
    112, 120, 124, 126–137,
    138, 149, 160–162, 165,
    168, 170, 171, 181–186,
    200, 213, 231, 244
Renaissance, European, 212
Republic, 203, 226, 232–243
Revolt of three viceroys, 215–216
Revolution, 190, 200, 225, 230
    cultural, 230, 234
Revolving bookcase, 109
Rhinoceros, 39, 151
Rhyme, 23, 185, 206
Ricci, 207, 212–213, 228
Rice, 4, 8, 27, 55, 66, 68, 150, 222
Richardson, Samuel, 230
Riots, 245
Ritual, 8, 15, 18, 19, 25, 26, 40,
    72, 157
Rituals, Rites (Book of), 51, 87,
    136
Roads, 27, 32, 34–35, 68, 97, 118,
    145, 166, 174, 175, 197,
    232, 235, 242
Roman Catholicism, 182, 212–213,
    228
Romance of Mu, Son of Heaven, 75
Rome, 30, 39, 42, 43, 81, 84, 99,
    138, 174, 178, 182, 212
Rugs, 41, 203, 220
Russia, 4, 21, 123, 152, 168, 172,
    174, 176, 178, 180, 196,
    212, 220, 224, 225, 238–
    240
Russian Turkestan, 101

Sachs, Curt, 105, 179
Saeki, 132
Safflower, 113

Saffron, 142
Sails, 77, 81, 151, 204
Saint-Denis, 179
St. Petersburg, 221
Sainte Chapelle, 179
Sakyamuni, 69
Salt, 40, 42, 96, 130, 199, 209
Saltpeter, 153, 179, 221
Salween River, 207
Samarkand, 167, 189, 192
San Francisco, 238
San kuo chih yen i, 210–211
San ts'ai t'u hui, 208
San Tzŭ Ching, 185
Sanskrit, 13, 28, 61, 65, 90, 105,
    111, 128, 137, 140, 160
Sapan wood, 151
Sassanid, 123
Saturn, 30
Sayyid Ajall, see Seyyid Edjell
Schall, 228
Schools, 72, 135, 168, 173, 233,
    236, 241, 244
    public, 155, 245
    technical, 231, 245
Science, 16, 23, 28, 30, 46–48, 70,
    149, 157, 159, 163, 180,
    205, 212, 233
Screens, 96
Sculpture, 17, 48–49, 62, 95, 103–
    104, 138, 154, 204
Scythians, 21, 28, 51, 64, 77, 100
Sea wall, 149
Seals, 50, 141, 157
Secret societies, 133, 190, 225
Sedan chair, 96–97, 150
Seismograph, 48
Sêng-hui, 65, 69
Seoul, 39, 196
Sesame, 113
"Seven Sages of the Bamboo
    Grove," 74
Seyyid Edjell, 176
Shadow play, 57

Sha-t'o, 143
Shahrukh, 192
Shallot, 113
Shaman, 170
Shang, 7–12, 15, 16, 18, 19, 29, 50
Shanghai, 54, 234, 235, 236, 240
Shansi, 5, 8, 80, 83, 90, 97–98, 101, 103–104, 125, 131, 146, 188
Shantung, 4, 8, 35, 39, 62, 66, 80, 91, 96, 103–104, 110, 125, 166, 172, 183, 195, 197, 199, 210, 235
Shanyang, 118
Shao-hsing, 80, 95, 137
Shao Yung, 159, 162, 163
Shastras, 89, 106
Sheep, 5, 15, 38, 56
Shên, 21
Shên Huai-yüan, 110
Shên Kua, 181
Shên Yüeh, 112
Shên-tsung, Emperor, 161
Shensi, 19, 31, 32, 67, 95, 103, 118, 184, 225, 234
Shih chi, 52
Shih huang-ti, 32, 36, 37, 38, 42
Shih Hu, 88
Shih Nai-an, 210
Shrines, 128, 129, 131, 197, 200
Shryock, 72
Shu, 95
Shu (Shu Han), 58–59
Shui hu chuan, 154, 185, 210–211
Siam, 86, 180, 190, 209
Sian, 8, 19, 20, 181, 236
Siberia, 2, 51, 104, 196, 220
Sicily, 159
Sikkim, 241
Silk, 7, 10, 17, 28, 29, 38, 39, 41, 42, 51–52, 82, 112, 127, 138, 148, 152, 160, 196, 220, 221, 222, 230, 242
Silla, 98, 123, 125

Silver, 29, 84, 113, 130, 148, 151, 174–175, 199, 203, 221, 223
Singapore, 152, 194
Sinkiang, 241
Sioux, 10
Six ministries, 216
Slavery, 16, 42, 56, 121, 131, 197
Smallpox inoculation, 159, 208
Snuff, 221
So Ching, 73
Society of Jesus, *see* Jesuits
Socrates, 24, 164
Sogdiana, 38, 39, 45, 62–65, 69, 76, 77, 105, 133
Soil erosion, 219
Somaliland, 159
Soochow, 54, 192, 211
Sorghum, 179, 202, 221–222
South America, 203
South Seas, 64, 76–77, 192
Sowing machine, 82
Soybean, 55, 222
Spain, 124, 196, 202, 203, 219, 221
Spanish America, 203, 219–220
Spear, 4, 16
Spear head, 18
Spherical trigonometry, 181
Spices, 192, 221
Spinach, 142
Spring and Autumn Annals, 51, 72, 87
Squash, 222
Sron-bcan-sgan-po, 121
Ssŭ-ma Ch'ien, 47, 52–54, 56
Ssŭ-ma Kuang, 110, 150, 156, 162–163
Stalin, 241, 243
Statues, 104, 105, 106, 128, 146, 164
Statutes, 216
Steamships, 231
Stele, 132
Stirrup, 100–101
Stramonium, 208

Stūpa, 62, 64, 65, 109, 146, 197
Su Shih, 156, 161
Su Sung, 159
Subhakarasimha, 129
Subotai, 172, 176
Sugar, 209
　beet, 142
　candy, 221
　refining, 180, 209
Sui, 86, 114, 115–119, 120, 126–142, 146
Sulphur, 71, 153, 192
Sumatra, 194
Sun Ch'ang-chih, 111
Sun Kuo-t'ing, 93
Sun Yat-sen, 226, 232
Sun Yen, 112
Sunday, 134
Sundial, 47
Sung, 89, 98, 119, 134, 146–163, 165–169, 172, 176, 182, 186, 188, 190, 201, 210
Sung Ying-hsing, 208
Sung Yün, 106
Sungari River, 190
Sūtra, 61, 65, 68, 91, 96, 103, 106, 109, 117, 141
Sweet potato, 202, 221, 222
Swingle, 205, 208
Synagogue, 182
Syphilis, 203, 208
Syria, 43, 120, 132
Szechuan, 19, 31, 45, 49, 60, 62, 66, 79, 82, 84, 88, 95, 114, 126, 131, 145, 161, 172, 181, 199, 234, 236

Ta-t'ung, 87, 104
Ta t'ung, 228
Tablets, 52, 73, 75, 135, 157
Tabriz, 178, 179
Tachen, 241

T'ai, see Thai
T'ai, siege of, 114
T'ai-p'ing, 219, 225, 230
T'ai-p'ing huan yü chi, 157
T'ai-p'ing kuang chi, 157
T'ai-p'ing yü lan, 157
Taiwan, 116, 195–196, 216, 220–225, 238, 240–241, 244–245
T'ai-yüan, 83
Takla-makan, 51
Talas River, 124
T'ang, 84, 93, 100, 115, 119–142, 143, 146, 148, 149, 150, 154, 165, 176, 181–182
T'ang-ming, 76
Tangut, 44, 147, 148, 150, 164–165, 167, 168, 171, 172, 173, 174
Tao-an, 88
T'ao Ch'ien, 92–93
Tao-tê-ching (The Way and Its Power), 109, 136, 184
T'ao Tsung-i, 186–187
T'ao Yüan-ming, see T'ao Ch'ien
Taoism, 26, 62, 66–71, 76, 87–89, 91–94, 102, 103, 109, 111, 126, 128, 129–130, 134–135, 136–137, 140–141, 145, 155, 159, 160, 162, 165, 167, 183–184, 188, 200–201, 210, 218
Tardu, 99, 115–116
Tarim, 2, 45
Tarsus, 137
Tartar, 80, 120, 165, 168
Tashkent, 116, 124
Taxation, 27, 32, 36, 40, 42, 102, 120, 130–131, 142, 145, 150, 168, 173, 198, 199, 201, 202, 219, 223, 242
Taxila, 104
Tea, 79–81, 96, 148, 150, 220, 221, 222, 242

Tea Classic, 80–81
Telegraph, 235
Telephone, 235
Temujin, *see* Jenghis
Temples, 8, 15, 17, 40, 61, 62, 69, 70, 88, 96, 102, 103, 105, 120, 128–131, 146, 158, 181, 183, 185, 197, 200, 206
Ten independent states, the, 143
Têng Ssŭ-yü, 139, 186
Terraces, 221
Terrestrial globe, 180
Textiles, 17, 56, 96, 123, 138, 150, 151, 179, 203, 221, 242
Thai, 86, 124, 125, 176
Thailand, *see* Siam
Therarada, 64
Thought, 24, 26, 48, 53, 88, 140, 149, 160–161, 162, 163, 200, 227
Thousand Character Classic, The, 110
Three Kingdoms, 58–82, 210
Tiberius, 42
Tibet, 13–14, 38, 80, 82, 116, 120–126, 148, 167–168, 181, 182, 183, 184, 186, 190, 195, 209, 220, 240
Tien hung K'ai wu, 208
T'ien-lung hill, 104
T'ien shan, 123, 124, 166, 189
T'ien-t'ai sect, 108–109
Tientsin, 241
Tiles, 49, 158
Timber, 192
Timur, 178, 190
Tin, 16, 154
Tito, 243
T'o-pa, 80, 82, 98–99, 101, 104
T'o-pa Chün, 103
T'o-pa Hung, 103
T'o-pa Ssŭ, 87
T'o-pa Tao, 99

Tobacco, 203, 221–223
Tokio, 226
Tombs, 17, 28, 46, 48, 49, 50, 62, 113, 157, 197
Tongking, 34, 43, 64, 75, 76, 84, 120, 125
Tools, 1, 2, 4, 5, 8, 17, 23, 29, 130, 203, 208
Tortoise shell, 10, 151
Toys, 5
Trade, 4, 28, 39, 41, 51, 56, 62, 64, 78, 80, 113, 116, 119, 123, 125, 127, 134, 137–138, 145, 150, 151–152, 158–159, 174, 192, 196, 219–221, 223, 233, 241–242
Trade routes, 45, 77, 79, 131, 134, 142, 150, 192, 194, 241
Translations, 61, 64, 65, 89, 90–91, 103, 106, 128, 137, 140, 160, 161, 167, 168, 170, 212, 213, 231
Travel, 27, 77, 90–91, 106, 113, 158, 174, 186, 207
Treaties, 38, 79, 220, 235, 236, 241
Tribute, 15, 16, 21, 39, 40–41, 15, 76, 86, 118, 150, 152, 164, 165, 169, 174, 192, 194
Tripitaka, 90, 127, 145, 161, 167, 200
Tripod, 5, 17, 157
Truman, Harry S, 240
Ts'ai Hsiang, 158
Ts'ao Chih, 105
Ts'ao Hsüeh-ch'in, 230
Ts'ao Ts'ao, 46, 67, 74
Tsar, 212
Tsin, 58, 77, 78, 79, 82, 84, 86, 92, 95, 96
Tsinan, 8, 172

Tso chuan (*Tso Chronicle*), 72–73, 75, 136
Tsong-Kha-pa, 183, 195–196
Tsu Ch'ung-chih, 111
Ts'ui Hao, 87
Ts'ung-shu, 205
Tu Fu, 139
T'u-chüeh, 101
Türküt, *see* Turks, eastern
Tu Yu, 140, 157
T'u-yü-hun, 84, 98, 116
Tului, 172
Tun-huang, 73, 90, 96, 103, 104, 133, 134, 141
Tung Cho, 45, 46
Tung Hu, 37
Tung Tso-pin, 7
T'ung chien kang mu, 163
T'ung chih, 157
T'ung oil, 153
T'ung Tien, 140
Tungus, 82, 84, 98, 124, 148, 168
Turfan, 64, 190
Turkestan, 101, 124, 172
Turkey, 209, 222
Turks, 82, 84, 98, 101–102, 119–120, 123, 136, 167, 180
  eastern, 101, 115–116, 120–121
  western, 115–116, 121, 123
Turkic, 98
Turquoise, 17, 84
Tzŭ chih t'ung chien, 156
Tzŭ-hui, 209

Uddiyana, 108
Uigur, 13, 14, 123, 124, 125, 133, 144, 160, 165, 167, 174, 182, 210
Ulan Bator, 49
Ulugh-beg, 192
United Nations, 223, 238, 239, 240, 241
United States, 220, 225, 231, 235, 236, 237, 238, 241, 245
Upanishads, 89
Ural Mountains, 2, 101

Uriangkatai, 176
USSR, 237, 241–243
Utopian ideas, 93, 227

Vajrabodhi, 129
Vasco da Gama, 203
Vedas, 89
Vehicles, 7, 40, 96, 209
Venetians, 178
Verbiest, 228
Vernacular, 139, 140
Vietminh, 240
Vietnam, 47, 240, 241
Violet Tower, 181
Vocabularies, 87, 209–210
Voltaire, 220

Waley, 54, 139
Wallpaper, 220
Walls, 4, 26, 28, 32, 35, 60, 149, 153, 171, 197
Walnut, 50
Wan-li period, 212
Wang An-shih, 155, 156, 161–162, 175
Wang Ch'i, 208
Wang Ching-wei, 237
Wang Ch'ung, 48, 53, 57
Wang Fu, 157
Wang Fu-chih, 227
Wang Hsi-chih, 93–95, 97
Wang Hsien-chih, 94
Wang I-t'ung, 143
Wang Mang, 42–43, 47, 66
Wang Pi, 74
Wang Shih-chên, 198
Wang Shou-jên, 198, 200, 205
Wang Ssŭ-i, 208
Wang Su (195–256), 73
Wang Su (464–501), 79
Wang Wei, 139
Wang Ying-lin, 185
Washington, D.C., 7, 235, 239
Water buffalo, 27
Water clock, 47, 164

Water mill, 81
Waterways, 27, 32, 34, 149, 161, 175, 197, 206, 231, 244
Weapons, 2, 4, 5, 8, 10, 12–13, 16, 23, 28, 30, 99, 100, 114, 152–153, 169, 172, 208–209, 233
Week, seven-day, 133
Wei, 58, 72–76, 78, 98–99, 103, 104, 106, 109, 112, 184
Wei Po-yang, 70
Wei Shou, 102
Wei shu, 104
Wei Shuo, 94
Wei Wên-hsiu, 111
Wei Ying-wu, 139
Weights and measures, 32
Wên-ch'êng, 121
Wên hsien t'ung k'ao, 157
Werckmeister, 207
West River, 34, 207
Western Heaven, 89
Wheat, 4, 8, 27, 202, 222
Wheel, 7, 8, 29, 32, 81
Wheelbarrow, 81
Wilbur, Dr. C. M., 56
William of Rubruck, 164, 183, 186
Windmill, 204
Windows, 96
Wine, 38, 42, 50, 56, 74, 79, 80, 179
Woodblocks, 138, 154, 158, 179, 206, 207, 208
Woodcuts, *see* Woodblocks
Wright, Arthur, 88
Writing, 5, 7, 10–14, 34, 54, 65, 73, 88, 93–94, 98, 165, 167, 169, 243
  origin, 10
  style of, 73
Writing tools, materials, implements, 10, 11, 13, 29, 51, 52, 75
Wu, 18, 21, 54
  of three kingdoms, 58, 64, 76
Wu, Empress, 128

Wu (first emperor of Liang), 53, 103, 106
Wu-ch'ang, 58, 230
Wu Ch'êng-ên, 210
Wu Ching-tzŭ, 230
Wu Han, 243
Wu pei chih, 208
Wu Tao-hsüan (Wu Tao-tzŭ), 138
Wu-chou, 75
Wu-t'ai shan, 131
Wu-ti (Emperor Wu), 38–41, 42, 43, 50, 51, 53, 66, 99–100, 106
Wu-ting, King, 8
Wu Yüeh, 146
Wylie, 180–181

Yalu River, 240
Yang Chien, 115–116
Yang Chu, 24
Yang Fu, 79
Yang Hsüan-chih, 110
Yang Kuang, 115–119
Yangchow, 117, 118, 119, 129, 137, 154, 176
Yangtze, 18, 21, 23, 34, 54, 61, 79, 84, 86, 88, 95, 100, 117, 133, 148, 150, 169, 195, 197, 207, 211, 234, 237
Yao Ch'ung, 128
Yao Hsin-nung, 187, 211
Yellow Emperor, *see* Huang-ti
Yellow River, 2, 4, 5, 7, 12, 19, 32, 38, 43, 60, 84, 86–88, 98, 117, 148, 166, 167, 168–169, 171–172, 186, 238
Ye-lü Ch'u-ts'ai, 173–174, 182, 185
Ye-lü Ta shih, 166–167
Yen, 190
Yenan, 234, 237
Yenching, *see* Peking
Yen-mên, 119
Yen Shih-ku, 139
Yen Yüan, 227

Yin, 7
Yin-li-p'u, 7
Ying tsao fa shih, 158
Yugoslavia, 243
Yü Fa-k'ai, 92
Yüan, Emperor, 86
Yüan dynasty, 134, 166, 171–189, 198, 210, 211
Yüan Shih-k'ai, 173
Yüeh, 18, 21–23, 137
Yüeh-chih, 37–38, 45, 61
Yüeh Shih, 157
Yüeh ware, 80, 137
Yung-chêng reign, 226–227

Yung-lo reign, 190, 192, 195, 204
Yung-lo ta-tien, 204–205
Yünnan, 43, 60, 125, 148, 176, 181, 189, 192, 197, 202, 221, 223, 225, 27
Yünnanfu, 23

Zanzibar, 150
Zebra, 194
Zero, 48, 159
Zinc, 71
Zither, 55, 57, 179
    bowed, 180
Zoroastrianism, 67, 125, 131–132

A CATALOG OF SELECTED
DOVER BOOKS
IN ALL FIELDS OF INTEREST

A CATALOG OF SELECTED DOVER
BOOKS IN ALL FIELDS OF INTEREST

CONCERNING THE SPIRITUAL IN ART, Wassily Kandinsky. Pioneering work by father of abstract art. Thoughts on color theory, nature of art. Analysis of earlier masters. 12 illustrations. 80pp. of text. 5⅜ x 8½.   23411-8

ANIMALS: 1,419 Copyright-Free Illustrations of Mammals, Birds, Fish, Insects, etc., Jim Harter (ed.). Clear wood engravings present, in extremely lifelike poses, over 1,000 species of animals. One of the most extensive pictorial sourcebooks of its kind. Captions. Index. 284pp. 9 x 12.   23766-4

CELTIC ART: The Methods of Construction, George Bain. Simple geometric techniques for making Celtic interlacements, spirals, Kells-type initials, animals, humans, etc. Over 500 illustrations. 160pp. 9 x 12. (Available in U.S. only.)   22923-8

AN ATLAS OF ANATOMY FOR ARTISTS, Fritz Schider. Most thorough reference work on art anatomy in the world. Hundreds of illustrations, including selections from works by Vesalius, Leonardo, Goya, Ingres, Michelangelo, others. 593 illustrations. 192pp. 7⅛ x 10¼.   20241-0

CELTIC HAND STROKE-BY-STROKE (Irish Half-Uncial from "The Book of Kells"): An Arthur Baker Calligraphy Manual, Arthur Baker. Complete guide to creating each letter of the alphabet in distinctive Celtic manner. Covers hand position, strokes, pens, inks, paper, more. Illustrated. 48pp. 8¼ x 11.   24336-2

EASY ORIGAMI, John Montroll. Charming collection of 32 projects (hat, cup, pelican, piano, swan, many more) specially designed for the novice origami hobbyist. Clearly illustrated easy-to-follow instructions insure that even beginning papercrafters will achieve successful results. 48pp. 8¼ x 11.   27298-2

THE COMPLETE BOOK OF BIRDHOUSE CONSTRUCTION FOR WOODWORKERS, Scott D. Campbell. Detailed instructions, illustrations, tables. Also data on bird habitat and instinct patterns. Bibliography. 3 tables. 63 illustrations in 15 figures. 48pp. 5¼ x 8½.   24407-5

BLOOMINGDALE'S ILLUSTRATED 1886 CATALOG: Fashions, Dry Goods and Housewares, Bloomingdale Brothers. Famed merchants' extremely rare catalog depicting about 1,700 products: clothing, housewares, firearms, dry goods, jewelry, more. Invaluable for dating, identifying vintage items. Also, copyright-free graphics for artists, designers. Co-published with Henry Ford Museum & Greenfield Village. 160pp. 8¼ x 11.   25780-0

HISTORIC COSTUME IN PICTURES, Braun & Schneider. Over 1,450 costumed figures in clearly detailed engravings–from dawn of civilization to end of 19th century. Captions. Many folk costumes. 256pp. 8⅜ x 11¾.   23150-X

STICKLEY CRAFTSMAN FURNITURE CATALOGS, Gustav Stickley and L. & J. G. Stickley. Beautiful, functional furniture in two authentic catalogs from 1910. 594 illustrations, including 277 photos, show settles, rockers, armchairs, reclining chairs, bookcases, desks, tables. 183pp. 6½ x 9¼.   23838-5

AMERICAN LOCOMOTIVES IN HISTORIC PHOTOGRAPHS: 1858 to 1949, Ron Ziel (ed.). A rare collection of 126 meticulously detailed official photographs, called "builder portraits," of American locomotives that majestically chronicle the rise of steam locomotive power in America. Introduction. Detailed captions. xi+ 129pp. 9 x 12.   27393-8

AMERICA'S LIGHTHOUSES: An Illustrated History, Francis Ross Holland, Jr. Delightfully written, profusely illustrated fact-filled survey of over 200 American lighthouses since 1716. History, anecdotes, technological advances, more. 240pp. 8 x 10¾.
                                    25576-X

TOWARDS A NEW ARCHITECTURE, Le Corbusier. Pioneering manifesto by founder of "International School." Technical and aesthetic theories, views of industry, economics, relation of form to function, "mass-production split" and much more. Profusely illustrated. 320pp. 6⅛ x 9¼. (Available in U.S. only.)   25023-7

HOW THE OTHER HALF LIVES, Jacob Riis. Famous journalistic record, exposing poverty and degradation of New York slums around 1900, by major social reformer. 100 striking and influential photographs. 233pp. 10 x 7⅞.   22012-5

FRUIT KEY AND TWIG KEY TO TREES AND SHRUBS, William M. Harlow. One of the handiest and most widely used identification aids. Fruit key covers 120 deciduous and evergreen species; twig key 160 deciduous species. Easily used. Over 300 photographs. 126pp. 5⅜ x 8½.   20511-8

COMMON BIRD SONGS, Dr. Donald J. Borror. Songs of 60 most common U.S. birds: robins, sparrows, cardinals, bluejays, finches, more—arranged in order of increasing complexity. Up to 9 variations of songs of each species.
                                    Cassette and manual 99911 4

ORCHIDS AS HOUSE PLANTS, Rebecca Tyson Northen. Grow cattleyas and many other kinds of orchids—in a window, in a case, or under artificial light. 63 illustrations. 148pp. 5⅜ x 8½.   23261-1

MONSTER MAZES, Dave Phillips. Masterful mazes at four levels of difficulty. Avoid deadly perils and evil creatures to find magical treasures. Solutions for all 32 exciting illustrated puzzles. 48pp. 8¼ x 11.   26005-4

MOZART'S DON GIOVANNI (DOVER OPERA LIBRETTO SERIES), Wolfgang Amadeus Mozart. Introduced and translated by Ellen H. Bleiler. Standard Italian libretto, with complete English translation. Convenient and thoroughly portable—an ideal companion for reading along with a recording or the performance itself. Introduction. List of characters. Plot summary. 121pp. 5¼ x 8½.   24944-1

TECHNICAL MANUAL AND DICTIONARY OF CLASSICAL BALLET, Gail Grant. Defines, explains, comments on steps, movements, poses and concepts. 15-page pictorial section. Basic book for student, viewer. 127pp. 5⅜ x 8½.   21843-0

THE CLARINET AND CLARINET PLAYING, David Pino. Lively, comprehensive work features suggestions about technique, musicianship, and musical interpretation, as well as guidelines for teaching, making your own reeds, and preparing for public performance. Includes an intriguing look at clarinet history. "A godsend," *The Clarinet*, Journal of the International Clarinet Society. Appendixes. 7 illus. 320pp. $5\frac{3}{8}$ x $8\frac{1}{2}$. 40270-3

HOLLYWOOD GLAMOR PORTRAITS, John Kobal (ed.). 145 photos from 1926-49. Harlow, Gable, Bogart, Bacall; 94 stars in all. Full background on photographers, technical aspects. 160pp. $8\frac{3}{8}$ x $11\frac{1}{4}$. 23352-9

THE ANNOTATED CASEY AT THE BAT: A Collection of Ballads about the Mighty Casey/Third, Revised Edition, Martin Gardner (ed.). Amusing sequels and parodies of one of America's best-loved poems: Casey's Revenge, Why Casey Whiffed, Casey's Sister at the Bat, others. 256pp. $5\frac{3}{8}$ x $8\frac{1}{2}$. 28598-7

THE RAVEN AND OTHER FAVORITE POEMS, Edgar Allan Poe. Over 40 of the author's most memorable poems: "The Bells," "Ulalume," "Israfel," "To Helen," "The Conqueror Worm," "Eldorado," "Annabel Lee," many more. Alphabetic lists of titles and first lines. 64pp. $5\frac{3}{16}$ x $8\frac{1}{4}$. 26685-0

PERSONAL MEMOIRS OF U. S. GRANT, Ulysses Simpson Grant. Intelligent, deeply moving firsthand account of Civil War campaigns, considered by many the finest military memoirs ever written. Includes letters, historic photographs, maps and more. 528pp. $6\frac{1}{8}$ x $9\frac{1}{4}$. 28587-1

ANCIENT EGYPTIAN MATERIALS AND INDUSTRIES, A. Lucas and J. Harris. Fascinating, comprehensive, thoroughly documented text describes this ancient civilization's vast resources and the processes that incorporated them in daily life, including the use of animal products, building materials, cosmetics, perfumes and incense, fibers, glazed ware, glass and its manufacture, materials used in the mummification process, and much more. 544pp. $6\frac{1}{8}$ x $9\frac{1}{4}$. (Available in U.S. only.) 40446-3

RUSSIAN STORIES/RUSSKIE RASSKAZY: A Dual-Language Book, edited by Gleb Struve. Twelve tales by such masters as Chekhov, Tolstoy, Dostoevsky, Pushkin, others. Excellent word-for-word English translations on facing pages, plus teaching and study aids, Russian/English vocabulary, biographical/critical introductions, more. 416pp. $5\frac{3}{8}$ x $8\frac{1}{2}$. 26244-8

PHILADELPHIA THEN AND NOW: 60 Sites Photographed in the Past and Present, Kenneth Finkel and Susan Oyama. Rare photographs of City Hall, Logan Square, Independence Hall, Betsy Ross House, other landmarks juxtaposed with contemporary views. Captures changing face of historic city. Introduction. Captions. 128pp. $8\frac{1}{4}$ x 11. 25790-8

AIA ARCHITECTURAL GUIDE TO NASSAU AND SUFFOLK COUNTIES, LONG ISLAND, The American Institute of Architects, Long Island Chapter, and the Society for the Preservation of Long Island Antiquities. Comprehensive, well-researched and generously illustrated volume brings to life over three centuries of Long Island's great architectural heritage. More than 240 photographs with authoritative, extensively detailed captions. 176pp. $8\frac{1}{4}$ x 11. 26946-9

NORTH AMERICAN INDIAN LIFE: Customs and Traditions of 23 Tribes, Elsie Clews Parsons (ed.). 27 fictionalized essays by noted anthropologists examine religion, customs, government, additional facets of life among the Winnebago, Crow, Zuni, Eskimo, other tribes. 480pp. $6\frac{1}{8}$ x $9\frac{1}{4}$. 27377-6

FRANK LLOYD WRIGHT'S DANA HOUSE, Donald Hoffmann. Pictorial essay of residential masterpiece with over 160 interior and exterior photos, plans, elevations, sketches and studies. 128pp. 9¼ x 10¾. 29120-0

THE MALE AND FEMALE FIGURE IN MOTION: 60 Classic Photographic Sequences, Eadweard Muybridge. 60 true-action photographs of men and women walking, running, climbing, bending, turning, etc., reproduced from rare 19th-century masterpiece. vi + 121pp. 9 x 12. 24745-7

1001 QUESTIONS ANSWERED ABOUT THE SEASHORE, N. J. Berrill and Jacquelyn Berrill. Queries answered about dolphins, sea snails, sponges, starfish, fishes, shore birds, many others. Covers appearance, breeding, growth, feeding, much more. 305pp. 5¼ x 8¼. 23366-9

ATTRACTING BIRDS TO YOUR YARD, William J. Weber. Easy-to-follow guide offers advice on how to attract the greatest diversity of birds: birdhouses, feeders, water and waterers, much more. 96pp. 5³⁄₁₆ x 8¼. 28927-3

MEDICINAL AND OTHER USES OF NORTH AMERICAN PLANTS: A Historical Survey with Special Reference to the Eastern Indian Tribes, Charlotte Erichsen-Brown. Chronological historical citations document 500 years of usage of plants, trees, shrubs native to eastern Canada, northeastern U.S. Also complete identifying information. 343 illustrations. 544pp. 6½ x 9¼. 25951-X

STORYBOOK MAZES, Dave Phillips. 23 stories and mazes on two-page spreads: Wizard of Oz, Treasure Island, Robin Hood, etc. Solutions. 64pp. 8¼ x 11. 23628-5

AMERICAN NEGRO SONGS: 230 Folk Songs and Spirituals, Religious and Secular, John W. Work. This authoritative study traces the African influences of songs sung and played by black Americans at work, in church, and as entertainment. The author discusses the lyric significance of such songs as "Swing Low, Sweet Chariot," "John Henry," and others and offers the words and music for 230 songs. Bibliography. Index of Song Titles. 272pp. 6½ x 9¼. 40271-1

MOVIE-STAR PORTRAITS OF THE FORTIES, John Kobal (ed.). 163 glamor, studio photos of 106 stars of the 1940s: Rita Hayworth, Ava Gardner, Marlon Brando, Clark Gable, many more. 176pp. 8⅜ x 11¼. 23546-7

BENCHLEY LOST AND FOUND, Robert Benchley. Finest humor from early 30s, about pet peeves, child psychologists, post office and others. Mostly unavailable elsewhere. 73 illustrations by Peter Arno and others. 183pp. 5⅜ x 8½. 22410-4

YEKL and THE IMPORTED BRIDEGROOM AND OTHER STORIES OF YIDDISH NEW YORK, Abraham Cahan. Film Hester Street based on *Yekl* (1896). Novel, other stories among first about Jewish immigrants on N.Y.'s East Side. 240pp. 5⅜ x 8½. 22427-9

SELECTED POEMS, Walt Whitman. Generous sampling from *Leaves of Grass*. Twenty-four poems include "I Hear America Singing," "Song of the Open Road," "I Sing the Body Electric," "When Lilacs Last in the Dooryard Bloom'd," "O Captain! My Captain!"–all reprinted from an authoritative edition. Lists of titles and first lines. 128pp. 5³⁄₁₆ x 8¼. 26878-0

CATALOG OF DOVER BOOKS

THE BEST TALES OF HOFFMANN, E. T. A. Hoffmann. 10 of Hoffmann's most important stories: "Nutcracker and the King of Mice," "The Golden Flowerpot," etc. 458pp. 5⅜ x 8½. 21793-0

FROM FETISH TO GOD IN ANCIENT EGYPT, E. A. Wallis Budge. Rich detailed survey of Egyptian conception of "God" and gods, magic, cult of animals, Osiris, more. Also, superb English translations of hymns and legends. 240 illustrations. 545pp. 5⅜ x 8½. 25803-3

FRENCH STORIES/CONTES FRANÇAIS: A Dual-Language Book, Wallace Fowlie. Ten stories by French masters, Voltaire to Camus: "Micromegas" by Voltaire; "The Atheist's Mass" by Balzac; "Minuet" by de Maupassant; "The Guest" by Camus, six more. Excellent English translations on facing pages. Also French-English vocabulary list, exercises, more. 352pp. 5⅜ x 8½. 26443-2

CHICAGO AT THE TURN OF THE CENTURY IN PHOTOGRAPHS: 122 Historic Views from the Collections of the Chicago Historical Society, Larry A. Viskochil. Rare large-format prints offer detailed views of City Hall, State Street, the Loop, Hull House, Union Station, many other landmarks, circa 1904-1913. Introduction. Captions. Maps. 144pp. 9⅜ x 12¼. 24656-6

OLD BROOKLYN IN EARLY PHOTOGRAPHS, 1865-1929, William Lee Younger. Luna Park, Gravesend race track, construction of Grand Army Plaza, moving of Hotel Brighton, etc. 157 previously unpublished photographs. 165pp. 8⅞ x 11¾. 23587-4

THE MYTHS OF THE NORTH AMERICAN INDIANS, Lewis Spence. Rich anthology of the myths and legends of the Algonquins, Iroquois, Pawnees and Sioux, prefaced by an extensive historical and ethnological commentary. 36 illustrations. 480pp. 5⅜ x 8½. 25967-6

AN ENCYCLOPEDIA OF BATTLES: Accounts of Over 1,560 Battles from 1479 B.C. to the Present, David Eggenberger. Essential details of every major battle in recorded history from the first battle of Megiddo in 1479 B.C. to Grenada in 1984. List of Battle Maps. New Appendix covering the years 1967-1984. Index. 99 illustrations. 544pp. 6½ x 9¼. 24913-1

SAILING ALONE AROUND THE WORLD, Captain Joshua Slocum. First man to sail around the world, alone, in small boat. One of great feats of seamanship told in delightful manner. 67 illustrations. 294pp. 5⅜ x 8½. 20326-3

ANARCHISM AND OTHER ESSAYS, Emma Goldman. Powerful, penetrating, prophetic essays on direct action, role of minorities, prison reform, puritan hypocrisy, violence, etc. 271pp. 5⅜ x 8½. 22484-8

MYTHS OF THE HINDUS AND BUDDHISTS, Ananda K. Coomaraswamy and Sister Nivedita. Great stories of the epics; deeds of Krishna, Shiva, taken from puranas, Vedas, folk tales; etc. 32 illustrations. 400pp. 5⅜ x 8½. 21759-0

THE TRAUMA OF BIRTH, Otto Rank. Rank's controversial thesis that anxiety neurosis is caused by profound psychological trauma which occurs at birth. 256pp. 5⅜ x 8½. 27974-X

A THEOLOGICO-POLITICAL TREATISE, Benedict Spinoza. Also contains unfinished Political Treatise. Great classic on religious liberty, theory of government on common consent. R. Elwes translation. Total of 421pp. 5⅜ x 8½. 20249-6

CATALOG OF DOVER BOOKS

MY BONDAGE AND MY FREEDOM, Frederick Douglass. Born a slave, Douglass became outspoken force in antislavery movement. The best of Douglass' autobiographies. Graphic description of slave life. 464pp. 5⅜ x 8½.　　22457-0

FOLLOWING THE EQUATOR: A Journey Around the World, Mark Twain. Fascinating humorous account of 1897 voyage to Hawaii, Australia, India, New Zealand, etc. Ironic, bemused reports on peoples, customs, climate, flora and fauna, politics, much more. 197 illustrations. 720pp. 5⅜ x 8½.　　26113-1

THE PEOPLE CALLED SHAKERS, Edward D. Andrews. Definitive study of Shakers: origins, beliefs, practices, dances, social organization, furniture and crafts, etc. 33 illustrations. 351pp. 5⅜ x 8½.　　21081-2

THE MYTHS OF GREECE AND ROME, H. A. Guerber. A classic of mythology, generously illustrated, long prized for its simple, graphic, accurate retelling of the principal myths of Greece and Rome, and for its commentary on their origins and significance. With 64 illustrations by Michelangelo, Raphael, Titian, Rubens, Canova, Bernini and others. 480pp. 5⅜ x 8½.　　27584-1

PSYCHOLOGY OF MUSIC, Carl E. Seashore. Classic work discusses music as a medium from psychological viewpoint. Clear treatment of physical acoustics, auditory apparatus, sound perception, development of musical skills, nature of musical feeling, host of other topics. 88 figures. 408pp. 5⅜ x 8½.　　21851-1

THE PHILOSOPHY OF HISTORY, Georg W. Hegel. Great classic of Western thought develops concept that history is not chance but rational process, the evolution of freedom. 457pp. 5⅜ x 8½.　　20112-0

THE BOOK OF TEA, Kakuzo Okakura. Minor classic of the Orient: entertaining, charming explanation, interpretation of traditional Japanese culture in terms of tea ceremony. 94pp. 5⅜ x 8½.　　20070-1

LIFE IN ANCIENT EGYPT, Adolf Erman. Fullest, most thorough, detailed older account with much not in more recent books, domestic life, religion, magic, medicine, commerce, much more. Many illustrations reproduce tomb paintings, carvings, hieroglyphs, etc. 597pp. 5⅜ x 8½.　　22632-8

SUNDIALS, Their Theory and Construction, Albert Waugh. Far and away the best, most thorough coverage of ideas, mathematics concerned, types, construction, adjusting anywhere. Simple, nontechnical treatment allows even children to build several of these dials. Over 100 illustrations. 230pp. 5⅜ x 8½.　　22947-5

THEORETICAL HYDRODYNAMICS, L. M. Milne-Thomson. Classic exposition of the mathematical theory of fluid motion, applicable to both hydrodynamics and aerodynamics. Over 600 exercises. 768pp. 6⅛ x 9¼.　　68970-0

SONGS OF EXPERIENCE: Facsimile Reproduction with 26 Plates in Full Color, William Blake. 26 full-color plates from a rare 1826 edition. Includes "The Tyger," "London," "Holy Thursday," and other poems. Printed text of poems. 48pp. 5¼ x 7.　　24636-1

OLD-TIME VIGNETTES IN FULL COLOR, Carol Belanger Grafton (ed.). Over 390 charming, often sentimental illustrations, selected from archives of Victorian graphics—pretty women posing, children playing, food, flowers, kittens and puppies, smiling cherubs, birds and butterflies, much more. All copyright-free. 48pp. 9¼ x 12¼.　　27269-9

PERSPECTIVE FOR ARTISTS, Rex Vicat Cole. Depth, perspective of sky and sea, shadows, much more, not usually covered. 391 diagrams, 81 reproductions of drawings and paintings. 279pp. 5⅜ x 8½. 22487-2

DRAWING THE LIVING FIGURE, Joseph Sheppard. Innovative approach to artistic anatomy focuses on specifics of surface anatomy, rather than muscles and bones. Over 170 drawings of live models in front, back and side views, and in widely varying poses. Accompanying diagrams. 177 illustrations. Introduction. Index. 144pp. 8⅜ x11¼. 26723-7

GOTHIC AND OLD ENGLISH ALPHABETS: 100 Complete Fonts, Dan X. Solo. Add power, elegance to posters, signs, other graphics with 100 stunning copyright-free alphabets: Blackstone, Dolbey, Germania, 97 more–including many lower-case, numerals, punctuation marks. 104pp. 8⅛ x 11. 24695-7

HOW TO DO BEADWORK, Mary White. Fundamental book on craft from simple projects to five-bead chains and woven works. 106 illustrations. 142pp. 5⅜ x 8. 20697-1

THE BOOK OF WOOD CARVING, Charles Marshall Sayers. Finest book for beginners discusses fundamentals and offers 34 designs. "Absolutely first rate . . . well thought out and well executed."–E. J. Tangerman. 118pp. 7¾ x 10⅝. 23654-4

ILLUSTRATED CATALOG OF CIVIL WAR MILITARY GOODS: Union Army Weapons, Insignia, Uniform Accessories, and Other Equipment, Schuyler, Hartley, and Graham. Rare, profusely illustrated 1846 catalog includes Union Army uniform and dress regulations, arms and ammunition, coats, insignia, flags, swords, rifles, etc. 226 illustrations. 160pp. 9 x 12. 24939-5

WOMEN'S FASHIONS OF THE EARLY 1900s: An Unabridged Republication of "New York Fashions, 1909," National Cloak & Suit Co. Rare catalog of mail-order fashions documents women's and children's clothing styles shortly after the turn of the century. Captions offer full descriptions, prices. Invaluable resource for fashion, costume historians. Approximately 725 illustrations. 128pp. 8⅜ x 11¼. 27276-1

THE 1912 AND 1915 GUSTAV STICKLEY FURNITURE CATALOGS, Gustav Stickley. With over 200 detailed illustrations and descriptions, these two catalogs are essential reading and reference materials and identification guides for Stickley furniture. Captions cite materials, dimensions and prices. 112pp. 6½ x 9¼. 26676-1

EARLY AMERICAN LOCOMOTIVES, John H. White, Jr. Finest locomotive engravings from early 19th century: historical (1804–74), main-line (after 1870), special, foreign, etc. 147 plates. 142pp. 11⅜ x 8¼. 22772-3

THE TALL SHIPS OF TODAY IN PHOTOGRAPHS, Frank O. Braynard. Lavishly illustrated tribute to nearly 100 majestic contemporary sailing vessels: Amerigo Vespucci, Clearwater, Constitution, Eagle, Mayflower, Sea Cloud, Victory, many more. Authoritative captions provide statistics, background on each ship. 190 black-and-white photographs and illustrations. Introduction. 128pp. 8⅞ x 11¾. 27163-3

LITTLE BOOK OF EARLY AMERICAN CRAFTS AND TRADES, Peter Stockham (ed.). 1807 children's book explains crafts and trades: baker, hatter, cooper, potter, and many others. 23 copperplate illustrations. 140pp. 4⅝ x 6. 23336-7

VICTORIAN FASHIONS AND COSTUMES FROM HARPER'S BAZAR, 1867–1898, Stella Blum (ed.). Day costumes, evening wear, sports clothes, shoes, hats, other accessories in over 1,000 detailed engravings. 320pp. 9⅜ x 12¼. 22990-4

GUSTAV STICKLEY, THE CRAFTSMAN, Mary Ann Smith. Superb study surveys broad scope of Stickley's achievement, especially in architecture. Design philosophy, rise and fall of the Craftsman empire, descriptions and floor plans for many Craftsman houses, more. 86 black-and-white halftones. 31 line illustrations. Introduction 208pp. 6½ x 9¼. 27210-9

THE LONG ISLAND RAIL ROAD IN EARLY PHOTOGRAPHS, Ron Ziel. Over 220 rare photos, informative text document origin (1844) and development of rail service on Long Island. Vintage views of early trains, locomotives, stations, passengers, crews, much more. Captions. 8⅞ x 11¾. 26301-0

VOYAGE OF THE LIBERDADE, Joshua Slocum. Great 19th-century mariner's thrilling, first-hand account of the wreck of his ship off South America, the 35-foot boat he built from the wreckage, and its remarkable voyage home. 128pp. 5⅜ x 8½. 40022-0

TEN BOOKS ON ARCHITECTURE, Vitruvius. The most important book ever written on architecture. Early Roman aesthetics, technology, classical orders, site selection, all other aspects. Morgan translation. 331pp. 5⅜ x 8½. 20645-9

THE HUMAN FIGURE IN MOTION, Eadweard Muybridge. More than 4,500 stopped-action photos, in action series, showing undraped men, women, children jumping, lying down, throwing, sitting, wrestling, carrying, etc. 390pp. 7⅞ x 10⅝. 20204-6 Clothbd.

TREES OF THE EASTERN AND CENTRAL UNITED STATES AND CANADA, William M. Harlow. Best one-volume guide to 140 trees. Full descriptions, woodlore, range, etc. Over 600 illustrations. Handy size. 288pp. 4½ x 6⅜. 20395-6

SONGS OF WESTERN BIRDS, Dr. Donald J. Borror. Complete song and call repertoire of 60 western species, including flycatchers, juncoes, cactus wrens, many more–includes fully illustrated booklet. Cassette and manual 99913-0

GROWING AND USING HERBS AND SPICES, Milo Miloradovich. Versatile handbook provides all the information needed for cultivation and use of all the herbs and spices available in North America. 4 illustrations. Index. Glossary. 236pp. 5⅜ x 8½. 25058-X

BIG BOOK OF MAZES AND LABYRINTHS, Walter Shepherd. 50 mazes and labyrinths in all–classical, solid, ripple, and more–in one great volume. Perfect inexpensive puzzler for clever youngsters. Full solutions. 112pp. 8⅛ x 11. 22951-3

PIANO TUNING, J. Cree Fischer. Clearest, best book for beginner, amateur. Simple repairs, raising dropped notes, tuning by easy method of flattened fifths. No previous skills needed. 4 illustrations. 201pp. 5⅜ x 8½. 23267-0

HINTS TO SINGERS, Lillian Nordica. Selecting the right teacher, developing confidence, overcoming stage fright, and many other important skills receive thoughtful discussion in this indispensible guide, written by a world-famous diva of four decades' experience. 96pp. 5⅜ x 8½. 40094-8

THE COMPLETE NONSENSE OF EDWARD LEAR, Edward Lear. All nonsense limericks, zany alphabets, Owl and Pussycat, songs, nonsense botany, etc., illustrated by Lear. Total of 320pp. 5⅜ x 8½. (Available in U.S. only.) 20167-8

VICTORIAN PARLOUR POETRY: An Annotated Anthology, Michael R. Turner. 117 gems by Longfellow, Tennyson, Browning, many lesser-known poets. "The Village Blacksmith," "Curfew Must Not Ring Tonight," "Only a Baby Small," dozens more, often difficult to find elsewhere. Index of poets, titles, first lines. xxiii + 325pp. 5⅝ x 8¼. 27044-0

DUBLINERS, James Joyce. Fifteen stories offer vivid, tightly focused observations of the lives of Dublin's poorer classes. At least one, "The Dead," is considered a masterpiece. Reprinted complete and unabridged from standard edition. 160pp. 5$\frac{3}{16}$ x 8¼. 26870-5

GREAT WEIRD TALES: 14 Stories by Lovecraft, Blackwood, Machen and Others, S. T. Joshi (ed.). 14 spellbinding tales, including "The Sin Eater," by Fiona McLeod, "The Eye Above the Mantel," by Frank Belknap Long, as well as renowned works by R. H. Barlow, Lord Dunsany, Arthur Machen, W. C. Morrow and eight other masters of the genre. 256pp. 5⅜ x 8½. (Available in U.S. only.) 40436-6

THE BOOK OF THE SACRED MAGIC OF ABRAMELIN THE MAGE, translated by S. MacGregor Mathers. Medieval manuscript of ceremonial magic. Basic document in Aleister Crowley, Golden Dawn groups. 268pp. 5⅜ x 8½. 23211-5

NEW RUSSIAN-ENGLISH AND ENGLISH-RUSSIAN DICTIONARY, M. A. O'Brien. This is a remarkably handy Russian dictionary, containing a surprising amount of information, including over 70,000 entries. 366pp. 4½ x 6⅛. 20208-9

HISTORIC HOMES OF THE AMERICAN PRESIDENTS, Second, Revised Edition, Irvin Haas. A traveler's guide to American Presidential homes, most open to the public, depicting and describing homes occupied by every American President from George Washington to George Bush. With visiting hours, admission charges, travel routes. 175 photographs. Index. 160pp. 8¼ x 11. 26751-2

NEW YORK IN THE FORTIES, Andreas Feininger. 162 brilliant photographs by the well-known photographer, formerly with *Life* magazine. Commuters, shoppers, Times Square at night, much else from city at its peak. Captions by John von Hartz. 181pp. 9¼ x 10¾. 23585-8

INDIAN SIGN LANGUAGE, William Tomkins. Over 525 signs developed by Sioux and other tribes. Written instructions and diagrams. Also 290 pictographs. 111pp. 6⅛ x 9¼. 22029-X

ANATOMY: A Complete Guide for Artists, Joseph Sheppard. A master of figure drawing shows artists how to render human anatomy convincingly. Over 460 illustrations. 224pp. 8⅜ x 11¼. 27279-6

MEDIEVAL CALLIGRAPHY: Its History and Technique, Marc Drogin. Spirited history, comprehensive instruction manual covers 13 styles (ca. 4th century through 15th). Excellent photographs; directions for duplicating medieval techniques with modern tools. 224pp. 8⅜ x 11¼. 26142-5

DRIED FLOWERS: How to Prepare Them, Sarah Whitlock and Martha Rankin. Complete instructions on how to use silica gel, meal and borax, perlite aggregate, sand and borax, glycerine and water to create attractive permanent flower arrangements. 12 illustrations. 32pp. 5⅜ x 8½. 21802-3

EASY-TO-MAKE BIRD FEEDERS FOR WOODWORKERS, Scott D. Campbell. Detailed, simple-to-use guide for designing, constructing, caring for and using feeders. Text, illustrations for 12 classic and contemporary designs. 96pp. 5⅜ x 8½.
25847-5

SCOTTISH WONDER TALES FROM MYTH AND LEGEND, Donald A. Mackenzie. 16 lively tales tell of giants rumbling down mountainsides, of a magic wand that turns stone pillars into warriors, of gods and goddesses, evil hags, powerful forces and more. 240pp. 5⅜ x 8½. 29677-6

THE HISTORY OF UNDERCLOTHES, C. Willett Cunnington and Phyllis Cunnington. Fascinating, well-documented survey covering six centuries of English undergarments, enhanced with over 100 illustrations: 12th-century laced-up bodice, footed long drawers (1795), 19th-century bustles, 19th-century corsets for men, Victorian "bust improvers," much more. 272pp. 5⅜ x 8¼. 27124-2

ARTS AND CRAFTS FURNITURE: The Complete Brooks Catalog of 1912, Brooks Manufacturing Co. Photos and detailed descriptions of more than 150 now very collectible furniture designs from the Arts and Crafts movement depict davenports, settees, buffets, desks, tables, chairs, bedsteads, dressers and more, all built of solid, quarter-sawed oak. Invaluable for students and enthusiasts of antiques, Americana and the decorative arts. 80pp. 6½ x 9¼. 27471-3

WILBUR AND ORVILLE: A Biography of the Wright Brothers, Fred Howard. Definitive, crisply written study tells the full story of the brothers' lives and work. A vividly written biography, unparalleled in scope and color, that also captures the spirit of an extraordinary era. 560pp. 6⅛ x 9¼. 40297-5

THE ARTS OF THE SAILOR: Knotting, Splicing and Ropework, Hervey Garrett Smith. Indispensable shipboard reference covers tools, basic knots and useful hitches; handsewing and canvas work, more. Over 100 illustrations. Delightful reading for sea lovers. 256pp. 5⅜ x 8½. 26440-8

FRANK LLOYD WRIGHT'S FALLINGWATER: The House and Its History, Second, Revised Edition, Donald Hoffmann. A total revision—both in text and illustrations—of the standard document on Fallingwater, the boldest, most personal architectural statement of Wright's mature years, updated with valuable new material from the recently opened Frank Lloyd Wright Archives. "Fascinating"—*The New York Times.* 116 illustrations. 128pp. 9¼ x 10¾. 27430-6

CATALOG OF DOVER BOOKS

PHOTOGRAPHIC SKETCHBOOK OF THE CIVIL WAR, Alexander Gardner. 100 photos taken on field during the Civil War. Famous shots of Manassas Harper's Ferry, Lincoln, Richmond, slave pens, etc. 244pp. 10⅝ x 8¼.　　22731-6

FIVE ACRES AND INDEPENDENCE, Maurice G. Kains. Great back-to-the-land classic explains basics of self-sufficient farming. The one book to get. 95 illustrations. 397pp. 5⅜ x 8½.　　20974-1

SONGS OF EASTERN BIRDS, Dr. Donald J. Borror. Songs and calls of 60 species most common to eastern U.S.: warblers, woodpeckers, flycatchers, thrushes, larks, many more in high-quality recording.　　Cassette and manual 99912-2

A MODERN HERBAL, Margaret Grieve. Much the fullest, most exact, most useful compilation of herbal material. Gigantic alphabetical encyclopedia, from aconite to zedoary, gives botanical information, medical properties, folklore, economic uses, much else. Indispensable to serious reader. 161 illustrations. 888pp. 6½ x 9¼. 2-vol. set. (Available in U.S. only.)　　Vol. I: 22798-7
Vol. II: 22799-5

HIDDEN TREASURE MAZE BOOK, Dave Phillips. Solve 34 challenging mazes accompanied by heroic tales of adventure. Evil dragons, people-eating plants, blood-thirsty giants, many more dangerous adversaries lurk at every twist and turn. 34 mazes, stories, solutions. 48pp. 8¼ x 11.　　24566-7

LETTERS OF W. A. MOZART, Wolfgang A. Mozart. Remarkable letters show bawdy wit, humor, imagination, musical insights, contemporary musical world; includes some letters from Leopold Mozart. 276pp. 5⅜ x 8½.　　22859-2

BASIC PRINCIPLES OF CLASSICAL BALLET, Agrippina Vaganova. Great Russian theoretician, teacher explains methods for teaching classical ballet. 118 illustrations. 175pp. 5⅜ x 8½.　　22036-2

THE JUMPING FROG, Mark Twain. Revenge edition. The original story of The Celebrated Jumping Frog of Calaveras County, a hapless French translation, and Twain's hilarious "retranslation" from the French. 12 illustrations. 66pp. 5⅜ x 8½.　　22686-7

BEST REMEMBERED POEMS, Martin Gardner (ed.). The 126 poems in this superb collection of 19th- and 20th-century British and American verse range from Shelley's "To a Skylark" to the impassioned "Renascence" of Edna St. Vincent Millay and to Edward Lear's whimsical "The Owl and the Pussycat." 224pp. 5⅜ x 8½.　　27165-X

COMPLETE SONNETS, William Shakespeare. Over 150 exquisite poems deal with love, friendship, the tyranny of time, beauty's evanescence, death and other themes in language of remarkable power, precision and beauty. Glossary of archaic terms. 80pp. 5³⁄₁₆ x 8¼.　　26686-9

THE BATTLES THAT CHANGED HISTORY, Fletcher Pratt. Eminent historian profiles 16 crucial conflicts, ancient to modern, that changed the course of civilization. 352pp. 5⅜ x 8½.　　41129-X

THE WIT AND HUMOR OF OSCAR WILDE, Alvin Redman (ed.). More than 1,000 ripostes, paradoxes, wisecracks: Work is the curse of the drinking classes; I can resist everything except temptation; etc. 258pp. 5⅜ x 8½. 20602-5

SHAKESPEARE LEXICON AND QUOTATION DICTIONARY, Alexander Schmidt. Full definitions, locations, shades of meaning in every word in plays and poems. More than 50,000 exact quotations. 1,485pp. 6½ x 9¼. 2-vol. set.
Vol. 1: 22726-X
Vol. 2: 22727-8

SELECTED POEMS, Emily Dickinson. Over 100 best-known, best-loved poems by one of America's foremost poets, reprinted from authoritative early editions. No comparable edition at this price. Index of first lines. 64pp. 5³⁄₁₆ x 8¼. 26466-1

THE INSIDIOUS DR. FU-MANCHU, Sax Rohmer. The first of the popular mystery series introduces a pair of English detectives to their archnemesis, the diabolical Dr. Fu-Manchu. Flavorful atmosphere, fast-paced action, and colorful characters enliven this classic of the genre. 208pp. 5³⁄₁₆ x 8¼. 29898-1

THE MALLEUS MALEFICARUM OF KRAMER AND SPRENGER, translated by Montague Summers. Full text of most important witchhunter's "bible," used by both Catholics and Protestants. 278pp. 6⅝ x 10. 22802-9

SPANISH STORIES/CUENTOS ESPAÑOLES: A Dual-Language Book, Angel Flores (ed.). Unique format offers 13 great stories in Spanish by Cervantes, Borges, others. Faithful English translations on facing pages. 352pp. 5⅜ x 8½. 25399-6

GARDEN CITY, LONG ISLAND, IN EARLY PHOTOGRAPHS, 1869–1919, Mildred H. Smith. Handsome treasury of 118 vintage pictures, accompanied by carefully researched captions, document the Garden City Hotel fire (1899), the Vanderbilt Cup Race (1908), the first airmail flight departing from the Nassau Boulevard Aerodrome (1911), and much more. 96pp. 8⅞ x 11¾. 40669-5

OLD QUEENS, N.Y., IN EARLY PHOTOGRAPHS, Vincent F. Seyfried and William Asadorian. Over 160 rare photographs of Maspeth, Jamaica, Jackson Heights, and other areas. Vintage views of DeWitt Clinton mansion, 1939 World's Fair and more. Captions. 192pp. 8⅞ x 11. 26358-4

CAPTURED BY THE INDIANS: 15 Firsthand Accounts, 1750-1870, Frederick Drimmer. Astounding true historical accounts of grisly torture, bloody conflicts, relentless pursuits, miraculous escapes and more, by people who lived to tell the tale. 384pp. 5⅜ x 8½. 24901-8

THE WORLD'S GREAT SPEECHES (Fourth Enlarged Edition), Lewis Copeland, Lawrence W. Lamm, and Stephen J. McKenna. Nearly 300 speeches provide public speakers with a wealth of updated quotes and inspiration–from Pericles' funeral oration and William Jennings Bryan's "Cross of Gold Speech" to Malcolm X's powerful words on the Black Revolution and Earl of Spenser's tribute to his sister, Diana, Princess of Wales. 944pp. 5⅜ x 8⅜. 40903-1

THE BOOK OF THE SWORD, Sir Richard F. Burton. Great Victorian scholar/adventurer's eloquent, erudite history of the "queen of weapons"–from prehistory to early Roman Empire. Evolution and development of early swords, variations (sabre, broadsword, cutlass, scimitar, etc.), much more. 336pp. 6⅛ x 9¼. 25434-8

AUTOBIOGRAPHY: The Story of My Experiments with Truth, Mohandas K. Gandhi. Boyhood, legal studies, purification, the growth of the Satyagraha (nonviolent protest) movement. Critical, inspiring work of the man responsible for the freedom of India. 480pp. 5⅜ x 8½. (Available in U.S. only.)　24593-4

CELTIC MYTHS AND LEGENDS, T. W. Rolleston. Masterful retelling of Irish and Welsh stories and tales. Cuchulain, King Arthur, Deirdre, the Grail, many more. First paperback edition. 58 full-page illustrations. 512pp. 5⅜ x 8½.　26507-2

THE PRINCIPLES OF PSYCHOLOGY, William James. Famous long course complete, unabridged. Stream of thought, time perception, memory, experimental methods; great work decades ahead of its time. 94 figures. 1,391pp. 5⅜ x 8½. 2-vol. set.
Vol. I: 20381-6　Vol. II: 20382-4

THE WORLD AS WILL AND REPRESENTATION, Arthur Schopenhauer. Definitive English translation of Schopenhauer's life work, correcting more than 1,000 errors, omissions in earlier translations. Translated by E. F. J. Payne. Total of 1,269pp. 5⅜ x 8½. 2-vol. set.　Vol. 1: 21761-2　Vol. 2: 21762-0

MAGIC AND MYSTERY IN TIBET, Madame Alexandra David-Neel. Experiences among lamas, magicians, sages, sorcerers, Bonpa wizards. A true psychic discovery. 32 illustrations. 321pp. 5⅜ x 8½. (Available in U.S. only.)　22682-4

THE EGYPTIAN BOOK OF THE DEAD, E. A. Wallis Budge. Complete reproduction of Ani's papyrus, finest ever found. Full hieroglyphic text, interlinear transliteration, word-for-word translation, smooth translation. 533pp. 6½ x 9¼.　21866-X

MATHEMATICS FOR THE NONMATHEMATICIAN, Morris Kline. Detailed, college-level treatment of mathematics in cultural and historical context, with numerous exercises. Recommended Reading Lists. Tables. Numerous figures. 641pp. 5⅜ x 8½.　24823-2

PROBABILISTIC METHODS IN THE THEORY OF STRUCTURES, Isaac Elishakoff. Well-written introduction covers the elements of the theory of probability from two or more random variables, the reliability of such multivariable structures, the theory of random function, Monte Carlo methods of treating problems incapable of exact solution, and more. Examples. 502pp. 5⅜ x 8½.　40691-1

THE RIME OF THE ANCIENT MARINER, Gustave Doré, S. T. Coleridge. Doré's finest work; 34 plates capture moods, subtleties of poem. Flawless full-size reproductions printed on facing pages with authoritative text of poem. "Beautiful. Simply beautiful."–*Publisher's Weekly.* 77pp. 9¼ x 12.　22305-1

NORTH AMERICAN INDIAN DESIGNS FOR ARTISTS AND CRAFTSPEOPLE, Eva Wilson. Over 360 authentic copyright-free designs adapted from Navajo blankets, Hopi pottery, Sioux buffalo hides, more. Geometrics, symbolic figures, plant and animal motifs, etc. 128pp. 8⅜ x 11. (Not for sale in the United Kingdom.)　25341-4

SCULPTURE: Principles and Practice, Louis Slobodkin. Step-by-step approach to clay, plaster, metals, stone; classical and modern. 253 drawings, photos. 255pp. 8⅛ x 11.　22960-2

THE INFLUENCE OF SEA POWER UPON HISTORY, 1660–1783, A. T. Mahan. Influential classic of naval history and tactics still used as text in war colleges. First paperback edition. 4 maps. 24 battle plans. 640pp. 5⅜ x 8½.　25509-3

THE STORY OF THE TITANIC AS TOLD BY ITS SURVIVORS, Jack Winocour (ed.). What it was really like. Panic, despair, shocking inefficiency, and a little hero-ism. More thrilling than any fictional account. 26 illustrations. 320pp. 5⅜ x 8½.
20610-6

FAIRY AND FOLK TALES OF THE IRISH PEASANTRY, William Butler Yeats (ed.). Treasury of 64 tales from the twilight world of Celtic myth and legend: "The Soul Cages," "The Kildare Pooka," "King O'Toole and his Goose," many more. Introduction and Notes by W. B. Yeats. 352pp. 5⅜ x 8½.
26941-8

BUDDHIST MAHAYANA TEXTS, E. B. Cowell and others (eds.). Superb, accu-rate translations of basic documents in Mahayana Buddhism, highly important in his-tory of religions. The Buddha-karita of Asvaghosha, Larger Sukhavativyuha, more. 448pp. 5⅜ x 8½.
25552-2

ONE TWO THREE . . . INFINITY: Facts and Speculations of Science, George Gamow. Great physicist's fascinating, readable overview of contemporary science: number theory, relativity, fourth dimension, entropy, genes, atomic structure, much more. 128 illustrations. Index. 352pp. 5⅜ x 8½.
25664-2

EXPERIMENTATION AND MEASUREMENT, W. J. Youden. Introductory man-ual explains laws of measurement in simple terms and offers tips for achieving accu-racy and minimizing errors. Mathematics of measurement, use of instruments, exper-imenting with machines. 1994 edition. Foreword. Preface. Introduction. Epilogue. Selected Readings. Glossary. Index. Tables and figures. 128pp. 5⅜ x 8½. 40451-X

DALÍ ON MODERN ART: The Cuckolds of Antiquated Modern Art, Salvador Dalí. Influential painter skewers modern art and its practitioners. Outrageous evaluations of Picasso, Cézanne, Turner, more. 15 renderings of paintings discussed. 44 calligraphic decorations by Dalí. 96pp. 5⅜ x 8½. (Available in U.S. only.) 29220-7

ANTIQUE PLAYING CARDS: A Pictorial History, Henry René D'Allemagne. Over 900 elaborate, decorative images from rare playing cards (14th–20th centuries): Bacchus, death, dancing dogs, hunting scenes, royal coats of arms, players cheating, much more. 96pp. 9¼ x 12¼. 29265-7

MAKING FURNITURE MASTERPIECES: 30 Projects with Measured Drawings, Franklin H. Gottshall. Step-by-step instructions, illustrations for constructing hand-some, useful pieces, among them a Sheraton desk, Chippendale chair, Spanish desk, Queen Anne table and a William and Mary dressing mirror. 224pp. 8⅛ x 11¼.
29338-6

THE FOSSIL BOOK: A Record of Prehistoric Life, Patricia V. Rich et al. Profusely illustrated definitive guide covers everything from single-celled organisms and dinosaurs to birds and mammals and the interplay between climate and man. Over 1,500 illustrations. 760pp. 7½ x 10⅛.
29371-8

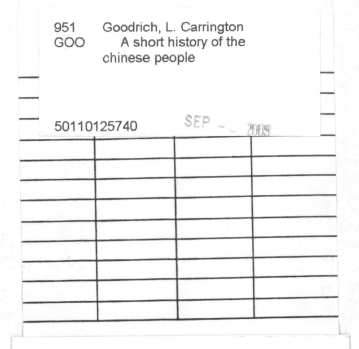